CAREER ALTERNATIVES FOR BANKERS

CAREER ALTERNATIVES FOR BANKERS

■■■

*How to Use Your
Background in Banking
to Find Another Job*

William B. King
Dean Graber
Rebecca Newton

MAGELLAN PRESS, INC.

Nashville, Tennessee

Career Alternatives for Bankers:
How To Use Your Background In Banking To Find Another Job
Second Edition

William B. King, Dean Graber, and Rebecca Newton

© 1998 Magellan Press, Inc.

Published by Magellan Press, Inc., P.O. Box 121075, Nashville, Tennessee 37212.
Printed in the United States of America.

To order additional copies of Career Alternatives for Bankers, call the publisher at 800/624-5359. Quantity discounts are available to volume buyers.

Book design by Bruce Gore, Gore Studio, Inc., Brentwood, Tennessee
Printed by Vaughan Printing, Inc., Nashville, Tennessee

Library of Congress Catalog Card Number: 97-69887

ISBN: 0-9634403-2-2

CONTENTS

SECTION IV. APPENDIX

ABOUT THE AUTHORS

William B. King has worked with banks and bankers for more than thirty years. Careers, Inc., of which he is chairman, maintains an online database of thousands of jobs in the banking industry and works with many of the nation's largest banks in finding jobs for displaced bankers. King is also chairman of *Bank Director* magazine and of Private Business, Inc.

Dean Graber is a freelance journalist who lives and works in Austin, Texas.

Rebecca Newton is a Nashville, Tennessee-based writer and editor who frequently reports on business.

PREFACE

When I began working with banks and bankers on a daily basis some twenty years ago, banking would have headed almost anyone's list of safe and secure professions.

Then, if you went into banking as a career, your move up the career ladder was fairly predictable. Whether you worked in Boise or Boston, your career path looked pretty much the same. You came out of college, entered a training program at the bank, settled into "the loan side" or the "administrative side," and began building your banking career. You got your picture in the local paper a few years after you began your climb — you'd been named assistant vice president. Then, after you'd proven yourself for a few more years, you made your family proud again when the bank announced that you'd been named a vice president. For a few on the fast track, subsequent years expanded the title on the card to "senior vice president" and, later, "executive vice president." And for a smaller number of bankers who performed especially well, becoming president of the bank was the capstone of a distinguished career.

That was the heyday of banking in America. Banks were growing in number; by the early 1970s, the number of banks had passed 15,000. There were more than 6,000 savings and loans and more than 20,000 credit unions scattered over the U.S. banking map. Only the smallest communities lacked a headquarters bank, and many towns you and I never heard of had four or five separate, independent financial institutions competing for deposits.

Even with this abundance of banks on the landscape, they all did pretty well. They rarely got in trouble. They grew in deposits every year. They added branches. They added staff.

What they didn't do was fire anybody. Or, to be more precise, they never terminated anyone who was doing the job. Banks didn't have to. Profit margins were wide enough and growth was fast enough to absorb pretty much everybody. Your career path might slow; you might not get the officer title you craved. But you still had a place to go every morning and you still brought home a paycheck every week or two.

The memory of all that is growing faint these days. Thinning profit margins, increased competition from non-banks, a deregulated banking environment, mergers and acquisitions, and a host of other forces that are beyond the scope of this book have combined to create a new world in banking.

Many of the changes bankers are facing are among the most fundamental in our society. Twenty years ago, there were more than 15,000 commercial banks in the United States, along with around 6,000 S&Ls and more than 20,000 credit unions. No other country came even close. Today, the bank count is down to around 9,000, and there are barely 2,000 S&Ls and credit unions of a size even to have separate human resources departments. No one expects the decline in the number of banks to suddenly reverse, and some predict that the U.S. of the next century will look more like Great Britain, where five banks have 90 percent of the commercial bank business, or most other major nations where the number of banks rarely exceeds one hundred. A 1995 study by Deloitte and Touche predicted that as many as 450,000 banking jobs would be lost in the next decade. My own guess is that the Deloitte number is a good one, and that a slowing economy and rapidly progressing acceptance of electronic banking could accelerate the decline.

In this new world, a lot of bankers who grew up in the old one are finding that, through no fault of their own, they must look for new jobs. For many of them, it's the first time since high school or college that they've hit the streets in search of a new job. Looking for a job is always scary, but it's even more frightening when you're past the age when you thought you'd have to worry about such things. And it's scarier still when you have to find a new job to feed your family, educate your kids, pay the mortgage. In fact, it's tougher than the first time you looked for a job.

That's why we wrote *Career Alternatives for Bankers*. There are still opportunities for bankers and there's still a demand for banking skills, it's just that the opportunities are harder to find because they are more scattered and they aren't all in banking anymore. Today's opportunities for bankers may not look like traditional banking jobs. They are in banking-related industries with vendors that sell to banks and in quasi-banking institutions, including some of the companies competing with banks today. There are also many opportunities in businesses and industries that are totally unrelated to banking, but which need good people with banking skills.

In fact, the banking industry has been the greatest training ground ever for the development of many of the skills that are most in demand today. In other words, your tenure in banking has given you the best training available for some of the best jobs available as we head into the 21st century.

For example, most of the banking jobs that have been "lost" in the past five years haven't been lost at all. They've shifted. They've been replaced by jobs that are information-oriented, some in banks and some in the offices of bank outsourcers. Bankers who have been laid off or who are looking at a career change will find ready employment if they develop abilities that allow their businesses to respond consistently and rapidly to the staggering array of technological changes and software innovations that have transformed, not just banking, but all of American industry.

If there is a central message to this book, it is this: If you've been in banking at all over this past decade (and if you've been awake), you're in better shape to find a new job than you may think. As you read, I believe you'll see why.

I hired two researchers when I set out to write the first edition of this book, but they turned out such seamless copy that the changes I had to make were minimal. It just made sense to call them co-authors, since that's what Rebecca Newton and Dean Graber were and are.

I am grateful for the valuable help Lee Wilson, our superb editor, gave us at every stage of both the first edition and this brand-new second edition of *Career Alternatives for Bankers*.

I'd like to thank Carole Cunningham for her hard work in updating the first edition of the book and Devona Matthews for her work in the production of this edition. I'm also grateful to Dawn Freeman, Tiffany Bridgewater, and Lee Ann Shelton for their work in assembling the world's most complete directory of bank hiring executives; and to Blair Ryals, Julie Lampley, and Joan Susie for their work on the outsourcers directory; both of these directories are completely newly researched and appear in the Appendix of this book. I was surprised to find that there was no such list available for bankers who want to land another banking job, and it seemed worthwhile to put one together.

As we were working on this new edition of *Career Alternatives for Bankers*, an interesting thing happened. Wells Fargo and First Interstate announced their merger, as did Chase Manhattan and Chemical. Headlines were screaming that thousands of jobs would be lost, many of them in markets already suffering from high unemployment.

In response to those announcements, we began an experiment to see if there were any new jobs in the banking industry. Frankly, we wondered if, in this edition, we should steer people clear of banking altogether. As we surveyed an initial sample of fifty metropolitan markets, we found hundreds of jobs. As we expanded our survey to 150 markets, we located thousands of jobs either in banking or where a banking background would be useful. The problem? There wasn't a central source of information on jobs available in the banking industry, and in an era when information is everything — especially to those terminated as the result of a merger — one was desperately needed.

I am delighted to tell you that today a company with which I am involved called Careers, Inc. puts out a weekly publication of jobs in the financial services area. It's called *Jobs for Bankers* and it covers the whole United States. Many of the nation's largest banks provide this publication and a package of support materials to their terminated employees, so that they may find new positions quickly by being empowered with information. I am grateful for the feedback we have received from bank human resources professionals; it has been instrumental to the publication's launch and continued success.

And finally, to all the former and present bankers, employment psychologists, executive recruiters, and outplacement executives who shared their time and insights with us, I offer special thanks. Their contribution of front-line information from the job wars has, I think, made this book uniquely useful.

William B. King
Nashville, Tennessee
January, 1998

INTRODUCTION

There was a time, and it wasn't so long ago, when change was something that happened in other industries, not in banking. Banks dealt with each other on a friendly and genteel basis. Rarely adversarial, they sometimes seemed to be trying to avoid competition, meeting each other on rates and offering me-too products when another bank introduced something new.

As banking slid into deregulation in the eighties, we began seeing a change in products. Gone were the days when banks offered identical savings accounts with identical rates. Gone were free checking accounts and loans that changed uniformly and quietly, in neat sync with changes in the money market prime.

As deregulation proceeded to its next phase, when expense control and consolidation became commonplace, I suppose I expected to see more bankers on the job market. After all, as the airline and trucking and telecommunications industries deregulated, there were increases in unemployment in each.

Still, I did not expect the onslaught of resumes that followed. Never would I have expected the number of phone calls from banking clients and banker friends and acquaintances, who called with the news that they were "exploring new career opportunities" or had just been "caught in a downsizing" or had become "a victim of the merger" or, more directly, had just been "canned."

I found that I was spending more and more of my time conducting job interviews. The only problem was, I didn't have any jobs for bankers — times were tight for my company, too. I realized that what I was really doing was job counseling, a vocation for which I had no training or expertise.

I came to realize that few of these bankers were getting any real counseling or direction elsewhere in their job search. Most had been provided no outplacement services. Most hadn't searched for a job in years, maybe since college. And few had the slightest idea what they wanted to do with their lives, except that most knew that what they wanted to do first was to find some way to pay the mortgage.

So with few jobs and only some seat-of-the-pants advice to offer, I started ending these courtesy job interviews by giving these out-of-work bankers some photocopies of articles from *The Nashville Business Journal*, a local weekly whose counterparts have sprung up in cities all over the country. The articles I saved and copied were on low-profile, little-known companies that had either recently moved to Nashville or were obviously growing. Such companies, it seemed to me, might need good, new people with financial backgrounds.

The reason I did this was because, almost without exception, my job-seeking friends were doing only the obvious. They were knocking on the doors of the biggest employers in town, or of companies they had been acquainted with in the past, or of businesses where their friends were employed.

As a result, they were going to the same places every other unemployed Nashville banker was going. The irony was that these larger, better-known companies, just like the local banks, had also undergone bad times, mergers, or restructurings. They were the least likely places to have jobs available.

I knew that my packets of photocopied articles were only a primitive means of providing job-seeking bankers with help in a difficult and often depressing time. Surely, I reasoned, there were books available that could provide a road map for these people.

Surprisingly, I found that there were no such aids. There were plenty of self-help books — all sorts of "This is the first day of the rest of your life" approaches to finding a job. There were books on writing a resume. There were books on interviewing. And there were some very good general books on job hunting and career changes. Yet I could find nothing written specifically for and about bankers, nothing specifically directed to financial skills and their applicability outside the banking industry.

So I decided to create such a book. And, as an employer, I do have some biases about bankers and job searches. As a matter of fact, some of the professionals in outplacement with whom we talked offered observations that run counter to my own preferences. For example, one outplacement specialist thinks it is especially important for a job candidate's resume to spell out his or her accomplishments in more detail than I like. (I want to know from a resume what jobs the applicant has held, when he or she held them, and what the job descriptions were. If the candidate was really successful, it will show in the resume; I'll find out about the accomplishments when I ask the questions.)

There are some job-hunting methods that I want to emphasize, some which in my experience are so basic and so underused that, just by following them, you set yourself apart from the mass of bankers out there who are trying to re-start their careers. They are:

☐ *Know something about my company.*

It drives me nuts when I spend three-quarters of an hour with someone who hasn't a clue what we do. It's public information. There are brochures, annual reports, magazine articles, all sorts of ways the interviewee can learn about my company. For me it speaks to the applicant's initiative if no homework was done. A corollary to this is that you should get to know your librarian. The business reference librarian at a big library, or the librarian at a small one, invariably has a wealth of information available about local companies and can be incredibly helpful at putting you in front of the pack.

☐ *Call me when you say you'll call me.*

If you send me a cover letter and a resume, and if you tell me you'll call me Wednesday to set up an interview, then *call me Wednesday*. Call me Thursday, and you've started our relationship with a lie, albeit a small one.

☐ *Don't be shy about calling me directly.*

I believe that few people are offended that you call them directly, or that you keep calling if you don't get through the first time, or that you call again to confirm an appointment. I figure that if you are aggressive in getting *to* me about getting *with* me, you'll be aggressive on behalf of my company if we employ you.

☐ *Don't start off our relationship with a euphemism.*

I like to speak honestly with people who are looking for a job. But if someone calls me and says "I'm a little tired of banking and I'm considering a career switch" — and if I then find out he's been fired two months before — that's annoying. I have to tiptoe around this "career change" and pretend the applicant's situation is something other than I know it to be.

Personally, I'd rather be told "The bank cut back a lot of jobs, mine was one of them, I'm looking, and I'd like to talk with you in person even if you don't have anything right now."

☐ *Don't show me a resume with a typo in it.*

I've noticed that sloppy people tend to have sloppy resumes. I think correct spelling is important. It seems to me that if you're careless on *your own* behalf, you're unlikely to take special care on behalf of my company. (I say this, of course, knowing that it ensures that we'll overlook a typo or two in this book!)

☐ *Show me some extra initiative.*

A number of years ago a banker confided to me that he had signed a contract with my company because a young salesman of ours had left a key piece of sales literature in his car and had excused himself from the meeting to get it.

"I watched out my window," related the banker, "and I saw your salesman run across our parking lot, open his car door to retrieve the material, then run back to the bank. I was so impressed by his zeal that I just couldn't *not* sign that contract."

I've thought of that young salesman often over the years (he, predictably, went on to head a successful company of his own), and it has always struck me how often I do just what that client did. I tend to reward the person who works a little harder for the order or the promotion or the new job. You don't have to run across parking lots to show you care about winning, but making an extra effort will almost always pay dividends.

In a job search situation, your extra preparation and knowledge of the company or your sending an article about something you discussed with the interviewer or *any* action that sets you apart in a positive way from everyone else will be a worthwhile effort on your part. Before your interview, during it, and after it, you'll do well to demonstrate creativity, initiative, and just wanting the job so badly that you'll probably do an outstanding job once you've got it. A caveat: Don't make it silly. Sending out an orange resume because your interviewer went to the University of Texas doesn't demonstrate anything but a touch of goofiness that few employers are seeking. Be sure to demonstrate your go-the-extra-mile personality in a way that translates into probable excellence on behalf of the company with which you are interviewing. Or don't do it.

☐ *Show me you can improve my sales.*

"Nothing happens until you sell something."

It's an old business adage, but the *reason* it's an adage is that it is true. Selling makes businesses go. Even businesses that never used to think about sales are now busily creating "sales cultures." Accounting firms and law firms are turning up with marketing directors, banks are putting calling officers on commission, and sales is suddenly a glamour area.

If you're a banker to whom sales is an unpleasant thought, you're missing a lot of job opportunities. There are a million businesses out there that don't need a CFO or a human resources director, but there's not one that doesn't need more sales ability. If you can convince me that you can sell, or if you're willing to *try* to sell my product, you'll get my attention. And if you're willing to take a low salary or a draw, or if you can afford to just have your expenses covered for a while, and live mostly on commission, you'll find an eager listener.

This is especially true if you're interviewing with very senior managers or owners. Company heads, especially, tend to see sales as the lifeblood of their companies, and everybody else as a necessary evil. Oh, they recognize the need for good administrators and data processors and the rest, but they'd just as soon have as few around as possible. If you can position yourself as being able to increase sales — or at least as having the ability to increase the revenue side rather than upping expenses — you can count on a decidedly better reception.

☐ *Don't be afraid to make me a proposition.*

I've been approached more than a few times by bankers who have made a lot of money — $100,000 or more a year, occasionally a lot more.

Well, I don't *have* a lot of $100,000 jobs lying around. Actually, I don't have *any* $100,000 jobs for a new hire and probably never will. Around my place, those jobs have to be earned.

So I end up telling the banker that I just don't have anything. Or the banker ends up telling me that he or she will accept a lot less.

I'd much rather hear something like this: "Bill, I know you don't have anything available that pays even close to what I've been making, and I'm not too keen on taking a long-term step down. So here's what I propose:"

"You take me on for, say, $3,000 a month. And set me up on a bonus payable at the end of six months, based on 10% of the new business I bring in or personally sign. If I make you money, I make money. If I don't, you're not out much, and I'll be on my way."

Now how can I turn that down? An operations person could propose that sort of thing, but based on savings.

Or try something *really* creative. Someone who really studied my company might say, "Look Bill, you've got a great business, but with banks as your only market, you *must* be looking for new areas of growth. I'd like to work three months on a project basis. I'll look at opportunities for you in the health care area, or I'll look hard at any pet projects you may not have had time to explore fully."

These approaches won't always work, of course, even with me. It's really easy for me or any other employer to turn you down for a job — I can just say I don't have any openings that suit you. It's much tougher to turn down a creatively crafted proposition. Even if I do turn you down, I'll respect you for your ingenuity and I'll probably remember you if I have a project pop up for which I need an ingenious person or hear of a job opening that you might want to apply for.

So there you have it. Some preferences, prejudices, tips, and suggestions from someone who has talked jobs with a lot of bankers who found themselves in your shoes.

The biggest mistake you could make is to stop here, though, because Rebecca Newton and Dean Graber have spoken with outplacement specialists, employment psychologists, and scores of bankers whose collective experience can give you the edge as you go for a new job. And, as we say, all you need is one.

SECTION I

■■■

Getting Ready
To Succeed

1

PREPARING YOURSELF MENTALLY AND PHYSICALLY

■ ■ ■

When you chose banking as a career you probably thought your job would last for life, or at least for as long as you wanted it. It seems hard to believe today, but that's the way it once was. If you wanted a job, you worked for a corporation. If you wanted a career, you went into banking.

But since deregulation began in earnest, the banking industry has undergone changes that have left large numbers of bankers at all levels jobless, worried, and wondering what to do next. If you count yourself among those jobless (or soon-to-be-jobless) bankers, you can take some comfort that you're not alone. And, as we'll see, you're in a better position than most to market your skills.

As a banker, you have witnessed and participated in one of the rockiest eras in banking history, certainly the most unsettled period since the Great Depression. You have lived through deregulation, recession, mergers, and takeovers. These trends have eliminated thousands of banking jobs across the country, and now out-of-work bankers face a job market crowded with other skilled, competent bankers. But before you mail out hundreds of resumes and telephone everyone who has ever given you a business card, you must address the fact that you have lost your job. Before attempting to meet the considerable challenges ahead, you have some very normal feelings to deal with — feelings of anger, unhappiness, confusion, and loss. If you don't recognize the existence of those feelings (and they may be masked), and address them, you may make mistakes that will make it even more difficult to find a new job. Even the most time-honored job-search tactics can backfire if they are employed at the wrong time, or if you have not achieved the right frame of mind before you use them.

There are specific ways to attain the mindset needed to successfully undertake a job search. We'll examine what happened to three former bankers who failed to make the necessary mental preparation: Charles, who could not admit that he was unemployed and, therefore, could not bring himself to ask for a job; Larry, who admitted he had lost his job but failed to make the personal adjustments necessary to get a new one; and Rita, who plunged into a job search prematurely, while she was still seething over losing her previous position. All three were skilled bankers who, like thousands of others, were dismissed because of poor economic circumstances rather than poor performance. If their reactions to their dismissals had been different, they would have found it easier to find new jobs.

■ REACTIONS TO UNEMPLOYMENT

You may have heard the story of a New York investment banker who was fired from her job on a Friday afternoon and celebrated that evening by throwing a lavish party in a posh hotel bar. In contrast, you may know a banker who took his dismissal so hard that he was paralyzed with depression and spent several months on a psychiatrist's couch trying to salvage his self-esteem. These responses are extreme, but they illustrate the differing reactions of people dismissed from a job. Psychologists say that most people who lose their jobs respond with some degree of shock, anger, sadness, and confusion. Sometimes there is also depression.

"Responses to job loss vary. Most people handle it pretty well and tend to work things through in a reasonably short time," says Dr. James Terrill, consulting psychologist with de Recat and Associates, a San Francisco-based outplacement firm.

Several factors determine whether it takes you a weekend or a month to "get your head together" before you begin a job search: your personality, your financial situation, how you felt about your job, how your employer handled the dismissal, and what you plan to do next. For example, bankers who lose their jobs because of a merger often have more time to anticipate their dismissal and may be better prepared than those who are let go abruptly.

But even if the prospect of job loss has loomed over a banker's head for months, it still comes as a blow when it happens, says Dr. William Roiter, a psychologist whose Boston firm, APM/Hurst Management, operates employee assistance programs for New England banks.

"Just the thought of it is catastrophic," Dr. Roiter says. "The reality is that it stinks. Even if you believe you are going to lose your job, it still surprises you when it occurs. There is still a sense of shock."

"Obviously it is a major shock," says Larry DeMeyers, chief operating officer of Bankers First Savings Bank in Augusta, Georgia. "Someone has been working at the bank for five, six, seven, eight, or even ten years. Then all of a sudden you tell them they're unemployed. Banking used to be an industry with very little turnover. Once you did a good job, you got to keep your job."

Psychologists say the loss of a job can be one of the most stressful experiences in life. For some people, losing a job is almost as traumatic as losing a spouse. As Dr. Roiter explains, our lives are divided into three main areas: family life, work life, and our sense of ourselves. For many of us, particularly men, our work lives and sense of ourselves are intertwined, making the loss of a job a double blow. And since jobs in banking have a certain prestige, dismissal from a banking job can mean much more than the loss of income and routine. It can mean a sense of loss in terms of identity and self-esteem.

"The more senior people have been in a position of authority.

Many are Type A personalities. They are used to getting things done, and they are used to working all the time. All of a sudden, they don't have anything to do," says Fairfax Randolph, president of the outplacement firm de Recat and Associates, and a former banker.

Psychologists have identified five coping stages that many people go through as they adapt to major losses like the loss of a job. Although not everyone experiences all the typical symptoms in the same sequence, the successive stages of shock and denial, anger, depression, and adaptation commonly follow a major loss.

■ Shock and denial — One of the first responses to losing a job, and one of the most common and healthy, says Dr. Roiter, is to shut down one's feelings. You don't pretend that it didn't happen, but to ease the shock of losing a job, many people respond by not allowing themselves to think about it.

"Denial allows you to get through the day without feeling the pain," Dr. Roiter says.

Dr. Roiter describes one banker who loses his job and spends the next few days at home. After the shock wears off, the banker realizes that he has no job to return to. At this point, he starts worrying about making a living. He may feel anxious. His feelings may fluctuate. But, through denial, he shields himself from the pain by not letting himself think about his problem.

Dr. Roiter explains: "You may spend part of the day doing grocery shopping because you have the time. You go up and down the aisle not thinking about the job situation. And for twenty minutes or so, the thought of being unemployed doesn't cross your mind. Then you get to the cash register, and the bill is $158. That's when you pull out your wallet and the bad feelings rush in again. You begin to worry, How am I going to pay for it?"

Denial lets people recover their strength, Dr. Roiter says. Once that strength is recovered, though, people often start to feel angry.

■ Anger — Dr. Roiter views anger as a good sign because it means that the individual has some energy to do something. "It's important that the anger be directed in a positive way," he says. "Someone who's angry in a negative way can really burn bridges in a career."

Dr. Roiter uses the example of a terminated banker who resolves that he will end up in a better situation than he had before he was fired. *I'll show them*, the banker might think. Focusing on living well as a kind of revenge is more constructive than focusing on suing the bank or writing letters to the bank president to complain about the unfairness of the dismissal, Dr. Roiter says. Activities with a negative focus may allow a terminated banker to release tension, but they may also hinder advancement to a new job.

Dr. Terrill says recently dismissed employees frequently say they are fine and deny having any problems. But if you probe a bit, he says, it becomes obvious that they do feel some anger. It is better to express that anger early than to risk the chance that it will surface in a job interview, which is the worst time to vent anger.

"You do want the individual to ventilate and get in touch with his feelings, but you don't want it to go beyond a certain point," Dr. Terrill says. Some people get carried away with anger and tend to dwell on it. "At a certain point," he says, "it's important to get beyond your anger."

■ Depression — It's normal to feel a certain amount of sadness and hurt after the loss of a job. However, when a person loses all hope and is overcome by sustained feelings of worthlessness and defeat, he or she may be clinically depressed? Depression is a physical and mental condition that should be treated professionally.

Although most people experience only temporary feelings of sadness and loss after losing a job, depression does occur frequently enough in such situations that anyone who has lost a job should be aware of the symptoms of depression. Symptoms of depression include insomnia, thoughts of death and suicide, irritability, anxiety, low self-esteem, difficulty in concentrating and thinking clearly, and loss of interest in favorite activities.

"As with many illnesses, there are individuals who are prone to depression," Dr. Roiter says. "If you've experienced depression before or know that other members of your family have suffered from depression, it's important that you seek the support and assistance you need."

■ Adaptation — As anger begins to subside, people gradually move from defending themselves to adapting to their situations. They gain some sense of self-awareness and evaluate the reasons they were let go. They consider their strengths and begin generating and exploring options. This process can be accelerated when the person feels that he or she has adequate information and several options to consider.

Dr. Terrill says that most of the executives he sees at the beginning of outplacement don't need any follow-up counseling. Instead, he says, they make progress through working with career consultants. "For most people the contact with the career consultant, where the primary focus is not on how they're feeling, but rather on the job search, seems to carry them along," he says. "Depression, per se, is relatively rare."

Fairfax Randolph, the banker turned outplacement executive, says that bankers are professionals who recognize layoffs as an unfortunate reality of their industry. Most bankers deal mentally with the loss of a job after a relatively brief period, sometimes after only a few days. "They don't mourn it for long periods of time," he says. "They're not mentally ill. They're not emotionally ill. They're not psychologically wounded. They got kicked in the gut, and they confront it. They act professionally. They say, *I'm an executive. This is life in the fast lane. I've got to confront it.*"

No one should undertake a job search before adjusting to the fact of termination. Failure to do so can produce unfortunate results.

For example, if you begin your job search when your feelings are still "shut down," you may come across in a job interview as rambling and appear scattered and confused. If you are angry, you won't make a good impression, and if you're depressed, you may feel powerless and lack the energy you'll need to look for another job. For these reasons, you should contact other people for information about jobs only when you are able to make a good impression.

Dr. Roiter says looking for a new job before dealing with the loss of the old job is one of the worst things a terminated banker can do. Even the most logical steps toward getting a new job can backfire if they are taken too soon.

"We've seen people get out their Rolodexes and begin calling people even before they have cleaned out their desks," Dr. Roiter says. "They respond out of instinct and, perhaps, panic. Before they've digested and dealt with the loss of one job, they start to look for the next one. This gets the search off on the wrong foot. They remember the president of a manufacturing company who said, 'Charlie, you did a great job structuring the deal. If you ever leave the bank, give me a call.' A banker may receive several of these informal 'job offers' over the years. Those are given in appreciation instead of intended as real job offers," Dr. Roiter says. "But people tend to remember them."

Reaching for your phone directory and calling contacts before dealing with the trauma of losing a position may even sabotage a job search, he says. On the phone the banker may seem unfocused, emotional, and angry. "Very good contacts can become polluted by an inept approach," Dr. Roiter says. "The person who has lost his job tends to sound desperate, and the person on the other end of the phone thinks, *What's happened to the guy who's always been in control? He sounds kind of strange to me.* Instead of thinking of you as a competent person who's always in control, he thinks of you as an emotional person with a grudge."

Not only do you risk presenting yourself badly, Dr. Roiter says, but you may not even know *how* you are presenting yourself because you haven't had time to assess the situation. For this reason, he recommends that newly unemployed bankers take two weeks to get themselves in the right frame of mind before making any calls. He adds that some people will need to take more time.

Randolph concurs that bankers who send out their resumes and make phone calls as soon as they learn they have been let go are doing the right thing, but at the wrong time. It's important to take these actions, he says, when you know where you are headed. "Friends want to help you when they feel you are in control of your own destiny. People will not want to help you when you dump your problem in their laps," he says.

There are numerous practical steps bankers who have lost their jobs can take to resist stress, maintain control, and achieve the frame of mind necessary to undertake a successful job search.

- Focus on resisting stress and maintaining control — By resisting stress, you can maintain a sense of control that will allow you to make wiser choices about your job search. To maintain your sense of control, Dr. Roiter says, you should concentrate on the following questions:

  - *Am I comfortable with what I am doing now?*
  - *Is banking worth it to me? Did it have value to me?*
  - *What do I enjoy doing? What do I dislike doing?*
  - *If I'm not satisfied, can I change? Can I find a job that's more satisfying to me?*

- Get your resume in order — Putting together a resume can be a great tool for rebuilding damaged self-esteem. Resumes are not just for getting interviews that will lead to a job, says Stanlee Phelps, a vice president of the Lee Hecht Harrison outplacement firm in Irvine, California. "Seventy-five percent of the value of putting together a resume is to empower yourself," she explains.

Resumes remind people of accomplishments they may have forgotten. This raises self-esteem and helps guide and direct the job search in terms of their marketability.

■ Stay involved in tasks, and keep a routine — View looking for work as your primary task. Structure it like a job, and devote a certain number of hours to it each day. If you spend fewer hours one day, make up for those hours the next day. Develop a set of projects that lead to a goal. But set time goals so the projects don't last indefinitely. Talk to other people who have lost their jobs. Most of them will have found work in a few weeks or months. Find out how they did it.

Develop a routine you follow during the work week, such as setting an alarm clock and getting up at the same time each morning, even if you're depressed. Resist the temptation to sleep until noon and to stay in your bathrobe all day. These behaviors underline the disruption in your routine. You may not miss having to wake up early to commute to your job, or the hassles at work, but people do miss the structure jobs provide.

■ Involve family members in your job search — In most cases, spouses are supportive of a wife or husband who has been dismissed from a job. However, Dr. Terrill says that in marriages that are already experiencing difficulties, the stress of a job loss can add to existing friction. A spouse who is taking care of the children during the day rather than working outside the home may feel stress and uncertainty about his or her partner's job loss and feel less in control of the situation.

■ Maintain social contacts — If you have lost your job you may feel like avoiding social activities. You may be embarrassed around friends. You may want to skip regular tennis games because of the cost. Friends outside of work may call your old office and discover that you are "no longer with the bank." Friends from work may feel awkward around you, since "there is a sense that unemployment is contagious," Dr. Roiter says.

Even though your friends may be at work during the day, it is important for you to maintain some social support. Find out about local support groups that meet in churches and community centers. If you cannot join an existing support group, Dr. Roiter suggests that you start your own with two or three other people who have also lost their jobs.

Establish a routine within your group. For example, you could meet every week for lunch or coffee and compare the progress of your job searches. If someone in the group flies to another city for an interview, ask them to report back to the group about the job prospects in that city.

- Try to remember that losing your job is not the worst thing in the world — It's important to keep your loss in perspective, Dr. Roiter says. Listen to the news and stay informed about local and world events. Keep your mind occupied with things besides your own unemployment.

- Volunteer — Volunteering is a great activity for laid-off bankers with time on their hands. Volunteer work not only gives you a routine and social contact, but it also helps put your own challenges in perspective as you see the difficult times faced by others. Most organizations will be grateful for your expertise and enthusiastic about your contributions. In some cases, civic involvement may even open the way to a new job.

"There are a lot of bankers who can't sit around with people in a church basement and talk about their careers," Dr. Roiter says. "On the other hand, they may be able to help senior citizens with their tax preparation." Such volunteer activities give unemployed bankers contact with other people and let them apply their skills in useful ways. Although volunteer work may expose you to some career opportunities, Dr. Roiter warns that you should not go into volunteering with the idea that it is a way to find a job. Rather, you should go for the sense of accomplishment, the social contact, and a sense of perspective.

■ Maintain a sense of humor — Many of those who do well after losing their jobs are those who still appreciate humor, even if it's gallows humor.

Dr. Roiter recalls a woman who worked in a bank credit card department. In October she learned that her whole division was going to be contracted out in February. While this gave her a little advance notice, it cast a pall over her Christmas holidays.

For eleven years, the woman had been responsible for putting up the Christmas tree in the credit card department. "The year of the layoff, she decorated it with black bows," Dr. Roiter says. "She thought it was the funniest thing in the world. So did the other employees. They were acknowledging the reality of the situation and the fact that they felt bad about it." But humor helped them keep it in perspective.

■ Don't face it alone — Although outplacement is a fast-growing industry that is frequently used by banks to take care of their terminated employees, there are thousands of bankers who do not have access to outplacement. People who face their unemployment alone can experience tension, confusion, isolation, and depression.

"I think it is very important to try to develop some kind of substitute if you aren't given outplacement," Dr. Terrill says. Some churches are addressing the unemployment problem by forming support groups led by people with relevant expertise. There are also organizations like the 40 Plus Clubs with chapters nationwide as well as state-operated programs. Notices of meetings of such organizations are posted at public libraries, published in the *National Business Employment Weekly*, or available through your local employment office.

If these groups are not available, Dr. Terrill recommends consulting a counselor. Depending on your needs, you might seek a career counselor or psychologist. While counseling may be costly, it can be very helpful and can even be tailored to address specific needs on a short-term basis.

■ CONCENTRATE ON YOUR PHYSICAL WELL-BEING

All of us know by now that exercise relieves tension and stress and contributes to a general sense of well-being. It isn't surprising, then, that outplacement firms and psychologists routinely recommend that job seekers undertake a regular exercise program.

"Unemployed bankers need to guard against feeling guilty that they are out of work and feeling undeserving of new opportunities," says Stanlee Phelps. She says that frequently people who have maintained a regular workout schedule stop working out when they lose a job, even though they have more time for exercise. Some may feel too depressed to exercise or think they can't take time to work out when they should be out looking for a job. But Phelps insists that her clients exercise.

"A job candidate who radiates vitality, enthusiasm, optimism, and good health is a much stronger candidate than one who looks like he's been run over by a truck," Phelps says. "It helps to remember that you make an impression with your physical appearance. Of course, this doesn't mean that you have to be Mr. or Ms. America."

Almost any kind of exercise yields physiological and mental benefits. However, people who have been dismissed from their jobs often say they don't have the energy or motivation to exercise. "I absolutely insist that they go walking," Phelps says. "Walking motivates, clears your head, and stimulates your mind. And you sleep better." She adds that exercise increases oxygen intake and may help relieve insomnia.

Other experts suggest walking for people who don't have the energy for more strenuous exercise or who have not maintained an exercise regimen. "Set small goals," Dr. Roiter advises. "You don't need to run a marathon. Just walking around the block will feel good when you haven't been exercising at all. If I have a client who hasn't left the house in two weeks and who starts drinking at 2:00 in the afternoon, it's an improvement if I can get them to walk around the block a few times and wait until 6:00 to take their first drink."

Going to the gym or playing tennis or golf can lead to some good networking opportunities, Phelps adds. Many gyms around the country offer mixers geared to business networking.

■ THREE WHO DID IT WRONG

If you still are not convinced that to find another good job you must examine, assess, and adjust your mental state and physical condition, consider the stories of three unemployed bankers who did not.

Charles was a former bank CEO who lost his job due to a merger. He was trim, intelligent, experienced, and quite polished during an interview. He approached a company president with the confidence of a banker who hoped to finalize a large commercial loan.

Charles explained that he was "doing some consulting" and that he would be pleased to do some work for the president's company. The president nodded, remembering the many bankers who had come to his office with newly minted consultants' business cards who were really looking for a permanent position. The interviewer gave Charles the chance to sell himself and his skills, but Charles never made the effort. It was clear that Charles was not actually a consultant and just as obvious that he simply could not bring himself to ask for a job. He seemed to think that his credentials would speak for themselves, and that the president would be so impressed that he would create a place for him within the organization. Although Charles's attitude suggested that he expected the president to make him an offer, he failed to explain how he could be useful to the president's company.

The president doubted whether Charles had actually admitted to himself that he was unemployed and needed a job. He couldn't offer Charles any encouragement and explained that the company's budget for consultants was limited.

Most of the other prospective employers who interviewed Charles also perceived that Charles had not accepted the reality of his situation.

Charles was an unemployed banker who masqueraded as a consultant because he was too ashamed to ask anyone to give him a job. Employers recognized this, and they silently questioned Charles's judgment, his sense of reality, and his ability to deal with problems. As an executive with a new company, Charles would have been required to face difficult situations each day, and he would have had to do so with candor. When he interviewed, however, he couldn't even admit that he needed a job; that inability eliminated him from the interviewers' consideration. Charles's mental resistance to his joblessness sabotaged his job search.

Sometimes a job seeker's problems are both mental and physical. Consider Larry, a former bank vice president who worked for twenty years at a medium-sized bank in the Florida city where he grew up. Larry was intelligent and enthusiastic, but he had been let go when his bank merged with an out-of-state bank. Unlike Charles, who couldn't admit that he needed a job, Larry had accepted the fact of his unemployment. In fact, in an interview with the chairman of a financial services company, he volunteered that he had already had eighty unsuccessful interviews. Larry was convinced that his long job search was simply a result of the bad economy. The executive who interviewed him immediately knew that there were other reasons why Larry had had eighty fruitless interviews.

Early in the interview, Larry called his interviewer "buddy" in response to a question about his previous job. This expression, and his casual, joking demeanor, may have been acceptable in his hometown, but to his interviewer, they seemed much too familiar for an interview setting.

It was difficult for the interviewer to take Larry seriously. Although Larry seemed intelligent, the interviewer was distracted by Larry's gold ring and cuff links and the gaudy silk handkerchief protruding from his suit pocket. His outdated hairdo had been heavily misted with hairspray, which made him seem more out of touch than he actually was, and he was so out of shape that the walk from the parking lot and up one flight of stairs had left him winded.

Even more disturbing was the fact that Larry did not know what he wanted to say in the interview. He rehashed the merger of his bank and described some of his previous interviews. He failed to indicate that he was familiar with the interviewer's company, even though several articles about the company had been published recently in the local business press.

Larry had obviously enjoyed his hometown status as a banker, and he showed it. He gave the impression that he expected the interviewer to find — or create — a position for him within the organization.

The interviewer also questioned Larry's judgment for mentioning the fact that he had had eighty interviews. The interviewer thought, *There goes an intelligent man who has never functioned outside his hometown and doesn't have the foggiest idea how he appears to others or how to adjust himself to the world elsewhere. If I hire him when eighty others didn't, how smart can I be?*

Rita was another competent banker with a problem of a different sort. Rita's appearance and preparation for interviews were as impressive as her work history. She had begun her career as a teller at a midwestern bank while working her way through college at night. After two years she entered the bank's branch management training program and was eventually promoted to manager at a suburban branch.

She had completed half the courses required for her M.B.A. when she was let go. She had accepted the fact that she was no longer a banker, and recognized that she was interested in finance and marketing. In an interview with a large insurance company whose headquarters were near her home, Rita explained how her bank marketing experience qualified her for a marketing position at the company.

The interviewer was impressed that Rita had taken the time to study his company's literature and to make a thorough review of insurance industry trade publications. She was familiar with the company's niche, its competitors, and the issues facing the industry.

In her cover letter, she listed a half-dozen specific ways that her experience might benefit the interviewer's company, and she asked for an interview to discuss ways that her skills could apply directly to specific positions. She did not hesitate to expand on these points during the interview.

But Rita had failed to deal with her anger at being fired. While reviewing Rita's resume, the insurance company interviewer mentioned that bank mergers had forced many qualified people out of work. At the mention of her bank, Rita's face tightened, and she blurted, "My bank went about it totally wrong, and they're going to pay for it. They fired all the competent managers who knew how to run the place. Now they're stuck with inexperienced kids and corporate clones who don't have the brains or guts for anything else."

Rita's outburst shocked her interviewer. It obviously surprised her, too, because she apologized before she left. Although she was extremely qualified, the interviewer knew that he would never hire anyone who was so bitter. Rita had not dealt with her anger and it was still poisoning her. The interviewer didn't want it to poison his company.

These examples show three bankers who failed to make the mental preparations that are necessary for a successful job search. All three bankers could have done better if they had stopped to think about the "package" prospective employers would see. Each needed a little "repackaging" before hitting the job market.

Charles made a good impression, but he hadn't admitted to himself that he was jobless, and therefore he couldn't ask for a job. Larry admitted that he needed a job (in fact, he was too candid for his own good), but he had not repackaged himself appropriately for a corporate environment and had failed to educate himself about the job he sought. He delivered the wrong product. Rita delivered the right product but defeated herself with her own anger; however justified her complaints, her inability to let go of her grievances worsened, rather than improved, her situation.

Repackaging yourself involves assessing your skills and deciding which job opportunities you will pursue — not as "a banker," but as someone whose banking skills will transfer to new occupations. Your banking background gives you some advantages as you take steps toward finding a new job. People respect bankers, and they find banking mysterious and complex. It takes no leap of faith for a prospective employer to see that a banker has skills that may be transferable to his or her business. And you're in good company. With consolidations and bank failures, many bright, long-tenured senior bankers are having to make career changes. As a result, there's little stigma connected with looking for a job today.

The day is over when you could stay in one job your whole career; today, business people can expect to have several jobs. What is happening in banking today — jobs disappearing in one sector and reappearing in another — has always happened in some industries. In the advertising business, for example, when an ad agency loses a big account, everybody assigned to that account may be terminated. What happens then? They dust themselves off, update their resumes and portfolios, and go out and find other jobs. There is no shame to it, no embarrassment. Banking is not the advertising business, of course, but it's starting to resemble that business more and more. It's not a bad idea to try to react to events like a crusty ad agency vet. Roll with the punches. Get your head together. And move on.

2

ASSESSING YOUR APTITUDES

■ ■ ■

Once you have dealt with the fact that you have lost your job, you will be ready to search for another one — either in banking or another industry. This is the perfect time to reflect on your previous jobs, the skills you have acquired, and the type of job you would like to have. Your reflections about your work history, skills, interests, values, and personality will help you decide whether to stay in banking or switch careers, and, if you decide to make a change, which jobs are possibilities.

The good news is that your banking experience has given you more marketable skills than those acquired by people in many other industries, and these skills are transferable to many other professions and occupations. The bad news is that you may have to convince people outside of banking that you possess these valuable skills and that you are more than "just a banker" — that you are, rather, a professional manager who has worked in the banking industry.

"Banking requires very broad skills, skills that are generally applicable to a lot of other industries, a lot of other jobs. I don't think people understand that," says Trish Benninger, first vice president of human resources for Great Western Bank in Northridge, California.

Your job-search skills may need a little sharpening, too. It is probable that banking has been a uniquely stable industry throughout most of your career. This means that you may be out of practice in looking for a job. Consequently, you may have a harder time identifying the skills you do have.

If you want to stay in banking, there are a number of opportunities. Though the number of banks is shrinking, there are still more than 12,000 banks, 2,000 savings and loan institutions, and 15,000 credit unions in the United States. Alternately, if you want to go to work in another industry, your banking skills will serve you well. In fact, since many businesses operate more like banks than other businesses, you, as a banker, have a natural advantage.

Regardless of your decision, the importance of taking some time to assess your aptitudes cannot be overstated. There are many ways you can do so. Whether you go through an outplacement program, consult a career counselor, or perform your own self-assessment, it is important to consider several questions:

- *What kind of work have you done? What did you accomplish?*
- *What kind of work do you do well?*
- *What kinds of work do you like and dislike?*
- *Would you prefer to do something different? If so, what?*
- *How do your values and personality traits influence your work?*
- *What are your goals?*

These are the questions employers will ask you in interviews. You won't be able to answer them well if you haven't taken time to reflect on them beforehand.

■ THE IMPORTANCE OF ASSESSING YOUR APTITUDES

If you're not convinced of the importance of evaluating your aptitudes, consider the case of James, a forty-five-year-old North Carolina banker. James had lost his job as senior vice president of corporate banking when his bank was purchased by a larger, out-of-state institution. He ignored the self-evaluation step in the job-search process and launched his job search blindly, without a true sense of his strengths and weaknesses. As a result, he failed to recognize several positions for which he was qualified.

Like thousands of bankers, James entered banking right after college. He went through his bank's management training program and, during the years he worked there, was promoted several times. When the sale of the bank was announced, James had a gnawing feeling that his job was going to be eliminated. He clung to the hope that his twenty-three years of experience would be valued by the incoming management and that he would be able to remain aboard. Unfortunately, things didn't work out that way; James was dismissed with 100 other senior managers.

James got over the shock of losing his job fairly quickly. He knew he could not waste time being angry since so many bankers had been thrust into the job market at the same time he lost his job. Besides, he had a mortgage to pay and a seventeen-year-old daughter who would begin college in a few months.

His wife's earnings from a part-time catering business made up only a small percentage of the family's income. The couple's savings were designated for their daughter's college tuition and their eventual retirement. James didn't want to touch those funds unless he had to. He needed to get back to work as quickly as possible.

Since James wanted to find a new job without delay, he didn't stop to think about his skills and goals before beginning his search for a new job. He added a paragraph to his resume and plunged into the classified sections of his local newspaper and *The Wall Street Journal.*

When James found no listing in the paper for a position at his level with any local bank, he checked the classified sections of out-of-town newspapers at the public library. He also bought Sunday newspapers from all over the Southeast at a local bookstore. He found no listings for his job title in any of those papers, either.

There's just no job for me anywhere, he thought, after spending another Sunday poring over the classified sections of seven newspapers.

James began to feel defeated even before he had sent out his first resume. He could have avoided this discouragement if he had taken time to look before he jumped into his job hunt.

What James didn't realize was that there *were* jobs for him, and that many of these jobs were advertised in the papers he had searched. James simply didn't recognize that his skills were a good match for these jobs because the ads seeking applicants for the jobs did not say "Wanted: Senior Vice President of Corporate Banking." In fact, most of the advertised jobs for which James was suited were *nonbanking* jobs.

Several companies, including some in his own city, were seeking managers who possessed the skills that James had acquired as a banker. These companies sought general managers, corporate treasurers, and chief financial officers. James hadn't bothered to read these job descriptions because he was thinking in terms of job titles rather than job skills. He also failed to recognize that, even if nobody needed a banker, his skills were sought by other industries. If James had stopped to examine his aptitudes and then had looked for openings that matched his skills instead of his title, he might have discovered the available jobs for which he was qualified.

How to Assess Your Aptitudes

Self-examination can take various forms. You might use the suggestions in this and other books to do some assessment exercises on your own. Or you may wish to undertake more detailed tests that probe your interests and personality. If you don't have access to outplacement advisors who possess these resources, you can visit a college testing center or an independent career counselor.

Regardless of the method used, career advisors agree that some sort of self-assessment is an essential first step in a productive job search.

"The first thing a banker needs to do when he finds he's going to be out of work is to sit down and make an assessment of what he knows how to do," says Fairfax Randolph. Randolph is a former banker who is now president of de Recat and Associates, the San Francisco outplacement firm.

You need to identify what you know how to do, what you do well, what you like to do, and how you think those skills can transfer to other areas, Randolph says. You may start by listing the skills required by each of the jobs you have held. You should try to be as specific as possible and think in terms of concrete accomplishments.

When you break down your job in terms of specific responsibilities and accomplishments, you will discover that you have a variety of skills. These may include several skills, such as budgeting, calculating, negotiating, analyzing, controlling, planning, and supervising, that are transferable to many nonbanking jobs. You may have engaged in this type of self-assessment at earlier stages of your career. Even so, it is important to your job search to conduct a new self-assessment that is as specific as possible with respect to job skills and as expansive as possible with respect to targeted employment possibilities.

During the process of self-assessment, job seekers should also identify the tradeoffs they are willing to make. For example, a banker may be unwilling to move from a certain geographic area. He or she may think: *Okay, in order to stay in banking, I will have to relocate. Since I don't want to relocate, I may have to consider fields other than banking.*

Some bankers are willing to make compromises. Others are not. Whatever your viewpoint, it's important to look at your job search as a set of options and a series of choices.

"It's important to have a Plan B, as well as a Plan A," Randolph says. These plans function best when you attach specific time goals to plan components, he adds. For example, Plan A could involve trying to find a nonbanking job in the city where you live now. Plan B may involve trying to find a banking job somewhere else. The time you spend on Plan A before switching to Plan B is generally determined by your answer to the question: *How long can I afford to look for a job?*

Randolph says most of the executives he sees are realistic about making tradeoffs, particularly if they are more attached to their geographic area than to banking.

"If you are being realistic, you know that in order to get a senior-level job with a financial institution, you may need to be flexible geographically," he says. "For instance, if you want to stay in banking but refuse to leave the city where you live now, you may be in for a long search."

As you evaluate your skills and decide what is important to you, a new set of career options may become apparent. For example, if you decide not to move you may consider working for a smaller bank or in the financial services industry. That's fine, Randolph says. But what other options do you have? Outplacement experts agree that bankers should think of themselves in broad terms — not just as bankers, but as professional managers whose acquired skills are useful beyond banking.

"There are a lot of horizons that people can explore if they get out of the 'I am what I do' niche," Randolph says. For example, a laid-off senior banker like James could discover that he is qualified for several corporate financial positions by thinking of himself in the following manner: *I've been a lender. I've supervised the bank's corporate banking division. Maybe I could be a treasurer of a company, or maybe a CFO. When I worked as a senior vice president, 300 people reported to me. I've had profit-and-loss responsibility. Come to think of it, I'm a good general manager. I could run a company.*

Many bankers will be able to identify their skills quickly, while others may need to give it more thought. The self-assessment process will help bankers confirm known skills and recognize additional skills they may not have previously identified, says Don Stevens, executive vice president of Drake Beam Morin International, a leading outplacement firm. For example, a banker may be admired by colleagues for the ability to quickly digest and analyze financial data without realizing the value and uniqueness of this skill. He or she may assume everyone is able to analyze data as quickly.

Stevens suggests a simple self-assessment exercise. On a sheet of paper, list thirty to forty accomplishments. Include everything you feel you have achieved — both in and out of banking. Then create two columns and dissect those accomplishments. In one column, list the skills required to achieve them. In the other column, describe your degree of interest in each area of accomplishment and how you feel about it. For example, you may list as an accomplishment the ability to put together a commercial loan. In the next column, write the skills needed to put together a commercial loan. You may list:

- *Ability to "read" people.*
- *Ability to make a friend.*
- *Ability to analyze numbers.*
- *Ability to analyze a project as a whole.*
- *Ability to communicate with the borrower and the lending institution.*

Then, think about other professions in which these skills are important. This exercise can be enhanced by feedback from friends or colleagues, Stevens says. Bankers typically know their communities; as a result, they have access to people in a broad range of businesses. Bankers should use their networks to assist them in the self-assessment process.

For example, you might sit down with a colleague or friend whose knowledge and opinions you respect. Explain that you are not asking for a job but that you are doing some serious self-assessment and would like a friend's feedback. Then describe your evaluation of your accomplishments, skills, and interests and ask: "Does my assessment resemble me?"

This can be a very positive activity, Stevens says. Your friend will be flattered to be asked for his or her opinion. Your friend's agreement with your assessment of yourself may validate what you have already concluded. He or she may even be able to name additional traits that you haven't considered. After you have reviewed your accomplishments, skills, and interests with him or her, ask: "Do these skills match any job opportunities that you are aware of?" Sometimes, Stevens says, the answer will be "yes."

This type of exercise helped one banker find a job in education, a field that he had identified as an area of interest. The colleague who reviewed his aptitudes had recently heard that a prominent Connecticut college was searching for a treasurer. The banker applied for the job as a result of the lead and got it.

Stevens says the self-assessment process can also help you adjust psychologically by switching your focus from the loss of your job to the next stage of the job search process. Later, you will use the information you discover through self-assessment in resumes and interviews. As a job candidate, you will face difficult questions from hiring executives about your abilities. You won't be able to convince others of your abilities until you yourself know what they are.

"Think of it as bringing a product to market," Stevens says. "First, you have to know the product. Second, you have to know how to market and package this new product. Then you launch the sales process."

Remember James? When James evaluated his skills, he realized that a number of options were open to him. Sitting in his living room, he asked himself these questions:

- *What kind of work have I done?*
- *What are my specific skills and accomplishments?*
- *What were the written and unwritten requirements of my previous jobs?*
- *What did I like and dislike about my previous jobs?*
- *Would I like to do something different?*
- *How do my values and personality traits influence my work?*
- *What sacrifices am I willing to make to get another good job?*

The act of evaluating his previous jobs and responsibilities empowered James by reminding him of his accomplishments and skills. He considered the specific responsibilities outlined in his job description: managing a division of 300 employees, overseeing all aspects of corporate banking, preparing the financial documents necessary to satisfy federal regulators, etc.

He also considered some other tasks, including mentoring and training new employees, which were not part of his formal job description. He then identified those aspects of his job that he had liked and disliked. He assessed his personality and reviewed the notes he had made about himself.

Meanwhile, James and his wife decided that staying in North Carolina near their families was more important than James's staying in banking. They decided that James would spend two months searching for a job in the city where they lived before enlarging his search to include jobs within a sixty-mile radius of their home.

When James next reviewed employment ads he discovered that there were several nonbanking jobs that he would enjoy and could perform well. He decided to apply for the following four:

- Senior finance manager of a utility company in his city. "Successful candidate will have ten to fifteen years of experience in a diversified financial management position, including accounting, budgeting, cash management, and annual audit preparation; a B.A. degree in finance or a related field; and excellent communication and interpersonal skills."
- Branch manager of a small data processing corporation twenty miles from his home. "You will assist our president in managing our expanding branch operations. Responsibilities include branch profitability and personnel supervision and training. You must have a college degree in business and more than eight years profit-and-loss responsibility in a service company. A hands-on person who can assist our president in the administration of a rapidly ex-

panding service company will find this position very rewarding and promotions rapid."

■ Credit and cash manager for a large appliance manufacturing plant located on the outskirts of his city. "Reporting to the CFO, the successful candidate will maintain the credit operation in the central finance department and be responsible for the central cash management function. Additional duties include cash-flow forecasting, corporate cash management, and long and short-term investments. Candidates should have a thorough knowledge of cash management systems and previous experience in banking or corporate treasury."

■ Chief lending officer of a small bank in his wife's hometown, thirty miles away. "We are seeking a candidate who is knowledgeable in all types of lending, with significant commercial lending experience."

As James pursued these jobs, he concentrated on packaging and presenting himself in a new way. He realized that he would not be given a new job simply because he was a former senior banker. Instead, he presented himself as a professional manager whose banking experience and skills could be valuable in other settings. His presentation was effective. James was offered the banking job in his wife's hometown and the job as finance manager of the utility company. He decided to take the finance manager position. It paid nearly 10 percent more than the other job he was offered. He also liked the fact that he would not have to move his family or endure a long daily commute to take it.

■ FINDING JOBS THAT USE YOUR APTITUDES

Allen Heimer is a banker who performed a thorough self-assessment and used the information he gathered to make a successful career change. He now holds a financial management position with a real estate development and construction firm in Michigan, and his earnings have nearly doubled.

Heimer had worked in banking for two decades in Kansas and Colorado after stints in the military and in manufacturing. In the early 1990s, Heimer was hired to turn around the commercial loan department of a bank in Pontiac, Michigan. But when the Resolution Trust Corporation (RTC) stepped in only six months after he had begun his new job as first vice president, Heimer knew it was time to start looking for another job. He spent several weeks reviewing his career and assessing his aptitudes. His approach followed three basic steps.

- He analyzed his current situation and the market conditions around him.
- He assessed his skills, aptitudes, and accomplishments and determined ways to employ them outside banking.
- He identified a few target industries and researched jobs in those fields.

Analyze the Current Situation and Market Conditions

Heimer had the advantage of being able to look for a job while he was already employed, but he felt some urgency because the RTC had already stepped in. He was worried because he knew that he would be competing with lots of bankers who were unemployed. He had heard horror stories of bankers who were offered jobs at very low salaries, but he didn't take these stories at face value because he trusted his skills and experience. Still, he decided to consider work in fields other than banking.

"I did not dislike banking," he says. "But what I saw coming was an end to banking as we know it. I didn't think my future was in banking. I made a conscientious effort to define my skills and take those skills outside banking."

Heimer also remembered and applied a maxim he had heard early

in his career: "The only report card for a company is its financial statement." Heimer knew that no one can adjust that report card better than
a banker.

Assess Skills and Aptitudes

Heimer set out to analyze his career in terms of specific tasks and
accomplishments. He spent several weeks on the project and was as
thorough as possible.

"I pulled out the job descriptions for the last three or four jobs I'd
had and went through and identified the skills they required and then
identified the experience level of each of those skills," he says.

As he reviewed his career, Heimer realized that he had developed
a broad base of skills, both in and out of banking. He had been drafted
into the Army in 1965 when he was a college student. After his dis-
charge from the military and his graduation from the University of Nebraska, he worked in management at a potato chip plant in Kansas.
But he disliked the work and switched to banking at the suggestion of
a former Army superior, who referred him to a banker friend.

Heimer went through a management training program at the
Kansas bank and did graduate work in commercial lending. Later, he
transferred to Colorado and took over the commercial lending department of a bank there. Then he switched banks and headed the marketing department of a competing bank. After six years as a vice president and commercial lender, he moved to Denver and worked as a
special assets lender at a bank for three years. From there he went to
work for the FDIC in Denver for two years before being hired to turn
around the commercial loan department of the Michigan bank.

On paper, Heimer listed specific skills he had acquired during his
career, such as commercial lending, special assets and loan review, experience in cash management, trusts, marketing, and economic analysis. Although he didn't consider himself strong in computer skills, he
had a working knowledge of computers and listed them as a skill. He

had much better marketing skills and liked marketing. He described his skills as: "Computers: minus, Marketing: plus."

Heimer defined his style of management and his approach to dealing with people. He also analyzed the interests and activities he had pursued outside of work. After spending several weeks outlining his professional life, Heimer asked a few friends to review his thoughts and to tell how they viewed his abilities. As a result of such sessions, Heimer was able to determine how he could apply his skills to other industries.

Identify Target Industries

Based on his assessment of his skills and aptitudes and his discussions with colleagues, Heimer thought he might be able to transfer his skills to a financial management position in manufacturing or education, or to a law or accounting firm.

He researched each potential field of employment in the library and read the trade publications pertinent to each. He contacted people he knew who worked in each area and set up meetings with them to discuss how he could find job vacancies.

Heimer's research paid off and led to several interviews. He interviewed for positions at an automotive component manufacturing plant and at accounting and law firms that were seeking administrators with his financial background. He interviewed for a bank president's job and for the position of community relations director at a small California university. Meanwhile, he was approached by a real estate development firm that was seeking someone with his financial experience. Although real estate development wasn't one of the industries that Heimer had targeted, he considered the idea. Key to his decision was the fact that his earnings would increase 70 percent.

Heimer took the real estate job in January 1992 and began studying construction, since he knew little about this industry except its financial side. Today he handles project financing and is the project manager for two projects. He negotiates with attorneys and government agencies, attends planning commission and city council meetings, and handles other cash management functions for the company.

Heimer says bankers must consider tradeoffs. Although his salary increased dramatically with his new job, the benefits were a "major change," he says. "Bankers have a lot of time off. But in the real world, you don't." While Heimer used to have four weeks' annual vacation as a banker, now he has only one.

Heimer believes that many bankers could transfer their skills to rewarding jobs outside banking. "Once they consider the fact that a manager is a manager, a lot of people in banking could go out and make more money working in other sectors. I think they might find that if they will take the time to do a self-assessment and not brood over the past, they may be very pleasantly surprised," he says.

■ CHANGING CAREERS

Heimer is a banker who was able to channel his banking skills into a new career. However, it took more than a simple self-assessment to do so. Heimer was motivated, determined, and confident that his skills could transfer to another industry.

Most displaced bankers continue to search for jobs within banking. Don Stevens estimates that while 37 percent of banking candidates look at other industries, only 15 percent actually make an industry change. Many bankers who switch careers later view their exit from banking as a blessing in disguise. But bankers don't always experience a smooth transition.

Melissa Webb, who recruits bankers for Dunhill, Inc., an executive search firm in Kalamazoo, Michigan, says many displaced bankers want to leave banking because its security has vanished. But, she says, they discover that employers tend to be wary of them because they aren't immediately qualified to work in another field.

"Sometimes bankers are seen as being ultraconservative," she says. "There is a perception that bankers, as a group, can analyze things but can't make a decision. I think bankers need to demonstrate that that is not the case. They need to demonstrate that they have sales skills as well as analytical skills, and that they can make good decisions."

Fairfax Randolph says that bankers need "a certain amount of repackaging and marketing" in order to switch careers. "If you move from banking and want to market high-tech products and electronics, a hiring official will ask, 'What do you know about our product?' That's a hurdle to overcome, and people have to understand how to bridge that gap. They should also realize that when they try to switch industries, that other industry may have some preconceptions about bankers that need to be addressed and overcome," Randolph says.

"When people think of bankers, what comes to mind is a commercial loan officer," he continues. "But bankers run the gamut of disciplines, as with any industry. These range from management of information systems to human resources, marketing, general management, and finance and control. All those disciplines are parts of banking, too."

Bankers can make successful transitions to new careers, but there are several important considerations inherent in making a career change. Dr. William Roiter, the Boston psychologist, estimates that a displaced banker will spend at least four to six months finding a new banking job and twice that amount of time if he or she changes careers.

"If you really want to make a career change, think about it while you're still a banker," he advises. "You may need to reorganize your finances. You may need retraining or more education. If you can plan your career change while you still are employed, you can save the money you might need to fund a career switch," he says. "You can also acquire the education you will need, and spend your vacation time going to national conferences related to the new field."

"People can change careers at any point, but it's not easy," says Nancy Seever, vice president in charge of First Chicago's career consulting center. "They really have to have the determination and the energy to do it. If somebody said to me, 'Three years from now I want to drastically change careers,' I would say, 'Save your money so you don't have to work for a year. And plan on spending the year pounding the pavement. Look at yourself physically; be sure to present the image you want. Start making friends in other industries. But don't wait until you've lost your job to do it.' If you are good at your job, you need to look at what you did well, and then look for industries that can use those skills," she says.

Unfortunately, many bankers receive little advance notice of their dismissal and, therefore, have little time to plan. This doesn't make it impossible to change careers, however. If you are an unemployed banker who wants to make a career change, you might compromise by taking a short-term, "transitional" banking job that allows you to support yourself while you acquire the skills and education needed to implement your career change. Deborah, a Texas banker who had specialized in marketing, did just that.

Throughout the 1980s, Deborah regretted that she had not gone into healthcare administration, considered one of the hottest career paths of that decade. As she watched healthcare evolve into a highly specialized field, Deborah realized that to switch into healthcare administration she would need to obtain more education and experience. When she was laid off from her job at a Texas bank, she took a job at a smaller bank. Her plan was to stay there for two years while acquiring the skills necessary to enable her to switch to a job with a healthcare center. Although she took a 12 percent cut in pay, she was happy to get another job with fewer responsibilities and more flexible hours that would allow her to devote the necessary time to her class work.

Deborah enrolled in night courses at a local college and studied hospital management and healthcare economics. She used her contacts to help arrange informational interviews and lunches with administrators from each of the hospitals in her area. She also volunteered to serve on the board of a community health center in a low-income neighborhood. Throughout the process, Deborah was conscious of the need to network, and she took advantage of every opportunity that presented itself to expand her list of contacts.

When she was assigned to write papers for her courses, Deborah chose topics that she felt would expand her knowledge of the health-care job market. These also gave her an excuse to introduce herself to hospital executives who might be in a position to hire her eventually. For one class assignment, she evaluated the marketing campaigns for four major hospitals in Houston. Instead of doing an analysis of the advertisements, she decided to meet the executives who created the campaigns. She wrote a letter to the presidents of all four hospitals, explaining her project and asking them to expect a call from her. When she telephoned, she was referred to the appropriate executive in each hospital's marketing department.

When, during her interviews, Deborah made it a point to mention that she was planning a career change, her interviewers were generous with information. Some even referred her to hiring executives at their hospitals.

Deborah followed up on this networking. At the end of her research, she wrote to the president of each hospital to share the results of her study. The project earned her an "A" for the class and expanded her network of contacts in the healthcare industry.

As her knowledge, experience, and network of contacts grew, Deborah applied for positions as credit manager of a health maintenance organization, administrator of a six-person orthopedic practice, and assistant marketing director of a hospital. When she was offered the job at the medical practice, she accepted it because she felt it would make the best use of her skills and provide a good opportunity to enter the healthcare field.

Deborah's networking skills, tenacity, and creativity paid off. When she was ready to change careers, her preparation and contacts led her to the executives who had the authority to hire her. As we will see in the next chapter, it only takes one such contact to land a job.

3

ALL IT TAKES IS ONE

■ ■ ■

Banking employment statistics, at least at first glance, are depressing. Tens of thousands of bankers have already been dismissed from their jobs, and some analysts predict that banks may eliminate 250,000 additional jobs by the end of the decade. It is discouraging to search for a job when the forecast is so negative. But you don't need thousands of jobs. You need only one.

Despite the statistics, many banks are still hiring. In fact, most banks are still hiring, at least in specific areas and departments. If you have evaluated your aptitudes and have decided to stay in banking, you can start your search for a new job by consulting the "Geographic Directory of the 500 Largest U.S. Banks" in the Appendix section of this book, which lists, by state and city, the names, addresses, phone numbers, and hiring executives for the top 500 U.S. banks.

Your decision to stay in banking is not unusual. As we have seen, bankers who transfer their skills to other industries are the exceptions and not the rule. Don Stevens, executive vice president of Drake Beam Morin International, the country's largest outplacement firm, estimates that only 15 percent of displaced bankers will switch industries.

Whether you stay in banking or switch to a nonbanking job, you probably will be tempted to start with a list of the ten largest employers in the geographic area or industry you prefer and submit resumes to them. This is not a bad idea, of course, but you should remember that everybody else may be doing the same thing. Realize, too, that in the current employment environment, many larger employers are cutting back on personnel or, if not cutting jobs, shrinking by attrition.

For these reasons, you should include in your job search the healthy small and medium-sized companies that abound in most parts of the country. Small companies are especially promising for former bankers because they grow. When they do, they find that they need financial types like treasurers, comptrollers, accountants, and bookkeepers.

Remember that although you need to find only one job, in order to do so, you will need to make your job search as expansive as possible. If you have worked as a banker for some time you probably have lost touch with the job-search process. Therefore, you should plan your strategy carefully.

You can't wait for the jobs to come looking for you; you must actively search for them. Job hunting involves much more than applying for jobs advertised in the newspaper and waiting for your phone to ring. You need to keep as many irons in the fire as possible and make your job search as creative as you can.

"I've always had a hard time getting bankers to be more expansive in terms of the job search," says Joe Meissner, president of Power Marketing, a San Francisco outplacement firm. "I find that bankers are too conservative in terms of the numbers of contacts they are willing to make in the marketplace, too conservative in the number of options they consider, and too quick to say that something's not going to work," he says.

Meissner, a former Texas Tech University marketing professor, teaches job seekers to approach the job search as if they were trying to market a product for Procter and Gamble.

"It can be difficult to get a banker to use a high-exposure, wide-ranging marketing campaign that goes through a number of channels," Meissner says. Bankers, by the nature of their profession, are averse to taking risks and generally not adventurous enough in their job-seeking strategy, he says. "I think the first thing job-seeking bankers need is complete retraining in the area of risk," he says. "The problems I have with bankers result from the fact that they are too tentative and conservative."

Avoiding risk may have helped a banker succeed as a lender, but a banker needs to be willing to take risks during a job search, Meissner says. He encourages his job hunters to develop creative, innovative approaches. Consider the tactic used by one of Meissner's candidates, a corporate executive who learned that his job would be eliminated in a few months. The executive drove his car across the San Francisco Bay Bridge to his job downtown each day. Like other Bay Area commuters, he frequently picked up passengers so that he could use the bridge's special express lane for carpoolers. He turned these carpools into job networking opportunities. Each morning the executive stopped outside the Bay Area Rapid Transit station, where the carpools assembled, and tried to select two successful-looking executives for his carpool. As they drove to San Francisco, the executive told his passengers that he was looking for a job and asked if they knew of any opportunities. The passengers provided several job leads, and his network of San Francisco business contacts mushroomed within weeks. Two of the leads from passengers resulted in job offers. He eventually accepted one of them, for a position with a shipping company.

You may be impressed with this executive's creativity, but as the job market fills with former bankers looking for jobs, most job hunters will have to develop innovative strategies, Meissner says.

Consider another of Meissner's ideas, which, he admits, is unconventional. He proposes that displaced bankers use their severance packages to finance a career change.

"Why not use your former employer's money to fund your next career move?" he asks. You could employ such a strategy whether you choose to remain in banking, switch industries, or start your own business, Meissner says. For example, if you decide to leave banking, choose the industry you want to work in, Meissner suggests. "Then, pick a small or medium-sized company and approach one of its executives. Make him or her a business proposition. Offer to work for a secretary's salary, or for free, for a certain length of time." This approach allows you to get your foot in the door of a company you hope will eventually employ you. Once you are in, you must negotiate a full-time position at a fair salary, but you can live off your former employer's money until you do, Meissner says.

"The smart banker is going to cut his losses really early. He's going to have to work for ridiculous wages at first, but he's going to be ahead of the pack in the long run."

Another option is to use your severance pay to launch your own business, Meissner suggests. "Take your thirty to sixty days to decide that you're not going to be a banker any more. Then spend the next thirty days doing your due diligence. Go out and find that franchise, or use your severance to fund that business."

Regardless of the approach you use, Meissner says you shouldn't "spend six months floundering around and getting stale, or you'll end up beating your head against the wall." You can afford to be adventurous when you are still being paid by your former employer, but you can't afford to be as adventurous after you've been jobless for several months and have spent most of your severance pay, he warns.

Of course, there are ways to get your foot in a company's door without working for free or transporting strangers in your car. You can also apply a creative approach to traditional job-searching activities like researching and networking.

■ REVIEWING RESEARCH SKILLS

Many bankers and executives from other industries have rusty research skills. This is a serious drawback, because in the information age, the best jobs will go to the candidates who are best informed. There are many ways to obtain information for a job search, and even a single item of information can result in a job lead, an interview, and, finally, a job offer. Again, it takes only one.

Allen Heimer, whom we met in chapter 2, is an example of a banker who used the resources of his public library to research prospective employers. Heimer read widely in newspapers, business magazines, trade journals, and industry newsletters. While researching jobs in education, for example, Heimer read the *Chronicle of Higher Education* and found a lead for the position of community relations director of a small California university. The lead resulted in an interview. Although Heimer was not chosen for this position, his research skills helped him land other interviews in each of the industries he had targeted.

Unfortunately, most bankers lack Heimer's research skills. Consider the case of Forrest, who was a vice president of a large regional bank. Forrest went to the library but he didn't know where to find the material that could have helped him, and he was too embarrassed to seek a librarian's help. As a result, he ended up "on safari" in the library.

Forrest had spent most of his career in an office tower only three blocks away from the library, but he had rarely visited it. Although he read two or three newspapers a day, plus the banking magazines and newsletters that came across his desk, he had done little research for himself. The library was unfamiliar territory.

In the main lobby of the library, which had once housed the card catalog, Forrest saw people punching information into computer terminals. In the reference department, he found machines for reading microfilm and microfiche and more computers. Forrest felt intimidated by this technology and his lack of familiarity with it. Instead of seeking help from the reference librarian, who was helping four students, he retreated to the periodicals section and browsed through some business magazines. Then he left.

Later, Forrest's daughter quizzed him about his experience. "Did you use the Infotrac?" she asked. "Infowhat?" he responded.

Forrest's daughter explained that Infotrac is an automated system that enables users to access a large number of magazines and business publications. If you are researching credit unions, she explained, you can find dozens of articles by typing "credit unions." Infotrac will then produce a list of titles of magazine articles about credit unions. The user can select interesting articles and view them on microfilm cartridges.

Computerized information systems, available in many public libraries, index several hundred publications and eliminate the need for a job seeker to spend hours poring through magazines for information about a specific company. Many job seekers use Infotrac to research companies and industries. The really good news is that a librarian can teach you to use the system in less than five minutes.

By avoiding the librarian, Forrest isolated himself from the person who could have helped him most. Librarians say they see many people like Forrest — educated professionals who don't use the library and, therefore, don't realize how it can help them.

"A lot of people don't know what the library has to offer. The library is probably the best resource for their job search," says Cheri Gay, of the Detroit Public Library's Career and Employment Information Center.

Although many people are familiar with their nearest branch library, they may feel lost and intimidated when they go to the main library. The Detroit Public Library is one of several libraries around the country that have special departments and librarians for job seekers. But all public libraries can help a job seeker find information about companies, industries, and other career-related topics.

Some materials serve as basic tools in any informed job search. These materials, most of which can be found in any sizable library, fall into several categories:

■ General career guides. This category includes general job-search handbooks; the *Directory of Occupational Titles*, published by the U.S. Department of Labor's Employment and Training Administration; the *Job Hunter's Sourcebook*, a comprehensive guide to sources of information about industries and careers; and *The Encyclopedia of Careers and Vocational Guidance.*

■ Resume and interviewing books. There are a number of books that deal specifically with the preparation of resumes and cover letters and interviews. (chapters 4 and 5 of this book also deal with these topics.)

At libraries with special career information centers, you may find a librarian who is qualified to critique your resume. This is not something that most libraries are prepared to do, however.

■ Business directories. Libraries will have a variety of information and lists about local businesses. They will also have more comprehensive guides to U.S. employers, such as *The Wall Street Journal Index*, the Moody's manuals, Standard and Poor's industry surveys, the *Thomas Register of American Manufacturers*, and the *U.S. Industrial Outlook.*

Library reference departments will also have specialized guides to corporations, manufacturers, government agencies, universities, and associations and organizations. Tell your librarian what you are seeking, and he or she will refer you to the appropriate guide or index.

Libraries may also have information about jobs in other communities. For example, if you are considering moving to another city, see if your library has any of the JobBank guides to eighteen major U.S. job markets. These books contain a great deal of information about key employers in each city. There are also a number of books available that profile companies according to certain criteria, such as *The 100 Best Companies to Work For In America,* and *The Best Companies for Women.*

■ Miscellaneous. Many job seekers use the out-of-town newspapers and telephone directories that are available at public libraries.

While both are valuable resources, it can often take hours to scour the classifieds for appropriate positions. In 1996, a publication was launched that solves this problem for people with a banking or financial services background. *Jobs for Bankers* calls itself "the banking industry's employment weekly," and contains a listing of positions available in banking and in jobs in which a banking background would be useful. It includes more than a hundred U.S. metropolitan markets. The publication also has an online counterpart, located at http://www.bankjobs.com. The online database contains thousands of jobs, and is updated twice each week so that positions stay current. Free sample copies of the print publication are available; call 800/999-6497 to request a copy.

In addition to daily newspapers and specialized employment publications like *Jobs for Bankers*, local business publications are a valuable but often overlooked resource. In the last few years, almost every city has spawned a weekly newspaper that does a better job of covering local businesses than most business sections of major city newspapers. These business journals generally excel in spotlighting companies that are doing very well and that are, as a result, hiring. The journals are also good sources for information on companies that are moving to town or expanding their facilities. And, because they tend to feature personalities, reading them may enable you to gain some useful information about the likes and dislikes of the company's management.

Another valuable feature of business newspapers is their business data pages that list new incorporations, building permits, new leases, and other information that can be helpful in a job search. Many out-of-town business newspapers are available on Infotrac.

In addition, telephone directories frequently contain information about a city and its businesses in special sections between the residential listings and the Yellow Pages. Valuable information can also be found in a library's vertical files. These files contain material that the library receives in the mail or through other sources. You may find brochures, articles, and clippings about a wide variety of topics in these files. Even if this information is outdated, you can contact the organization for more current information.

In addition, a typical major city library might refer readers to the following publications:

- *Places Rated Almanac: Your Guide To Finding the Best Places To Live In America*
- *Encyclopedia of Associations, Regional, State and Local Organizations*
- *Gale Directory of Publications*
- *The JobBank Guide to Employment Services: Comprehensive Listings for Executive Search Firms, Employment Agencies/Temporary Help Services, and Resume/Career Counseling Services*

■ Business guides. There are a number of books that are available to help a banker research a company or an industry. Corporate annual reports can be found in a library's business reference department. If you want to obtain a current report, contact the company directly.

Remember to rely on the professionalism, knowledge, and experience of your librarian, who will be glad to help you locate the information you need and will teach you to use the library's resources. But don't expect a librarian to do your research for you. "We're happy to steer people in the right direction," Cheri Gay says. "But it does require some work on their part." Here are some additional tips for library use:

■ Much of the material a job seeker will use is located in the reference department and does not circulate. Therefore, Gay says, you should plan to spend some time in the library.
■ Pay attention to library bulletin boards. The library is a good source of information about community services and activities. You may find notices for support groups that help white-collar workers cope with unemployment. These groups frequently meet in churches or community centers and are likely to post their meeting announcements in libraries.
■ Use trade journals to research industries and companies that you are

considering. An hour spent browsing through the periodicals racks will expose you to dozens of trade journals that you have probably never seen. The news stories, advertisements, and announcements in these publications may yield information that will be valuable to you in your job search.

■ Set concrete goals when using the library. It's O.K. to browse, but if you are going to spend several hours in the library, make sure you leave with some job leads or concrete information, and not just a stack of mystery novels.

■ If you want material that the library does not have, ask the librarian. The library might consider buying the book if funds are available and if the book is likely to interest other readers. Or, your library may be able to obtain the book from another library through an inter-library loan program. To use this service, you would pay the postage and perhaps a small fee to have a library book mailed from another city.

You should not limit your library research to public libraries. In most cities, libraries can be found in universities, government agencies, corporations, and other organizations. Although these libraries are rarely known outside the organizations that maintain them, they may contain specialized information that is not available at public libraries. Your public librarian may know which libraries are available to you.

Libraries at most public universities are open to all residents of the state. Phone the library to see how you can use such a library if you are not a student. You may have to present identification or proof of residency.

Don't rule out libraries of private colleges or universities. Some private institutions allow nonstudents to use their libraries on a limited basis. They may issue guest passes as a one-time courtesy. For more extensive use, some private universities sell visitors' library passes. Business school libraries subscribe to many periodicals and trade publications that are not available at public libraries. A visitor's pass will pay for itself if it enables you to obtain a productive job lead.

Gaining entry to a corporate library may be more difficult, but don't rule it out. For example, if you are interested in researching the computer software industry and there is a major software company located in your area, call to see if the company has a library and if you can arrange a visit. Company policy may prohibit such a visit, but you lose nothing by asking. If you know someone who works at the company, it might be easier to arrange a visit through him or her. Try to visit the coffee machine area; internal job openings may be posted on the bulletin board there.

State government agency libraries also can be valuable resources. Although they are generally open to the public, few people outside the agencies know that the libraries exist. Begin by calling the government agency in your state that handles economic and community development. This department will have a great deal of information about the industries, companies, and communities in your state. It may also have information about companies that are relocating or expanding in your area. If the agency doesn't maintain a library, contact its public information officers and ask how you might otherwise gain access to this information.

Other government agencies with libraries include state departments of planning, transportation, health and environment, and education. These libraries should be open to the public and will have books, periodicals, and documents that you may not be able to find elsewhere. You will also find librarians who are knowledgeable about their respective fields at these specialized libraries. Some libraries may only allow agency employees to check out books, but most will probably grant you reading privileges. To find these libraries, check the government pages of your phone book. Even if you don't find a listing, there still may be a library. Telephone the agency's main number and inquire.

Your library research will increase your knowledge of the job market and will help you gather information about the industry and companies you are considering. The information you gather will also help you to market yourself through networking and other approaches.

■ NETWORKING

Networking is one of the terms you will hear most often during your job search. It is the process of interacting with other people to build business relationships. Even if you didn't call it "networking," you have probably networked throughout your career.

"There are some people who are constantly making contacts as they go through life. They're always writing down names, addresses, and phone numbers. They're always networking. Then there are others who never reach outside of their own offices," says Larry DeMeyers, chief operating officer of Bankers First Savings Bank of Augusta, Georgia. "I have a feeling that if you're the kind of person who just doesn't network well, it's too late to start when you lose your job. We all have to decide who we are. Some of us network easily and some of us don't."

Joe Meissner, the San Francisco outplacement executive, notes that there is a strong correlation between a person's network of contacts and the time it takes to become re-employed. But many professionals — in banking and other industries — fail to realize the importance of networking.

"Basically, networking is selling, and most people are not salesmen," Meissner says. "It's fairly unusual to see a banker or any other candidate who has a ready-made network. The majority of candidates have been focused on their own company and their own industry, and they are not well networked when they start," he says. "Typically they have to start from scratch."

Social scientists have found that networking is such an effective force that most of us could use our personal contacts to help us reach a stranger anywhere in the country with relative ease. Consider what you would do if you were asked to mail a letter to a stranger in Yuba City, Arizona. You are given no address, and you don't know a soul in Yuba

City. You do, however, have an acquaintance in Phoenix. If you mail the letter to this person, there is a good chance that he knows someone in Yuba City, or at least knows someone who knows someone there. A letter traveling through this network could reach its destination quickly.

You can apply the same process to your job search. For example, you may not know the CEO of a company you wish to work for, but perhaps you know someone who knows the CEO and could help arrange a meeting. Similarly, you can gain information for a career change by consulting the members of your network. You may not know anyone who works in computer software marketing, but think of the people in your life who might.

Networking does not mean calling everyone you know and asking for a job. Nor does it mean going to every meeting you hear of, engaging in small talk with whoever will listen, and collecting as many business cards as you can stuff into your pocket. Networking involves building business relationships with people and, in turn, giving them the opportunity to build business relationships with you.

As you may recall from Chapter 1, you should refrain from beginning your networking until you have adjusted to the idea that you have lost your job and you have decided where you are headed in your job search. Classic networking employs some or all of the following approaches:

- Determine what you hope to accomplish through networking. For example, do you want information about a specific company or industry? Would you like a personal introduction to the CEO of a certain bank? You can network for several things at once, but you should keep your networking goals in mind.
- Identify the people in your network who might help you achieve your job-seeking goals. Your immediate network consists of friends, relatives, neighbors, past and present co-workers, people you do business with, play tennis with, worship with, etc. Include

your spouse, your parents, your spouse's parents, your spouse's friends, your parents' friends, etc. Also include your college alumni association and members of professional associations to which you belong. Don't rule out anyone. There are stories of people being referred to job contacts by unlikely sources such as barbers, dentists, and elevator operators. Even strangers at the right place at the right time can become part of your network, as illustrated by the San Francisco executive who networked with his carpool passengers.

- As you consult your network, think carefully about people you have served as a banker. For example, if you are considering a career change, think about the companies with which you conducted business. "Think about which industries you understand. And, if you're a lender, whom you know in that industry. Go talk to those people. This is part of developing a progressive network," says Fairfax Randolph, of the de Recat and Associates outplacement firm.

- Consider former suppliers. "If you want to change careers, the vendors are a good place to look," Meissner says. "Whatever you buy from your vendors, you know the problems of installing, using, and working with that kind of product. You can turn the tables. You can go out and sell, support, service, and train people to use that product."

  Meissner recalls a banker who had specialized in systems applications for a commercial lending unit. This banker had developed many contacts in the banking software area. After she lost her job, she found work as a customer service representative, demonstrating and installing software and teaching its use. Within two years, she was earning twice her salary as a banker.

- Communicate with the people in your network. You must communicate clearly and specifically with your network contacts so that they will be able to describe you accurately to the people in their networks. Tell your networking contacts what type of job you are seeking. Don't make vague statements like "I'm looking for anything. Call me if you hear of anything." You increase the chances that your networking will bring positive results if you are specific.

- When you call on a contact, don't ask for a job. Ask instead for information and more contacts. Remember, your purpose in networking is to obtain information and job leads that eventually will steer you to people who have the authority to hire you. Many candidates ask for referrals to three other individuals who might be able to help them expand their networks. You will be surprised how rapidly your network grows if you follow such an approach.

- Stay organized during networking. Record information from your networking contacts in a list or in a notebook. When you receive someone's business card, take a minute to write notes on the back that will jog your memory about that person. Review your notes and business cards regularly to recall who is in your network. It does no good to have a desk drawer full of business cards if you can't recall the people who gave them to you. Be organized in your approach, whether it's by phone or in person. You may want to prepare a networking "script" to help you get to the point in a polished, professional way.

- Stress the mutuality and reciprocity of networking. "Give as well as get," Stanlee Phelps of Lee Hecht Harrison says. Have something to offer, whether it's an article that may be of interest to them or a personal introduction. "Many people are uncomfortable with networking because they feel that they are begging," she explains. "But if they redefine networking, they will see that it is a mutual and reciprocal process, which has potential to help both parties."

- Aim for face-to-face meetings. Just because somebody says "send me a resume" doesn't mean you should leave it at that. Make an effort to get together with that person. "It's much more powerful face-to-face," Phelps says.

■ Do follow-up after each networking contact. Send a thank-you note after every meeting. This is different from the type of letter you would send after an interview. A networking follow-up can be a handwritten note or a postcard, Phelps says. Keep in touch with each of your contacts to tell him or her the results of each referral.

■ Think of networking as a continuing process. You should view networking as an important tool for building relationships that should continue throughout your career. People need to understand that they should never stop networking, Phelps says. As soon as you get a job, it's important to continue networking. It's an important tool in your professional development and advancement. And if current business trends continue, you may change jobs several more times during your career.

Many executives are natural networkers who meet people and share information on their own. Others find it more difficult and less natural to network. Many of these differences are related to gender. One of the differences between men and women is that women network to build relationships, but men network for specific purposes, Phelps says. She observes that when men have what they want, they tend to drop the relationship or association instead of developing it further. Phelps says, "Men are more interested in 'What can you do for me today?'"

"Men are much more terrified than women at the prospect of networking. They see themselves as leaders who are more used to giving help than asking for it," she maintains. Phelps conducts networking workshops for clients at the Lee Hecht Harrison outplacement firm. She says it is difficult for men to pick up the phone and announce to associates that they are looking for a job. "It's embarrassing for men. The prospect of having to get on the phone and ask somebody for something is horrifying to them. It feels like they've lost their power. It feels like they are begging. And they hate the thought of that."

"I think for men there also is still such a thing as the old boy network," Phelps says. "It's not built necessarily on personal relationships. It's more strategic. It's like, 'You scratch my back, I'll scratch yours.' The way men approach networking is that they call someone if they want something. They feel O.K. if they feel they are in a position to give something back right away. But if they are out of a job, the whole ball game changes." Phelps says women are more relationship-oriented and tend to personalize their experiences more than men. Therefore, they have larger networks. They don't see it as humiliating to admit that they are looking for a job.

Networking Meetings: Working a Room

In addition to networking with people you already know, plan to attend meetings and gatherings held specifically for the purpose of networking. These meetings are announced in the business sections of local newspapers, the *National Business Employment Weekly*, newsletters of professional organizations, and bulletin boards of public libraries and universities.

Consider whether the people who are likely to attend these meetings would be good networking contacts for you. If so, attend the meetings and learn to "work the room." Meissner suggests the following methods:

- Set some personal objectives before attending a networking meeting. These might include gaining job-search leads or learning more about a company, industry, or profession. View a networking meeting as an opportunity to gather job leads, rather than as a social and educational gathering.
- Arrive early and attach your name tag. If there are other tags lying on a table, read them to see who is attending. Target key people you wish to meet.
- Keep moving. Don't stay in one place, and resist the tendency to congregate with people you already know. Of course, you will greet your friends and colleagues, but the purpose of a networking

meeting is to expand your network. Ask your friends to introduce you to anyone you might enjoy meeting, and do the same for them.

■ It is easiest to approach people who are standing alone. Make eye contact, smile, offer your hand, introduce yourself, and tell what you do. Usually, two people will each make their "pitch" and exchange business cards. When deciding how much time to spend with one person, weigh the value of your time against the value of the information you are getting. Meissner generally tries to meet as many people and obtain as many business cards as possible on the assumption that he can develop relationships in follow-up calls. If you find yourself trapped in a non-productive conversation, offer your hand and say "Nice to meet you." Then walk away. Or play the role of a host, and introduce the person to someone else.

■ Even if you are unemployed, make sure you have business cards to distribute. It's not professional to use your old business card with the phone number scratched out. Go to an office supply store or printer and order a simple card with your name, address, and phone number. If you wish, include your profession, such as "marketing specialist." But don't overdo it. "Johnson and Associates, Consultants" may be a little grandiose if you're Johnson, you have yet to perform your first consulting job, and you *have* no associates.

■ OTHER STRATEGIES

Networking is an effective tool that results in many job contacts, but there are other approaches that a candidate should consider. For example, Meissner estimates that about 18 percent of his outplacement clients find their jobs as a result of an introduction or other efforts initiated directly by his firm. Some 22 percent of his candidates find jobs directly through networking contacts. Meanwhile, 25 percent find jobs through classified ads; 15 percent through executive recruiters; 5 percent through targeted mailings; and 2 percent through intermediaries. Some alternatives to networking are described below.

Classified Ads

Lots of people believe that most jobs are found through networking and that only a relatively small percentage of jobs are found through classified ads. In reality, classified ads are one of the best resources for a job search, and it is a mistake to omit them.

You should read the ads in many publications: local newspapers, *The Wall Street Journal*, the *National Business Employment Weekly*, trade publications, and industry newsletters. Read the entire classified section, A through Z, because you never know where an ad will be placed, Meissner says. "Be expansive in terms of the ads you answer," he says. "Answer those that you seem overqualified for, those that you seem underqualified for, and those that seem right on the money." Remember, you are trying to be included — not excluded — as a candidate for jobs.

Classified ads frequently generate more responses than a hiring executive will have time to read. Often the responses are handled by an assistant who has been told to screen the responses according to the qualifications described in the ad. Candidates who appear to have the desired qualifications go in the "Yes" pile. Those who don't will end up in the "No" pile. You can increase your chances of landing in the "Yes" pile if you analyze the ad and tailor your response to reflect the desired job qualifications, Meissner says. "Formulate your response so that the recipient will see that you're a clear match for the job," he says. "We spend a lot of time teaching our candidates how to rewrite an ad response. As transparent as it sounds, it seems to work."

Executive Recruiters

An executive recruiter, or "headhunter," is a consultant who receives his or her fee from an employer who is seeking a candidate with specific skills. You wouldn't expect a company to pay a recruiter to find a candidate whose skills are not proven. For this reason, you should not expect a recruiter to help you change careers. However, although the drop in banking employment has altered the banking recruiting business, if you try to remain in banking, you may still want to work through a recruiter.

Melissa Webb has recruited bankers since 1986 for Dunhill of Kalamazoo, Inc. Because of the decline in banking positions, she has developed a second recruiting specialty; she now also recruits candidates for the environmental engineering and health and technology fields. "When I started in the banking industry in 1986, I was probably taking an average of three new job orders a week. Now it's maybe one every three weeks, if that," she says. Her searches are now evenly divided between banking and technology positions.

Webb says it's important for a candidate to be candid with recruiters. "If a candidate has already blanketed a certain geographical area with resumes, it is important for them to share that information with a recruiter," she says. Nothing is more embarrassing for a recruiter than to phone the hiring official of a company to discuss a candidate, only to discover that the candidate has already sent his or her resume directly, Webb says. "It makes the candidate look ridiculous, and it angers the placement consultant because the candidate is not being up front with them," she says.

Webb says recruiters also have obligations to be candid and to tell a candidate: "I haven't seen anything in your particular field for three months. But I will keep you in my active file in case such a position becomes available."

Meissner cautions bankers against limiting their contacts to two or three recruiters. "You don't get lots of shelf space if you're limiting your exposure to a few people," he says.

Direct Mail

Mailing resumes to a list of targeted companies and following up with phone calls is a time-consuming approach, Meissner says, but it is frequently effective and accounts for 5 percent of his candidates'

job placements. If you decide you want to work in a certain manufacturing industry, obtain a list of 100 manufacturers and write to the
CEO — or the executive you feel would be in a position to hire you —
of each of those companies. Saturate the market, he says. And when
possible, use a "hook" line such as "I recently read about your company in *Inc.* magazine."

Meissner says one risk manager from a utility company did a mailing to all the CEOs of the Fortune 1000 Companies and followed up
with phone calls. He was hired for a job with a subsidiary of one of
the companies that had initially turned him down. The candidate's persistence landed him one of the few available risk manager jobs in the
country, Meissner explains, since companies have been shedding risk
managers instead of hiring them.

Phoning a CEO may bring mixed results. You may find that you
cannot get past the receptionist and the executive may be "in a meeting" every time you call. You won't know if your tenacity is viewed as
an annoyance or if it distinguishes you from the dozens of other people who sent in their resumes but failed to follow up. If you call before
or after business hours, a CEO may answer his or her own phone. Or,
if you are persistent and polite, the secretary may sympathize with you
and make sure the boss returns your call.

Meissner says he gets several unsolicited resumes in the mail each
week. He doesn't have time to respond to each of them, but he keeps
them in a "slush pile" in a credenza behind his desk.

"When someone calls, I can take out their resume and read it for
the first time. I try to help them with a job lead if I can. Occasionally,
maybe once a year, I'll hire somebody," he says. In cases like this,
sending a resume isn't enough to make the connection. Following up
with a phone call makes the resume — and the candidate — come to
life.

Intermediaries

Remember Allen Heimer, the banker who took a job with a real estate development company? His job connection was made through the company's lawyer, who served as an intermediary. When the lawyer learned his client company was seeking someone for a financial management job, he recommended Heimer, a business acquaintance.

Many professional firms that serve a broad base of clients, such as law firms, accountants, investment bankers, and venture capital firms, often know when a client is seeking someone for a position. Their recommendation of a candidate can carry weight. If you present yourself to these intermediaries, it may pay off. Meissner says accounting firms frequently compile lists of available job candidates and available openings at client firms. "If you know one of the partners, he can get you into that pool," Meissner says.

In addition, remember that accounting firms and law firms also could be potential employers. When Heimer was looking for a job, he found that several accounting and law firms were seeking candidates with financial management experience for positions in their own firms.

SECTION II

■ ■ ■

Success Is the
Best Solution

4

YOUR RESUME

■ ■ ■

A resume won't get you a job, but if it presents your accomplishments and skills in a favorable way it can land you a job interview. You may have kept your resume current throughout your career, but does it portray you in the most favorable light? If you're like most executives, it could probably stand some improvement.

Take a good, long look at your resume — think of it as a sales brochure for your job search. When you last updated it, you probably thought it was a flattering summary of your qualifications. You were probably satisfied with it. But did you consider it from an employer's perspective?

Try reading your resume as though you were a potential boss evaluating a stranger. Would your resume impress someone who didn't know you? Does it explain how you can make your boss's life easier, and how his or her company could benefit by hiring you? Would it make him or her want to interview you? If not, your resume needs to be overhauled.

Peter Veruki has reviewed thousands of resumes — as a former recruiter for Chemical Bank and in his current position as director of career planning and placement for Vanderbilt University's Owen Graduate School of Management.

"A good resume should do two things up front," Veruki says.

"First, it should tease the reader to know more about you. It should not, and cannot, tell the whole story. It has to grab the reader's attention. Like the headlines in *The New York Times*, it should tease the reader. A resume should entice a reader to pick up the phone."

"Second, the resume should guide the reader," Veruki says.

Does your current resume tease or entice a reader to find out more about you? Does it guide the reader through your objectives and accomplishments, and does it suggest what you could accomplish for a future employer?

If you're like most professionals, your resume and cover letter are weak in some areas. Employment managers and career counselors say effective resumes and cover letters always share the following characteristics:

- Strong content that communicates to a prospective employer how your objectives, accomplishments, and skills could benefit his or her company.
- An attractive, professional appearance that will impress the prospective employer who skims it and encourage the employer to read it carefully and arrange an interview.
- A thoughtfully conceived strategy that targets your resume to specific companies, achieved by the skillful use of cover letters that tailor your abilities to the requirements of a particular job.

In your haste to become re-employed, you may be tempted simply to tack a paragraph onto the top of your trusty college resume. Don't let your anxiety to find another job cause you to underestimate the importance of a resume and the need to spend time improving it.

"Every time you do a resume, you may need to redo the whole thing," advises Lynn Nemser, a former corporate employment manager who is president of Partners in Performance, a human resources consulting firm in Pittsburgh. "You'll see some excellent resumes and some absolutely horrid resumes," Nemser says. "Some people don't realize how important the resume and customized cover letter are."

As you redo your resume, remember that you need to do more than portray your work history in an organized, attractive fashion. You must present your accomplishments in such a way that they will convince a reader that your skills could transfer directly to a job with his or her company.

Tom Markovich is a former banker who made a successful career change after managing bank branches in suburban Chicago. After fourteen years of banking, Markovich became dissatisfied with the profession and decided to switch careers. He realized that banking had given him a strong base of management skills, and he sought a job in business. He was first hired as the administrator of an accounting firm. A year later he became a policy analyst for the National Association of Realtors in Chicago. Markovich networked heavily during this time with people in other industries. His contacts helped him learn how to convince prospective employers that he was more than just a banker.

"I firmly believe that no matter how impressive your resume or how varied your skills, you tend to be pigeonholed in a certain field," he says. "My resume reeked of banking. It definitely looked like banking in spite of the fact that I had sales skills, human resources skills, and other management skills."

When Markovich applied for the position with an accounting firm, he revised his resume and played up his accounting background, quantitative skills, and course work toward his M.B.A. This emphasis helped employers think of him in a broader light.

Your resume is the tool that enables you to communicate your skills more broadly. Before you review your resume with an eye to improving it, it is helpful to familiarize yourself with the structure and appearance of an effective resume and to consider how it will be evaluated.

■ HOW YOUR RESUME WILL BE USED

Imagine what happens to your resume when it arrives in the

office of a company that has advertised an interesting job opening. Remember, there are many qualified bankers and executives from other industries who are out of work, and your resume may be only one of hundreds that arrive in the mail in a given week. All these resumes will be skimmed quickly; those failing to convey the qualifications sought for a specific opening will be weeded out. Some companies employ large human resources staffs to review resumes or store them on computer for later evaluation. At other companies, resumes may be screened by individuals who have many additional responsibilities and little time to devote to resumes. Regardless of the system used, your resume may be judged in a matter of seconds, so it is essential that it makes a good first impression.

"You really don't have that many opportunities to impress an employer," Lynn Nemser says. "The resume and cover letter may be your only chance." When your resume crosses an employer's desk, if it doesn't ring a bell, it gets placed in a stack — never to be looked at again.

"Most professionals will skim a resume in thirty seconds," Nemser adds. "That's a horrible fact for people to hear, but it's true."

Your qualifications may be strong, but if they do not leap off the page in thirty seconds, your resume may not get a second look. No one will linger over your resume and try to imagine how your skills will match up with his or her organization. It is no easy task to decide which of your skills and accomplishments will interest someone who doesn't know you.

"Writing a resume can be a very threatening process," Nemser says. "It's like being asked to put your whole life on paper. For people who are used to having plaques on the wall and their accomplishments written about in the newspaper, it can be very difficult to put their life on one page."

Fortunately, you can study basic resume structures and modify them to fit your purposes.

■ WHICH TYPE OF RESUME — CHRONOLOGICAL OR FUNCTIONAL?

There are two basic resume structures: chronological and functional. You probably are most familiar with the chronological resume format. This type of resume outlines your work history and education over a specific period of time. A functional resume, which is the type frequently employed by career changers, emphasizes your specific skills and achievements instead of when and where you attained them.

Although the chronological resume format is most widely recommended for displaced workers who are initiating a job search, you should examine various resume structures used by friends, colleagues, and people in your network. There are several good books about resume preparation that will suggest modifications of the two basic formats, as well as more creative approaches to resumes. As you evaluate various resume formats, try to determine which structure will work best for *you*.

As your job search advances, you will learn that different types of resumes can help you achieve different goals. For example, your initial goal is to get interviews, and your first resume should be designed for that specific purpose. Once you have arranged an interview, you can write an expanded resume to present your qualifications to an interviewer in greater detail. In this expanded resume, you can focus on the skills you feel are most pertinent to the position for which you are applying. Similarly, if you are applying for jobs in several industries, you may wish to prepare a resume for each industry. For example, if you are considering jobs in banking, you may prepare a "banking resume" that would play up your experience as a lender. For jobs in sales and marketing, you could prepare a "sales and marketing" resume that would play up the customer service aspects of your banking experience.

"The most important thing to do is to tailor your resume to the job you're applying for," Tom Markovich says. "I thought it was a joke when people said they had fifty different resumes on a floppy disk and could alter them according to the job they were interviewing for, but that's exactly what you have to do."

The chronological resume is recommended if you are beginning your job search because it will help the person who skims it determine what you are doing now and what you have accomplished in recent years. If you are invited to interview, it is appropriate to give the interviewer a functional resume, organized by skill categories instead of chronologically, Peter Veruki of Vanderbilt University says.

"A short, hard-hitting resume is what you lead off with," Veruki says. "This is what you do your fishing with, and what you pass along to people in the job market. It should be one, or maybe one and a half pages, but not more than two or three pages. After you've hooked them a little bit, there's a place for a more detailed curriculum vitae. This can be a three-page resume that you can present in an interview."

"I reviewed resumes for twenty years and I have always preferred a chronological resume," Veruki says. "I never liked having to figure out, *Where is this person now?* With a functional resume, you read through a person's accomplishments, but you still don't know what the person is doing *now* — whether he is working, or going to graduate school or what. The person reading your resume will want to know quickly what you are doing now."

Veruki says interviewers may be flexible in their expectations of the structure of a resume, but they particularly value brevity. "They don't want to start reading paragraphs. They let their eye drop down the center of the page, and if they like the highlights they'll want to read more."

Nemser agrees. "One of the most common problems with resumes is that they're too long," she says. "People tend to ramble. Nobody's going to read your resume or cover letter if it's too long. If it is too long, it will get tossed aside. You want to entice people — to invite them to read your resume."

"Sometimes people write a book about themselves," she says. "Put yourself in the recruiter's position. Imagine their weary eyes late at night, and try to make it easy for them to read. I doubt that anyone should have more than a two-page resume. A one-page resume should be adequate for anybody with less than five years' business experience."

In some circumstances, you may be required to provide more information than a standard one- or two-page resume can contain. When Allen Heimer interviewed for a position as community relations director of a small California university, the administrators wanted specific details regarding Heimer's military career. These were details that had not interested his interviewers when Heimer applied for positions in banking and industry.

"When applying to a nonbanking industry, it's important for bankers to adjust to that industry's philosophy," Heimer says. "I found that bankers are used to making their resumes short and concise," he says. "I had to rebuild my resume for the education industry. My two-page resume with a cover sheet went to eight pages with a cover sheet."

If you don't know how long your resume should be, or if you need suggestions about how to organize your resume for an industry other than banking, you can consult a friend or acquaintance who works in that industry. Or telephone the personnel department of the company to which you are applying. They probably won't mind telling you what they expect to see on a resume, because it only increases the quality of the resumes they receive.

Components of a Resume

From top to bottom, the resume consists of a simple heading; an objective statement; a summary of your work experience and education that supports the objective; and an optional summary of personal interests.

■ Heading — The heading should enable an employer to contact you easily to ask questions or schedule an interview. It should include your name, address, and telephone number. Remember that if you don't have an answering machine, a prospective employer may not be able to reach you, and your resume may end up at the bottom of the stack.

■ Objective — A statement of your objectives is key to guiding a reader through your accomplishments, Veruki explains: "The objective should be very succinct and hard-hitting. It should not be something vague or hollow like: 'to find a challenging and rewarding position that utilizes my management and interpersonal skills.'"

"If your objective is to find a job in real estate finance, just state that without all the fancy words. The objective statement lets the reader know whether to read on," he says. After stating your objective, you will select the work and education experiences that relate to and support that objective.

"Your resume has to be developed in light of your objective," he adds. "Let's assume you are a banker who is going into marketing. You have ten years' experience as a lending officer. The way you describe your lending experience for a marketing position is going to be different from the description you use when applying for other jobs in banking," he explains. "You would highlight the marketing aspects of lending, like client development, rather than financial and quantitative aspects."

■ Work experience — Although the summary of your work experience will account for most of your resume, you should not reproduce a detailed description of every job you have ever had. Choose only those accomplishments that are significant to prospective employers. Make it easy for them to find this information when they are skimming your resume. Remember, the employer will first skim your resume and will only read it carefully if he or she finds something in your resume that makes a careful reading worthwhile.

"I tell students to keep all the meat in the middle of the resume," Veruki says. "They should put dates in the left-hand column — 1990-94, for example. In the right-hand column, they should put the geography — Atlanta, London, New York, Seattle — wherever they've worked."

"You keep the dates and geography out to the sides. That way, readers can see them easily if they want to. But the meat belongs in the middle of the resume. It should consist of hard-hitting statements that use action words. They don't have to be complete sentences, and they don't have to be punctuated like sentences. For example: 'Developed capital budgets'; 'Managed quality control programs'; and 'Saved $50,000 through efficiency studies.'"

Remember, you are not making a list to inform the reader where you have spent your time. You are trying to show a reader what you have accomplished and what you might accomplish for his or her company.

"Too many people think when they describe their work history on a resume, they should use the job descriptions from their previous positions. That's probably the worst thing they can use," Veruki says. "What is important is: What did you really accomplish that you could accomplish in your next job, too?"

"Your accomplishments are what sell you to your next employer," Nemser says. "To list just what you were responsible for gives an impression of passiveness. I always encourage people to use as many verbs as possible. You want to make your resume as active as possible, focusing on your accomplishments, and make it more than a simple list. More and more in the 1990s, employers are looking for people with initiative, ideas, and creativity. If your resume is a list, it just doesn't show that creativity."

Example:

1990-1994   First National Bank   Portland, Oregon

Senior Vice President, Commercial Lending

- Developed division from $200 million in commitments and $85 million in deposits to $380 million in commitments and $100 million in deposits.

- Negotiated loan agreement for Oregon Paper Company's $80 million purchase of Columbia Timber.

Veruki suggests a solution for presenting yourself in a chronological resume if you lost your bank job several months ago and have been working temporarily outside your field. He cites the example of a former Citicorp banker who lost his job and did substitute teaching and temporary accounting work for six months. Although these were the banker's most recent positions, they were not jobs that he wished to emphasize in the resume he prepared to send to businesses. So he modified the format of a chronological resume to meet his needs. Veruki points out that it was appropriate for this banker to lead with his most recent banking accomplishments. At the bottom of the chronology, he created a separate line that said, "Most recent six months, 1996-1997," in which he stated that he was working as a substitute teacher and doing temporary accounting work. This would satisfy an employer's curiosity to know what the banker was presently doing, but it didn't emphasize the banker's temporary teaching job over his banking career.

As you describe your accomplishments, remember that you should be able to justify everything on your resume. "If you put something on your resume that's untrue, you're in big trouble," Veruki says. "There's no place for an untruthful or highly subjective resume. It's going to catch up with you sooner or later."

■ Education — Unless you have little professional expertise, you should list your education after your work experience. The education section of your resume should state the degree you earned, the school, and the date of graduation. Remember, the importance of your formal education will diminish with time, and you may wish to exclude your graduation year if you feel that fact will "date" you. If you think that other college accomplishments would be important to an employer, find a way to state them briefly. Remember, the basic resume structure can be altered in order to personalize the presentation of your credentials and abilities.

■ Personal information — Many job seekers try to "round out" their resumes by including personal items like marital status, health, weight, and birth date. This information usually is irrelevant to prospective employers, and many consider it to be an obsolete practice.

"There's no need for those details," Nemser says. "They take up valuable space in a resume. I don't care how tall you are, how much you weigh, how many children you have, or what church you go to. In the 1960s, employers might have wanted to see these types of things on a resume," she says. "Once employers viewed this sort of information as necessary to ensure that they were getting a well-rounded, family-oriented individual, but in the 1990s this information is no longer considered important on a resume," she says.

Veruki also advises candidates not to clutter their resumes with unnecessary personal details. But he says candidates can create a one-line category at the bottom of a resume to mention professional activities or hobbies. "You can take one line to humanize yourself as long as it's something significant about what you do in your spare time."

In addition to giving another dimension to your work experience, personal details can also provide a good icebreaker for the interview. An interviewer might scan your resume and begin the interview by saying, "I see you run marathons." Or, "I see you like the symphony." This is a nice way to get started in the otherwise stuffy environment of an interview. Too much emphasis on the personal may, on the other hand, create the impression that you've been more engrossed in your hobbies than in your career.

■ References. It is unnecessary to include references with a resume. At the very least, references take up space. At worst, the interviewer could phone your references and decide that he no longer wants to interview you. Many people unnecessarily announce "References available on request" on a resume. An employer assumes you will supply references when requested, as this is a customary stage of the hiring process. The list of references that you present upon request at an interview should include the name, address, phone number, and job title of each of your references and a brief description of your professional relationship. Before listing someone as a reference, contact the person. Ask permission to use the name of the reference and advise him or her of the types of jobs you are seeking so that your references' responses will support your presentation.

How to Improve the Appearance of Your Resume

If you have taken the time to assess your aptitudes and to present your skills in a positive light, don't let an act of carelessness sabotage your resume. One typo or misspelled word will immediately convey the wrong impression to a prospective employer. So will pink paper, green ink, an elaborate typeface, tape, coffee stains, photographs, or anything else that varies from the standard businesslike resume. Despite the fact that you should be creative in the presentation of your qualifications, prospective employers expect the resume that contains that creative presentation to be neatly produced on white or off-white bond paper. Resumes that deviate from these basic standards will be quickly eliminated from consideration.

"The visual presentation is the first thing I look at. Can I read the darn thing without straining my eyes?" says Joe Holland, president of Holland-Lanz Associates, a Longwood, Florida, executive search and outplacement firm that recruits top-level executives for several industries.

When reading a resume, Holland asks himself: *Is there white space? Can I read it? Are there margins? Is the resume free of smudges, cartoons, and written comments scrawled in the margins? Overall, does it give a serious, professional impression?*

"We see a lot of misspelled words, and we see resumes that require a microscope to read," Holland adds. "Regardless of what those resumes say, the presentation is poor."

Nemser agrees. "Lots of people have resumes that don't look good, and one of the simple things contributing to that is typos. It's hard to proof your own work. No matter how good a speller you are, you can always make mistakes. It may help to put your resume down and come back to it later."

If spelling, punctuation and grammar are not your strong points — and even if you think they are — ask someone who is competent in these areas to proofread your resume. Spell-checking devices can allow a misspelled word to slip through on a resume if it is an actual word. Even if you must use a dictionary to verify the spelling of every word on your resume, do it. Otherwise, your resume could be eliminated from competition.

Here are some additional hints for resume appearance:

- Stay away from colored paper unless you're in a very creative field like graphic arts or advertising. "Some professionals might value an unusual approach," Nemser says, "but for a banker, it's not appropriate."
- Pictures are inappropriate with resumes. But many job applicants still attach their mug shots to their resumes, as though it were an expected part of the application process. Attaching a picture to a resume shows an employer that you are out of touch with current hiring practices.
- Many employment managers dislike the cookie-cutter type of resume that reflects preparation by a third-rate resume writing service. For example, a company that was recruiting marketing exec-

utives in Arizona received three four-page resumes from applicants who lived in the same town. Each resume was printed on the same mottled beige stationery in bold, informal type that might have been appropriate for advertising a college keg party but was inappropriate for a resume. No doubt the resume service promised the applicants who sent these resumes that their resumes would "stand out." They did; and they were quickly culled from the stack. An employer expects to read a resume that stands out because of the candidate's qualifications, not because it looks like a menu.

"There are a lot of bad resumes out there because there are a lot of resume writers who are charging for resumes who have never written resumes before," Holland says.

■ Some candidates send their resumes via local courier or overnight express delivery services. It may be desirable to send a resume this way if you must meet a deadline. If not, the practice could have mixed results. On the one hand, the person receiving a resume might be impressed by your interest in the job. On the other hand, you may be viewed as an extravagant, wasteful person who spends ten dollars or more to send a document that could have been mailed for less than fifty cents. A prospective employer may wonder if you would waste his or her company's money. Further, it is unlikely that such expedited delivery will result in a quicker examination of your resume or more attention for it.

■ USING YOUR RESUME AND COVER LETTER AS MARKETING TOOLS

Constructing a resume will help you repackage your skills in a way that may convince an employer that you are a good match for his or her organization. But it is important to know how to use this important tool. The first thing you need to decide is whether to make a mass mailing of your resume or to target specific companies or industries.

Many career advisers say targeting specific companies to receive your resume increases your chances for success. Since you will mail only to companies you have identified as good prospects, this method increases the likelihood that the companies that receive your resume will view you as a desirable employee. This strategy combines the insights you gained through your self-assessment with the information you gathered through research and networking.

For this approach to work, however, your resume needs to do more than convince an employer that you are a well-rounded, capable, intelligent person. The objective of targeting is to present your credentials in a way that will make the employer think: *This resume seems to be written precisely for us. This sounds just like the person we're looking for.*

"Remember, you've got to know your market," Holland says. "The resume is a brochure that sells you. But you have to know something about the customer who is going to be reading your brochure. The best resume is one that interests me. It is the one that addresses the requirements of the job that we're trying to fill and explains the history, qualifications, and education of the candidate."

A strong cover letter can help fill in any gaps that may be left by the resume. An effective cover letter is more than just a simple letter that says, "I enclose my resume. I look forward to hearing from you." A customized cover letter can serve several important purposes, according to Nemser. First, it can help an employer identify your interests and experience. It should contain a personalized greeting that indicates that you have a genuine interest in the company. Second, it suggests a way for you to follow up with the employer. For example, in your cover letter, you may request an interview or inform the employer that you will call at a certain time.

"You're trying to make a better match with the cover letter," Nemser says. "What you don't want to do, though, is to restate everything that's on your resume. If you do, you're wasting the reader's time. You might, however, want to expand on something in the resume or frame it for the reader so it will fit into the context of the reader's business."

"Almost every cover letter should be limited to one page," Nemser says. "I've rarely seen a cover letter where more pages were necessary. After one page, people stop reading." And if you overdo the cover letter, she adds, you will not have as much to discuss during the interview.

Nemser instructs her assistant to staple the cover letters to the back of applicants' resumes. She, like many hiring executives, prefers to see the resume before the cover letter. But a good cover letter can link the resume to the reader.

"Most employers will read the resume first and the cover letter second. They're going to look at the resume to make sure there is pertinent experience. They will first skim the resume, rather than reading it. If you skim a resume that warrants further reading, you'll examine it more thoroughly. Next, you'll read the cover letter."

Here is an example of an effective one-page cover letter that a banker might use to request an interview with a nonbanking company.

Douglas Fontaine
129 Rosedale Road
St. Louis, Missouri 63115(314)
689-0647

October 21, 1997

Mr. Charles Greenlee, President
American Bottling Company
2000 Southwest Expressway
Kansas City, MO 64133

Dear Mr. Greenlee:

Eric Grainger of your St. Louis affiliate told me about your plans to consolidate your regional accounting operations in Kansas City and said that you are currently recruiting financial managers who have experience in the bottling industry.

I have negotiated financing for your St. Louis branch for nine years and arranged the loans for your St. Louis expansion, including the distribution center construction and fleet modernization. I think my knowledge of your operations and of the bottling industry could be valuable to American Bottling. I would like to discuss how my financial management skills could be of use to your company's accounting division.

I would like to meet with you in Kansas City during the week of November 10. I will phone you next week to schedule an appointment that is convenient for you.

Sincerely,

Douglas Fontaine

Notice how Fontaine tailored his presentation directly to the prospective employer. He informed the employer that he had been referred by a mutual business acquaintance. He displayed a knowledge of the company and suggested a next step — a phone call to schedule an interview.

But many job candidates underestimate the importance of a cover letter.

Consider the following excerpts, reproduced verbatim from actual cover letters. All contain insipid or inappropriate phrases that fail to enhance the applicant's qualifications:

- "Given the opportunity for an interview, I am confident you might agree I could offer your company a wealth of talent that would benefit you."
- "The enclosed resume is a brief guideline stating my accomplishments in Sales, Management, Leasing, Marketing and Property Management. I have never failed at any endeavor I've attempted and would like the opportunity to achieve results for your organization."
- "I would like to know more about the sales executive position that you have available in the area. My salary was $40,000. If I can be of assistance, please contact me."
- "To whom it may concern: After reading your advertisement in the classifieds, I elected to use a former resume and the only current small photograph available to expedite a return on your inquiry. The job you outlined is the first that has truly interested me in quite a while. I look forward to your call."
- "I am alert, eager, and accomplished — the result of carefully planned, day-to-day, methodical, well-thought-out personal productivity."
- "I work well alone and equally well with others at all levels, and under all conditions. I understand the inner complexities of the work environment."

How to Write Resumes for Target Companies

Tailoring your approach to the needs of a specific company or industry is very important to a successful job search. "You should first assess who you are and what you would like to do. Then you should target positions that you would like to have and that you would have a reasonable chance of being successful in," says Joe Holland, the Longwood, Florida, executive recruiter. Set reasonable goals, he says. "If you're forty-five years old and you've been in banking for twenty years, you're not going to direct the astronaut program."

When you have completed the self-assessment described in chapter 2 and used the networking and research skills described in chapter 3 to target the industries and companies that interest you, Holland suggests the following approach:

- Define the job description. "When I teach someone to be an executive recruiter, I tell them the first thing they have to do is to get a job description before they go out and search. An unemployed banker can do this on his own and try to develop a profile of the ideal candidate. When you learn about an opening, get the job description. If there is an opening in these companies, there is usually a written job description. All you have to do is simply ask them to send you a description of the job."

  "Instead of trying to guess what they're looking for and trying to construct a resume that may or may not have all the bullets in it, ask for the job description. Then try to construct a resume with the bullets that you'll need."

- Call the person who last held the position and ask him or her about the job. Holland suggests that you ask about the skills the job required. What were the politics involved? What should you watch out for? What are the company's prejudices? For example, if you smoke, will the company consider hiring you?

  Although you may be uncomfortable calling someone and inquiring about his or her former job, you may find that most people are willing to cooperate with such a request. And the information you gain will help you highlight the appropriate qualifications in your resume and later in an interview. "You construct the resume according to your legitimate experience, emphasizing those areas that seem to be required for a particular job," Holland points out.

■ Call a competitor and speak with someone in that organization who performs a job that is similar to the one you are seeking. You might say, "I'm considering working in your industry for another company. Would you please tell me what a person has to do on a daily, weekly, monthly basis? What types of skills are required? Who are your customers?" Holland has encountered little resistance to such requests. "People try to help each other," he says.

■ Call a trade association and speak with its executive director or someone who would be in a position to provide information about the industry you are considering.

Say, "I'm thinking about working in your industry, but I've never done it before. Can you give me some information?" Ask about training programs, meetings you could attend in your area, and people with whom you might talk. These calls could help you enlarge your network and find out about job leads.

Each of these steps should arm you with information that will help you make a favorable impression with your resume. The information you gather will also help you as you reach the crucial phase of the job search: the interview.

5

MAKING THE INTERVIEW WORK FOR YOU

■ ■ ■

Good jobs don't always go to the people with the best qualifications. They go to the candidates who present themselves most effectively in interviews. If you have conducted a thorough self-assessment, researched job opportunities that match your experience and interests, networked extensively, and written a resume that highlights your skills and accomplishments, you should be prepared to succeed in a job interview.

Although you have interviewed successfully during your career, you may not have had a job interview for several years. Now is the time to review your interviewing skills. One of the worst mistakes a job candidate can make is to approach an interview from his or her own perspective instead of tailoring the presentation to meet the employer's needs. You should strive during an interview to present yourself in a way that shows an employer how your skills can benefit the employer's organization. Your success will depend largely on your preparation.

■ PREPARING FOR THE INTERVIEW

You probably have gathered much of the information you will

need for interviewing through your self-assessment, research, networking, and resume preparation. Your ability to direct this information toward a specific employer will determine your success in an interview.

"I find that a weak interviewee typically knows nothing about the position, the company, the industry, the marketplace, or the kind of compensation that the job offers. They simply haven't done any homework," says Joe Holland, president of Holland-Lantz and Associates, a Longwood, Florida, executive search and outplacement firm.

The director of an Atlanta search firm says that by the time executives are forty years old, they are acquainted with proper interviewing technique, but that they may not understand the job market.

Preparation for an interview should help you achieve three basic goals. You should be able to:

- Arm yourself with information about the company, industry, position, and the person who will interview you;
- Identify skills you possess that would make you valuable to the company; and
- Organize your presentation to convince an interviewer that your qualifications match the requirements of the job.

Researching the Company

First, you should revisit the public library to review the literature about the company and the people with whom you will interview. "Locate a reference librarian and throw yourself on his or her mercy," advises Sam Sackett, an executive consultant in the Oklahoma City office of Bernard Haldane Associates, a national outplacement firm. A librarian can help you locate information about particular industries or companies with which you may be interviewing, Sackett says. For companies and industries, these resources include annual reports, business directories like *Standard and Poor's, Hoover's Business Profiles,* or *Dun and Bradstreet,* trade magazines, reference books, newspaper indexes, and computer databases. For information about specific executives with whom you interview, you should consult the library's "Who's Who" directories, regional or industrial biographies, and newspaper indexes.

But don't limit yourself to the public library. You should also seek information from the chamber of commerce, the Better Business Bureau, and trade associations. Another obvious but overlooked research method is to call the company's public relations department and ask its staff to provide information about the company. Companies that have web sites on the Internet often post recent press releases. These can be a great way to learn how a company wants to be seen, what concerns are important to the company, what sort of people have been recently promoted, etc.

After you review the available literature, you should use your network to gather additional information that could give you a competitive advantage over other candidates. Use your contacts to locate current employees, past employees, and people who do business with the company or know its operations. Seek information about the person who will interview you. Learn why the position is open and how long it has taken to fill it. Inquire about the company's goals.

A single item of information can prove valuable in an interview. Consider the case of Craig, a laid-off commercial lender who interviewed for a financial management position with a real estate development firm that had been profiled in a local business publication. Craig correctly assumed that other candidates had read the same article he had, so he dug for knowledge that his competitors lacked. Through networking he learned that the firm was bidding for contracts for building nursing homes in Canada and that the executive who would interview him had supervised a study of the Canadian market. Craig used this knowledge to his advantage. Early in the interview, he found an appropriate time to say, "I know that the firm is bidding for contracts to build nursing homes in Canada. During our discussion today, I would like to tell you about my experience with Canadian companies and my lending experiences with the nursing home industry."

Craig dominated the interview as a result of this information. During the rest of the interview he explained how his skills and experiences could benefit the organization. Craig was invited back for a second interview and received a job offer. Although the company had interviewed twelve candidates, Craig distinguished himself from the competition because he presented himself as "the candidate who could help with the Canadian projects."

Craig's experience illustrates the importance of gathering information about a company, but this should constitute only part of any candidate's interview preparation. Although Craig's knowledge of the company impressed the interviewer, he landed the job because he presented the set of skills that the employer needed. As a candidate, it is your responsibility to convince an interviewer that your skills will contribute to the success of that person's company. You cannot, however, expect an interviewer to make this connection for you. Nor can you assume that you will be spoon-fed the questions that will elicit your best responses. You must use your initiative to sell your skills to an employer.

"People go into an interview much too passively," says Ralph Plimpton, president of Plimpton Associates, a Denver executive search and outplacement firm. "They go into an interview as though it were out of their hands and out of their control. Not so! While it's true that the interview format usually consists of the interviewer asking questions, I believe the interviewee should go into an interview with a soft game plan."

Preparing an Interview Game Plan

Plimpton advises job candidates to consider the following question: "When people gather to compare notes on you, what is it that you want them to be saying and thinking about you?"

Plimpton says employers are likely to evaluate candidates on the following criteria:

- Does the candidate's personality mesh with the personalities of the key players in the department in which he or she would work?
- Does he or she fit in with the corporate culture?
- Assuming that the answers to the first two questions are satisfactory, will he or she be a long-term successful performer?

If you can envision the type of candidate a company is seeking, you should be able to present your skills accordingly. Plimpton instructs candidates to use the following strategy:

- Identify the unidentified needs of the organization and its key players. "These needs may not be articulated, but nevertheless, decisions are made based on these needs," he says. "Don't expect the interviewer to ask you the ideal questions," he warns. As you prepare for an interview, he says, put yourself in the interviewer's shoes and ask yourself, "What are the company's real needs?"

    For example, Craig learned through his research that the development firm needed an experienced financial manager who could negotiate deals with Canadian companies. The interviewer never asked, "Do you have experience negotiating deals with Canadian companies?" But Craig identified this need and addressed it during the interview. Consequently, he was offered the job.

- Anticipate which factors will really influence the hiring decision. Will the decision be based on a candidate's quantitative skills? Lending background? Knowledge of the construction industry? Ability to work with customers in a sophisticated city center as well as those in a small community? Once you know which factors will influence the hiring decision, develop five to eight themes about yourself that will match the factors sought by the company,

Plimpton advises.

Craig determined that the company's hiring decision would be based on a candidate's ability to do business with Canadian companies, knowledge of the nursing home business, strong quantitative skills, and ability to speak and read French. These were the themes he emphasized during his interview.

■ Overcome objections. "Objections may never be raised in an interview, but nevertheless, people make decisions based on objections," Plimpton says. A candidate needs to think: *If I were in that chair, what objections might that person have to me?* Once you have identified the objections, you should decide whether to address them during the interview.

The personnel director of a manufacturing company might be impressed by a banker's qualifications, but he might object to the banker's lack of experience in a manufacturing environment. The interviewer may or may not address this issue during the interview, but if a banker has identified this as a possible objection to his candidacy, he may wish to address the issue himself. He could do so by saying, "I realize that I haven't worked directly for a manufacturer, but I have considerable experience dealing with manufacturers as a banker, and I would like to tell you what I've learned."

■ Ask questions. In the course of the interview, the candidate should ask open-ended, probing questions about the job. Career counselors say an interviewee should pay careful attention to framing these questions. Don't ask anything that would indicate a lack of preparation. For example, if you interview for a job in a company that is publicly owned, you should avoid asking questions like "How were the company's profits last year?" or "What products does the company make?" This information is widely available and an employer will expect you to have done your homework.

You can use your questions to provide additional evidence of your skills. For example, the following is an example of the sort of questions and statements you can use to obtain information and show evidence of your management skills: "I enjoy managing a staff and have done so successfully in the past. When I managed my bank's commercial loan department, employee turnover dropped 30 percent, and absenteeism dropped 40 percent. How many people would report to me in this position?"

■ THE INTERVIEW

If you have researched the company and anticipated the points you would like to make about yourself, you will be better prepared than most candidates. But you must also pay attention to the other aspects of a successful interview.

You must make a good first impression. In order to manage the interview successfully, you must establish good rapport with the interviewer. You must handle difficult questions skillfully. Before you leave the interview, you must summarize your qualifications for the job and address any questions that might exist about your abilities to perform it. Finally, if you want the position, you should ask for the job before you leave the interview.

You cannot be passive in an interview. You must do more than respond well to the questions you are asked. Although the interviewer will establish the flow and format of the interview, it is your responsibility to convince the interviewer that you warrant a job offer.

Making a Positive Impression

An interviewer will judge you during the first few minutes — or seconds — of your meeting. If your appearance and demeanor fail to impress the interviewer, it will be difficult to develop good rapport. The first step to making a good impression is to examine the way you dress. Although you likely realize the importance of proper attire and grooming, you may not know how to dress if you are interviewing for a nonbanking job.

To find out the company's dress code, talk to current employees or make an informal visit to the company before your interview to observe how its executives dress. Most consultants say a banker's customary business attire — conservative, tailored clothes for both men and women — is a safe bet for most companies.

"Usually banking attire would be appropriate," says Sam Sackett, of Bernard Haldane Associates in Oklahoma City. "If you were applying for a CFO position at a company with a corporate culture more relaxed than a bank's, you might appear to be a little overdressed. But on the whole it's better to be one notch overdressed than one notch underdressed. In some companies a banker might look a little stuffy. But I think one of the things that a banker might want to think about is: would you feel comfortable working at a place where people feel you look stuffy?"

"Wear clothes that fit," adds Joe Holland. "Make sure that they are tailored and pressed and look fresh. Conservative, professional-looking clothes are always a safe option. Proper amounts of makeup for women and proper haircuts for men are essential. I think women do much better when they look professional but feminine and men tend to do better by looking professional but masculine," he adds. If you want more advice about colors, attire for specific industries, or regional styles, consult *Dress For Success* or *The Woman's Dress For Success*, both by John Molloy.

Most seasoned businesspeople will recognize the following suggestions as examples of good business etiquette, but their importance to a candidate who is preparing for an interview cannot be overstated, and they bear repeating.

■ Remember that you are being evaluated by a prospective employer from the moment you enter the building. You should be friendly and sincere to everyone you encounter. Hiring executives may ask receptionists and secretaries for their impressions of you.

- Be punctual. You can sabotage an interview by arriving late, regardless of your excuse. A late arrival destroys your confidence and gives the interviewer a poor impression of your personal habits. It is a terrible way to begin a business relationship. To avoid being late, confirm the time and location of the interview and determine how long it will take to get there. If you are unsure, drive to the interview site in advance. It is better to arrive early than to risk being late. Allow enough time to collect your thoughts and check your appearance before the interview. If you arrive more than ten minutes early, however, you may be perceived as desperate for a job.

- Be alert and rested when you interview. You may need to modify your sleeping, eating, drinking, and exercise habits the day before the interview.

- Try to develop poise by practicing before an interview. Some candidates practice in front of a mirror or with a friend or spouse. Others record or videotape their performance so they can study their voice and body language. If you have practiced interviewing, you probably will be less apprehensive about actual interviews.

  "I really urge people who haven't interviewed for a long time to go out and do some interviews whether they want the job or not," Plimpton says. "There's nothing better than a live interview to learn from."

- When the interview is scheduled, learn the name and title of the person who will interview you, and ask how much time you should plan to spend at the company. Pay attention to the name of each person you meet during the interview and write down their names for future use.

- Take to the interview a list of questions about the company and the job. Also take extra copies of your resume, a list of references, and letters of reference if you have them. Take a notepad and a pen or pencil to record important details that arise in the interview, but don't let note-taking distract you or the interviewer.

Making a good first impression is essential to establishing good rapport with an interviewer. Since interviewers make tentative decisions about a candidate during the first few minutes of the interview, there are no substitutes for basic interpersonal skills such as firm handshakes, sincere smiles, and direct eye contact. But after the greetings are exchanged, you can steer the interview in a positive direction if you are prepared.

"Most people in business respond favorably to establishing some type of personal relationship and then getting down to business," Sackett says. This means you should be prepared for a few minutes of casual conversation.

"I think the best thing to do is to find as much background on the interviewer as you can," Sackett says. "Sometimes this is difficult. You might find out something about him that might establish a point of common interest. For example, you might say, 'I noticed you're on the symphony board of directors. I sure enjoyed the last symphony.' Of course, you only say that if you've been to the last symphony. If you haven't, you're in trouble. Or you can say, 'I see you went to Texas Tech University. I grew up in Lubbock myself.'" Look for evidence of the interviewer's hobbies, but avoid family matters.

"Even if a person has pictures of people on his or her desk, I would leave those alone," he says. "There are too many unknowns." For example, your well-meaning references to an interviewer's family photographs may backfire. She could say, "Yes, those are my children. But their father has kidnapped them and I'm spending a fortune on detective fees trying to get them back." Or, "This is a photo of my brother. He was killed in a mountain-climbing accident two years ago."

Although a few minutes of casual conversation might help break the ice, you should not attempt to prolong the small talk or you will have less time to discuss your qualifications for the job. Experienced interviewers will get down to business quickly. "In a job interview, I think it is a good idea for a candidate to wait until the interviewer makes the first move," Sackett says. "But if the candidate has requested the interview and is going into it on a referral or informational basis, then it is definitely up to the candidate to make the first move."

During the first few minutes of an interview, you and the interviewer will try to "read" each other. The interviewer may give some cues that will help you determine how to implement your strategy. For example, some interviewers begin by explaining the responsibilities of the position and describing the qualifications of the ideal candidate. If an interviewer says the position requires strong analytical and computer skills, you will know to play up these qualifications.

Other interviewers will begin by asking questions about a candidate's resume or start with open-ended questions ranging from "What can I do for you?" to "Tell me why you think you are the person for this job."

Ralph Plimpton says he likes to begin an interview by asking a candidate, "Tell me about yourself." He says he likes to see how candidates deal with the question. He evaluates how much a candidate tells, what subjects he or she covers, how he or she expresses himself or herself, and whether the subjects are relevant to the job. Some candidates attempt to tell their whole life stories, but a response to this question should not take more than seven sentences, Plimpton says.

"Interviewers don't all interview the same way, and they don't all judge a candidate the same way," the director of an Atlanta search firm says. "When you get into an interview with a skilled interviewer, the best thing to do is to try to read the interviewer."

"The interviewer knows what he or she wants. They may or may not tell you. You have to read the cues. If the interviewer is elusive or doesn't communicate what he wants, you may have to take it upon yourself to find out. You might say, 'I know we have a limited amount of time. What would you like to know about me?'"

An interviewer will be reading your cues as well. Your eye contact, body language, and voice modulation can provide as much information as your responses to the interviewer's questions. For example, if you break eye contact with an interviewer after he asks you to explain why you lost your job, he will perceive your discomfort and may wonder if you are trying to hide something. Again, preparation and practice will help you present yourself well.

You can probably guess the basic questions that will surface during an interview. But many candidates perform poorly in interviews simply because they fail to anticipate questions they might be asked.

"The biggest problem is that they don't think through and develop four or five different ways of dealing with particular types of questions. And they don't practice. If they did, they would be in a better position to provide the optimum answers," Plimpton says.

"I'm not suggesting that the answers be canned," Plimpton says. "I am suggesting that job candidates think through several alternatives for dealing with a particular question."

For example, if you are unemployed, you should expect an interviewer to ask the obvious question, "How long have you been out of work?" You could answer tersely, "Five months." Or you could say, "I've been out of work for several months, and here's what I've been doing as part of my campaign to find another job." The latter answer illustrates your ability to deal with problems and seek solutions, and it gives additional behavioral evidence of how you think and act.

Tom Markovich, who managed bank branches in suburban Chicago for fourteen years, knew that employers in other industries would look at his resume and say, "You've been a banker for most of your career. What can you do for us?" Markovich prepared for this question. He conducted a thorough self-assessment, researched the companies and positions he had targeted, and anticipated the questions he might be asked. He was ready to answer the question: "What can you do for us?"

Markovich says that in an interview for an administrative position with an accounting firm, he responded to the question in the following way: "I have prepared to make a career change. I have completed 80 percent of the work for my master's degree, and I bring with me a host of skills." Then, he emphasized the quantitative skills, accounting background, and general management experience that he had acquired through banking. He was able to convince employers that he was more than "just a banker." He was hired as an administrator for the accounting firm and later as a policy analyst for the National Association of Realtors.

"I tried to sell myself as if I were selling a commodity," he says. "It really does take some soul-searching."

You should expect to be asked some difficult questions. An interviewer is not looking for a "right" answer. He wants to know how you think, reason, and express yourself.

"A number of companies use behavioral psychologists as part of an interview process," Plimpton says. "These people are trained to predict how a person is likely to perform in the future. The better interviewers today focus on trying to elicit evidence of a candidate's typical behavior and therefore to develop a pattern of their probable future behavior."

Your answers may reveal a great deal of information about you. For example, do you get bogged down in detail? Are you a strong conceptual thinker? Are you well organized? Do you possess strong analytical skills? How well do you relate to people? Do your answers fit the questions asked?

As you anticipate some of the questions you might face in interviews, consider the following commonly asked interview questions:

- Tell me about yourself.
- Why should we hire you?
- What have you accomplished?
- What are your weaknesses?
- What did you contribute to your former employer?
- How did you choose your career?
- Why are you making a change?
- What do you anticipate doing five years from now?
- If I were to sit down with your spouse or people who know you well, what would they say about you?

- Tell me about your favorite job and why you were successful.
- Tell me about your least favorite job and why it was difficult.
- What is the most innovative thing you have done?

Also consider these suggestions for responding to an interviewer's questions:

■ Talk about results and accomplishments in specific terms. The more factual the conversation the better. "If your field is personnel, don't just say that everyone loved working for you," the Atlanta recruiter says. "Say that absenteeism went down 30 percent and turnover declined 40 percent."

■ Highlight your specific accomplishments. For example, Craig might have said, "I understand that your company is trying to expand into Canada, and I can help you," but that wouldn't have been enough to convince an employer that Craig was the best candidate for the job. Craig's ability to present his skills in a way that matched the goals of the company secured his job offer. He told the interviewer, "I understand your company is bidding to construct nursing homes in Canada, and I think I could help you achieve this goal. I have helped my bank arrange deals for companies that were trying to expand into Canada. I have also made loans to the local operations of two Canadian-owned manufacturers. As a result of these relationships, I have cultivated some good Canadian business contacts, and I have made it a point to follow Canadian business trends. I also speak and read French fluently, which could be beneficial if the company does business in Quebec."

■ Be honest and sincere in the interview. Don't use clichés like "I'm a people person," or "I thrive on challenges." These tell an interviewer nothing about your ability to help his or her company achieve its goals. Highlight your presentation with specific accomplishments.

■ Steer the interview. If your interviewer gets sidetracked, redirect the discussion so it focuses on your qualifications. For example, if your interviewer notes that you are a graduate of the same university and launches into a spiel about your alma mater's football team, he or she is chiseling away valuable time from your presentation. You may have to leave the interview before you are able to convince the interviewer that you are the right person for the job. You can tactfully redirect the conversation by saying, "You know, I did enjoy college, and I joined First City Bank immediately after I graduated. Can I tell you how my career has progressed during the past ten years?"

■ SINS OF INTERVIEWING

While it is difficult to predict what will happen in an interview, or which questions an interviewer will choose to ask, there are some behaviors that are certain to impress interviewers negatively. Sam Sackett, the Bernard Haldane Associates consultant in Oklahoma City, describes some "venial sins" and "mortal sins" of interviewing:

Venial Sins

- Don't cross your legs with your ankle on your knees. "This gives what we call the crotch shot," Sackett says. It is acceptable to have both feet flat on the floor. If you must cross your legs, he says, do so knee-to-knee, or cross your ankles.
- Don't fidget with a pencil or pen. "As you're sitting there, you're going to be taking notes, which is fine," Sackett says. "But if you're nervous, you may start playing with your pencil or pen, and that can distract the interviewer's attention away from you to what you are doing."
- Don't use the interviewer's first name too early. Many people want to be called by their first name, but there are others who find such familiarity inappropriate, especially during an interview. Wait for

the interviewer to tell you explicitly, "Call me Charlie," Sackett says. "Even if the person starts calling you by your first name, wait for him to make it explicit to you that you may call him by his first name."

■ Don't invade the interviewer's space. "Some people come in with their portfolio and will set it down on the executive's desk and open it up. That desktop is part of the executive's space," he says.

■ Don't sit until you are asked. "Don't make yourself at home in someone's office before you are asked to do so. I tell my candidates that even if the interviewer sits down first, remain standing until he invites you to sit down. This might be difficult for a man who has been running a bank for twenty or thirty years to do," Sackett says.

■ Don't fail to maintain good eye contact. "In this culture, eye contact is seen as a sign of sincerity and honesty. Of course, almost everybody in talking to someone else has to take his eyes away sometime. It's very hard to think of the next thing to say while you're looking somebody right in the eye. But try to train yourself not to look too far away," Sackett says. "It can be distracting if you swerve your head ninety degrees. Instead, try to look at the tip of the interviewer's ear or the top of her glasses so it won't be so obvious."

Mortal Sins

■ Don't express a negative attitude toward anything. Sackett remembers a candidate who, when asked why he left his bank, replied that the bank was managed badly and was losing money. "Some people have a great deal of difficulty keeping their bitterness in bounds. But they shouldn't let their bitterness show in an interview," he says.

■ Don't give answers that are excessively long. Keep your answers short and to the point. Frequently, a candidate will answer a question and then, if the interviewer doesn't respond with another question, he or she will expand on the answer just given. "They may introduce all kinds of irrelevant details," Sackett says. And as they ramble, they may expose things that are better left unsaid. The moral of this? "Don't be afraid of silence," Sackett says. "Once you've answered a question, be quiet and wait for the next one."

■ Don't give answers that are too general. For example, you might be asked, "How do you respond to pressure?" Many candidates will simply say, "I respond very well to pressure." This answer is too vague. Instead, describe a specific work situation in which you handled pressure well. For example, you could respond to the same question with an anecdote that describes a pressure situation, the action you took, and the results of your action. Sackett gives this example: "You might say, 'There was one time when the bank needed to get out a report to the FDIC, and it looked as if there wouldn't be enough time to meet the deadline. So I organized my section into two teams and divided the report into two sections.' That would be a specific situation in which you don't tell but you show how you react to pressure," he says.

Concluding the Interview

Toward the end of the interview, the interviewer will ask you if you have any questions. "At that point, the candidate should have some questions, perhaps regarding something that's arisen previously in the interview," Sackett says. "If the candidate doesn't have any questions, it will raise the question: *How interested is this person in the job?*"

"For this reason, bring some questions to the interview, in case something doesn't strike you during the first part of the interview," Sackett says. "If you're not invited to ask questions, I advise candidates to say, 'I have a few questions about the position. Would it be appropriate for me to ask them at this time?'"

Vanderbilt University's Owen Graduate School of Management

suggests that students consider asking the following questions during an interview:

- How will my performance be measured at this company or for this position?
- Why did you choose to work here?
- If you were running the company, what would you do differently?
- When you visit with friends from work, what kinds of work-related issues keep coming up?
- What else do you need to know about me to make a hiring decision?
- What doubts or questions do you have about my qualifications? Then: Do you believe I have the skills you are seeking for this position?

As you reach the end of the interview, you should ask yourself whether you have convinced the interviewer that your skills, education, work experience, and personal characteristics make you the perfect candidate for the job. This is how you will be evaluated. Use the end of the interview to reiterate or introduce any points you have failed to make during the interview. A recruiter may be impressed by your qualifications but may reject you because he is not sure if you want the job, so you should communicate how you feel about the position.

"I don't think you should conclude by saying, 'I want this job,' but you want to signal that it is a perfect fit," says Peter Veruki, director of career planning and placement for the Owen Graduate School of Management. "Reassure the recruiter that you meet the requirements."

Before the interview is over, you should determine the next step in the hiring process. Sackett explains, "In a job interview, your next-to-last question should be: 'When do you plan to reach a decision on this position?' Your last question should be, 'If I haven't heard from you by then, may I give you a call?' The best way to close a referral or informational interview is to seek referrals to additional contacts. You might say, 'If you were in my position, who else would you talk to regarding information about your industry?'"

Following Up an Interview

Many people think the interviewing process is over when the actual interview has concluded. But you need to take certain follow-up steps if you want to be considered for the job.

First, make notes about the interview that might help you prepare for a second interview. Do this while the interview is still fresh in your mind. Use the notes you have taken during the interview to reconstruct the interview. Note those issues you handled well and identify those things that you feel you need to address in a second interview.

Second, writing a letter or note to the person who has interviewed you should be considered mandatory. Most candidates fail to write such a letter, but those who do make a good impression on the interviewer. More than one candidate has been hired because he or she followed up with a personal letter of thanks for the interview.

You can also use the note to include additional information, particularly if you want to reiterate something that was said in the interview or to include a point that you failed to make. You might say, "It occurred to me after the interview that I had not made it clear enough that I am willing to relocate to take the job with your company." Or you could say, "I think my thirteen years of experience in making commercial loans should be an advantage to your company."

Despite the rapport you may have established with an interviewer, don't be surprised if you don't hear from a company after you interview. Unsuccessful candidates are rarely advised of a company's hiring decision.

"Frankly, most of them are left hanging," Sackett says. "In the earlier days, when people were more polite and life was moving less rapidly, people took time to notify everybody. Nowadays, it seems to be the general rule that you're not notified."

If you are turned down for a job, following up after the rejection can be as important as following up after an interview. It is possible to reopen the door weeks or months after you have been rejected or after you have been told there is no job available. If you were particularly interested in the company, stay in touch with the person who interviewed you, and let the interviewer know you are still interested. Write a note or, if you established a particularly good rapport, a phone call may be appropriate. There are several reasons why it can be worthwhile for you to keep in touch with a company that rejected you:

- There is always a small chance that the candidate who was selected to fill the position will not take the job. If you were next in consideration and have continued to express your interest in the job, your persistence may pay off.
- If you continue to stay in touch with the person who interviewed you, you may be considered for future positions that become available within the company. Once you have identified a company that you would really like to work for, make it your business to keep in touch with your contacts. Even if it takes months or years, your persistence may be rewarded.
- Interviewers can become part of your network. If you keep in touch, your name will remain fresh in the interviewer's mind. If an interviewer is impressed by you but is unable to offer you a job, you may be referred to a person in the interviewer's network. Such a referral could lead to a position with another company.
- Interviewers can provide information that might help you improve your interviewing skills. For example, you may go through an extensive interviewing process at a company but come in second for the job. You might tell the interviewer, "I was very interested in the job with your company and appreciate your consideration. Would you be willing to tell me about the impression that I made?" You may learn something that can help your performance in future interviews.

SECTION III

■■■

*Using Your
Background in Banking
to Find Another Job*

6

JOBS WITH BANKING OUTSOURCERS

■ ■ ■

As you read this book and begin your job search, you will probably discover that the job market isn't nearly as bleak as you may have thought. You may even conclude that the discouraging statistics you have heard about banking jobs may be overstated, especially when you consider what is happening in banking today. The number of jobs in banks may be shrinking, but banking jobs and banking functions are to some degree merely shifting outside banks.

That is why you have heard so much in the last few years about banks "outsourcing" functions that were previously handled internally. You may have first encountered this trend in bank administration when you learned from management that your job would be eliminated because your division's functions were being taken over by a more cost-effective "outsourcer." Outsourcers have become major users of banking expertise and major employers of former bankers. This means that the bad news that your bank has decided to outsource your function could also be good news in disguise.

What is a "banking outsourcer"? Banking outsourcers do business all over the United States and beyond, but perform so many different functions that they defy simple definition. To many people in the banking industry, the term "outsourcer" means a service bureau or facilities management vendor. But with respect to the jobs available to former bankers, "outsourcer" means a company providing specialized professional services to financial institutions. They're not hard to find, because they serve both community banks and huge bank holding companies. Consequently, they may represent one of the most promising areas for the re-employment of displaced bankers.

One small Georgia outsourcer comprised of a dozen former bankers-turned-consultants concentrates on asset disposition; another firm in Ohio has provided hundreds of banks in the Midwest with specialized acquisitions, planning, and regulatory compliance services. The common thread among outsourcers is the marketing of a service that can reduce bank operating costs or position a bank more competitively with customers. This means that when considering whether your skills are marketable to outsourcers, you should keep in mind the reasons outsourcing exists. Evaluate whether the talents you cultivated in banking could mean enhanced profits to a prospective employer in outsourcing.

This chapter divides outsourcing opportunities for bankers into two categories: information systems outsourcing and general services outsourcing. Both outsourcing companies' revenue gains and the number of business start-ups indicate that these areas are growing, but no specific federal occupational data exists to tell former bankers where employment is strongest. Yet if the field is short on data, it's long on enthusiasm. When interviewed, many former bankers now in outsourcing report a rising demand for outsourcing specialties. They agree that the field is very promising.

"I think former bankers who don't just sit back and lick their wounds have a tremendous opportunity to take advantage of outsourcing trends," says Royce Chitty, a former bank marketing vice president who has chosen an entrepreneurial outsourcing career. "Banks are driven by efficiency and productivity, and if that's the case, why go against the trend? Instead, go with the trend and sell your productivity. Efficiency is really the essence of outsourcing."

The trend toward outsourcing services to the financial industry can be attributed, in part, to the tight budgets and restructuring caused by mergers and acquisitions. Ironically, the efficiency march, while it ousts many bankers from their jobs, creates the potential to replace those same jobs within outsourcing firms. Most eliminated jobs that migrate to outsourcing are in businesses that improve the performance of existing bank computer, management, and administrative systems.

■ INFORMATION TECHNOLOGY OUTSOURCING

Information systems consultants and researchers say that the outlook for data processing outsourcing companies is not just strong — it's skyrocketing. In a recent report on outsourcing published by the Yankee Group in Boston, the top nine financial services facilities management vendors had annual outsourcing revenues ranging from $31 to $900 million. Arthur Gillis, an outsourcing industry analyst based in New Orleans who studies the companies, says, "All vendors except IBM had smashing success in the early 1990s" in revenues and profits; and in the late 1990s, IBM has engineered a stunning revenue turnaround. A look at two leading vendors illustrates their success:

■ Electronic Data Systems Corporation in Dallas, founded in 1962, has operations in thirty countries and employs more than 95,000 people worldwide. EDS reported revenues of $12.5 billion in 1995. In 1984, EDS became an independently operated subsidiary of General Motors Corporation, but EDS's performance far outshines GM's. Services are provided to 5,000 financial institutions. An article in *Business Week* declares that the giant EDS is now "poised to grab the lion's share of the vast computer services market."

■ FIserv, based in Milwaukee, operates thirty-five data centers in the United States and abroad, maintaining integrated data processing services for more than 1,400 financial institutions. Employees number 3,800, and as of mid-1996, the company had achieved 42 consecutive quarters of record growth. Revenues for 1995 topped $703 million, a 21 percent increase over the prior year. In 1996, FIserv acquired UniFi, Inc. of Fort Lauderdale. Founded in 1983, UniFi offers clients a Windows-based mortgage loan origination system and a consumer loan origination system, both utilizing Unisys hardware and client/server technology. As part of the FIserv Mortgage Products Division, the UniFi group is closely aligned with the FIserv Data-Link Systems mortgage loan servicing business.

The performance of data processing outsourcers is expected to remain strong, says Richard M. Sullivan, executive director of the Bank Outsourcing Alliance and a consultant on the management of technology in the banking industry. "As loan portfolios get sorted out and banks' earnings reports continue to become more favorable — as the siege mentality ends — more executives of well-managed financial institutions will begin to appreciate the advantages of outsourcing," he says.

But does an increase in outsourcing of data processing by banks and thrifts translate into *more* available jobs for former bankers? Actually, the reverse may be the case, industry consultants and human resources professionals say. Sullivan explains that the advantages banks achieve by outsourcing data processing are primarily technological, meaning that as the number of outsourcing contracts increase, the total number of jobs necessary to perform the banking function shrink. Job hunters looking for a position with firms like EDS will need to have skills that are valued in a highly competitive and highly technical environment.

Does this mean bankers who want to move into outsourcing must already possess technological skills? Not necessarily, says Ted Shaw, who had twenty-three years of experience in the banking industry when he went to work for MTECH, a data processing company later acquired by EDS. Shaw says that he did not take advanced technical skills to his current job at EDS. Instead, he brought advanced banking managerial skills with him — pure operational know-how honed at First National Bank of Oklahoma City.

Operations Executive Crosses Desk Easily to Serve Bank Clients

"I grew up in the banking industry on the operational side, in data processing and correspondent banking, eventually managing all operational aspects," Shaw says. "I reached the position of president, then chief operating officer of the bank and vice chairman of the bank holding company, before the bank was acquired in 1986."

"With EDS I am vice president of the banking services division. I manage bank accounts in the United States with $5 billion in assets or less. We provide facilities management, service bureau processing, and other information technology services. I have profit and loss responsibilities for operations and customer service."

"The parallel I see between my banking experience and my current position is that both emphasize hands-on executive management experience. And my banking experience allows me in my position at EDS to put myself on the client's side of the desk — I ask myself what the banker needs and then, from the vendor side, determine how my company can supply items that meet the banker's needs. Understanding the terminology of bankers as well as the opportunities and challenges they face in their field gives me a distinct advantage in selling outsourcing services to these clients."

"Obviously if you've managed a sizable bank, or elements of it, you've been involved in strategic financial projections and customer service planning — these are skills I learned have a direct bearing on the business planning side of EDS. Certainly my network in the banking industry helps. When clients know you understand their business because you've been there yourself, you have an easier time gaining their trust and positioning your services as advantageous in a way they can relate to."

"I had a background managing data processing for the bank, but I was by no means a technologist. Former bankers seeking positions with a data processing company need an understanding of the applications and how they apply to customers. Many of today's bankers have that knowledge already because of modern banking's dependence on technology."

Shaw possesses several of the sought-after skills identified by recruiters in data processing outsourcing firms, skills that may be common among former bank executives: operations knowledge, comprehensive banking experience, and strong interpersonal sales abilities. His career change demonstrates the potential to creatively apply professional banking experience to meet the needs of data processing outsourcers. Among general services outsourcers, the job possibilities are far more numerous.

■ GENERAL SERVICES OUTSOURCING

"Finding a job with a general services outsourcer may be easier in service areas where banks need expertise, not a full-time staff," Shaw says. Indeed, many former bankers furnish that expertise as consultants with outsourcers. Ted Shaw reports: "There are people doing commercial loan servicing, compliance, general consulting, cost-cutting, reengineering. I believe a lot of exbankers possess those specialty skills and, by hooking up with others who have complementary skills, could sell their services to banks. Because of turnover and staff shrinkage in the banking industry, banks are looking to hire or buy those lost services from outside vendors rather than staffing to provide them internally."

Like the growth seen in data processing outsourcing, the expansion of general services outsourcers has been driven by cost-cutting initiatives within the industries they serve. Prospective employees and independent contractors will do well to keep cost-consciousness at the forefront of their effort to join the general services outsourcing market. Staff reductions that follow downsizing or acquisitions have actually been a boon to the consulting business "across the board," says Ed Hendricks, president of the Association of Management Consulting Firms. "They're looking for people who can come in and show them how to do the same amount of work with fewer employees working smarter and more productively. Alternately, they may want to outsource the whole function to consultants," he says. Hendricks contends that bankers who have gone through downsizing themselves "can probably transfer the lessons of that experience to other organizations going through downsizing."

Bankers with skills they know are marketable to financial institutions may be positioned to start their own entrepreneurial venture with other service providers. Trish Benninger, first vice president in human resources at Great Western Bank in Northridge, California, knows of some bankers who lost their jobs but continued to do the same work for the banks that let them go: "They just moved their department outside the bank and kept going." These entrepreneurs turned the circumstance that cost them their jobs to their own advantage: the bank wanted the service without the overhead and that's a need these exbankers knew they could meet outside the bank. Although this transition to self-employment sounds simple, the reality of making a job for yourself requires a sharp change of direction, self-examination, and careful planning.

Yet a growing number of jobless professionals choose to generate their own income by serving clients like their former employers (see chapter 14). And it appears that bank outsourcing has become a prime ground for growing your own business. Small firms like Young and Associates in Kent, Ohio, which provides specialized services to community bank clients, have experienced rapid success. Founded in 1978 by Gary Young, former director of marketing and personnel for United National Bank and Trust, the company now employs sixteen people and has grown from its Ohio base to other Midwest locations.

Specialization in Planning Focuses on Community Banks

"Planning was always the part of my banking background I liked the most," Young says. "A career path specializing in planning meant I kept moving to larger and larger financial institutions. But I really liked working with small financial institutions."

"So when I started my own consulting practice in 1978, the goal was to provide my specialized skills to a large number of small financial institutions, and that's where I've made my niche. Our consultants meet the needs of independent community banks that find us less expensive than maintaining the expertise on staff. About the only areas of banking that we are not involved in are legal work and certified audits. Our key areas are planning, expansion, branch or bank acquisitions, compliance, marketing and market research, loan review, and regulatory enforcement. We have people who specialize in all of these banking functions."

"Of the sixteen people on staff, eight are exbankers. We provide the services banks need more efficiently and a lot less expensively than banks could in-house."

Young adds, "I think the use of outsourcing will steadily increase over the next ten to twenty years. It's a matter of market and regulatory change, and the advent of tremendous opportunities. By controlling operating expenses through outsourcing, small banks can effectively compete with larger banks."

Another former banker, Royce Chitty, launched his own outsourcing company in Orlando. While optimistic about his chance for success, he is also realistic about what it will take to establish his own outsourcing business. The financial payback, he knows, may be slow, and a great deal of self-direction, salesmanship, and travel may be required.

Marketing VP Plans to Take Expertise Back to Banks

"I have twenty-five years of banking experience," Chitty says. "In my last position, I was responsible for an advertising budget of about $2 million, product development, pricing, market research, advertising, site selection and assessment — the full gamut of marketing. I have a B.S. in economics and business administration, and I've attended the graduate schools of banking at the University of Colorado and at the University of Chicago. I started out as a typical college graduate in the bank training program, going through operations, trust, and lending. Finally, because marketing was obviously what I enjoyed most in banking, I ended up staking my career in this area."

"I was not invited to stay on as part of the management team when our company was acquired. I spent sixty days looking for another job, then realized there was an opportunity here. I chose to go into business for myself. I quickly discovered that American businesses are increasingly outsourcing certain staff functions that were formerly performed in-house. I'm finding a market exists serving community banks that feel they cannot afford or justify a full-time, highly qualified marketing staff. I consider the market to be local banks, generally under $500 million in deposits, but well run. Their desire to control costs lends itself favorably to the proposition I have to offer."

"The only thing that I can sell and be confident in selling is what I do. But selling this kind of service just doesn't happen overnight; you have to develop some trust relationships with these clients and demonstrate that you can do what you say you're going to do. If you're a new company, there's really no track record to go on except what you've done with the banks you've worked for."

"What I'm trying to sell to any client is exactly what I did as marketing director of a single bank, and my focus is on five quality clients. In addition to community banks, larger banks can augment their marketing efforts and achieve a high degree of objectivity by hiring an outside firm such as mine. I think that's what you sell with the big banks — objectivity — and with the smaller banks, you can sell more than one service and do very well."

"I will have to do some traveling, and there is some front-end expense. You have to promote yourself; you have to be out there in the market where your client is. I'm probably happier than I've ever been because I'm doing something that I wanted to do all my life. Getting my company to the point that it provides a monetary return is another thing — it will take a little while. But if there's a nonfinancial benefit, then I'm enjoying it right now."

■ The Skills Bankers Bring to Outsourcing

"We have hired people in key departments who have banking backgrounds, and they don't necessarily have data processing backgrounds," says Bob Bellinger, senior vice president of human resources at FIserv. He believes that former bankers may indeed possess advantages over others for positions in outsourcing — "primarily the people who have had client experience, operational experience." But the chief skill he identified as desirable is banking industry knowledge.

"People who've been in banking know how a bank works; they know the banking culture. And, secondly, they know which products financial institutions use and what they need," Bellinger says. Knowledge of banking is also valued by general services outsourcers like Young and Associates, says Gary Young. But Young warns that too much experience can also be "the biggest disadvantage" when consulting firms are looking for innovative ideas. "Needing that fresh outlook is why clients turn to outsourcers," Young adds.

Other skills bankers possess may be exactly what is required for a career change to outsourcing. After all, outsourcing is, to a great degree, banking that occurs outside the bank. "I really believe that all banking skills are valuable," states Young. "A person with an investment background could provide outsourcing services on investments; a person in lending can provide services as well. You name a position in a bank, and it can be sold by an outsourcer."

Total Operations Savvy

"The areas in outsourcing that are most in demand are those that involve a total understanding of how a bank operates. As so many banks keep growing, more people who go into banking simply stick to their niche, never really learning how it all works. But because the banks have grown so large, the need for people with total banking understanding has become more critical," says Ted Shaw, the former banker now with EDS.

Systems Expertise

Richard Sullivan, with the Banking Outsourcing Alliance sees a growing demand for knowledge niches in information systems that involve high technological content. Among these are cash management and treasury management services, image statements, compliance, and network management. "What banks need to create a marketable program in these areas is not so much resources as expertise," Sullivan points out. He predicts that "in the cash management and treasury services area, you will see small boutique firms springing up."

Of course with large data processing outsourcers, systems experience may make it easier for former bankers to transfer their skills, explains Bellinger: "Because banking and technology are so closely aligned, anyone who has been in banking probably can find opportunities in the data processing field, provided they have some knowledge of technology." Programming, operations, product development, analysis, networking — outsourcers supply the full spectrum of systems responsibilities. Outsourcers are assuming a growing share of item processing and, Bellinger suggests, more data processing outsourcers are using the experience of former bankers in administering these services.

Sales Acumen and Contacts

"Pure sales skills" rank high on Bellinger's list of abilities in demand at FIserv. "We have a high level of hiring in sales, practically all of it from the financial industry because they have to know the product. We always look for good salespeople," he reports. Former bankers with strong relationship marketing, retail, or commercial account experience may have the job skills companies like FIserv seek.

Former bankers with many years in the industry may bring another valuable asset to outsourcing — their contacts. Whether or not one's banking experience required sales ability and client relationships, access to the circle of contacts surrounding the banking business is marketable to firms seeking banks as clients.

Lending and Asset Disposition Finesse

"Loan workout and lending is a promising area in outsourcing, but will demand innovative solutions," says Gary Young at Young and Associates. "The banking industry has struggled with the new Community Reinvestment Act requirements, and it takes someone with a tremendous amount of creativity to determine: How can I solve this problem in a low-cost, professional way? And it's not good enough just to be able to design the program; you must also sell the program."

■ WHERE ARE THE JOBS IN OUTSOURCING?

Jobs in some outsourcing disciplines can be found almost everywhere in the United States; in other disciplines, they are centered mainly in a few corporate offices. Bellinger at FIserv says that the company's employee roster fluctuates from approximately 3,800 to 4,000 people because of acquisitions, and it has offices and remote sites located in most states. "They are totally independent facilities," he says. Job applicants can contact the human resources or administrative officers at any of the FIserv locations, or the corporate office.

Other large data processing providers have processing centers dotting the country and remote sites in addition to corporate headquarters. The number of people employed outside central offices varies.

Yet the fact that a data processing outsourcer has remote locations may not mean that the likelihood of finding a job improves. Neither do satellite sites assure an applicant that a position will be available nearby. At FIserv, Bellinger says, "We're not constantly out there recruiting for bankers. Because acquiring companies is our current means of growth, we obtain a large number of talented people through acquisitions, and we try to promote and move people up from within. Occasionally, we will need those with specialized skills in certain bank products and will then look to candidates from the banking industry." Others monitoring the data processing industry report similar trends: significant growth in revenues and contracts, personnel added through acquisitions, and an emphasis on "raising their own."

Former bankers and human resources professionals in the data processing field acknowledge that employment with a large data processing company can require, in addition to a change in residence, moving to a radically different work environment.

"The data processing business has a substantially different culture than banking," explains Bellinger. "And I think it's very important for bankers who leave banking to understand the rapidity with which this industry has grown and is growing. It's a culture shock because it's a dynamic, fast-growing, highly competitive industry. It's a different ball game. Data processing is volatile because of S&L and some bank failures, so you have to be adaptable and you have to be creative."

Jobs with small and medium-size outsourcers that serve banks may be easier to find than positions with the large data processing outsourcers because the smaller firms can be found nearly everywhere. "You find general bank outsourcers all over the nation, but I think there are some locations where it wouldn't work," advises Gary Young. "You need a base of banks around you that will support the service you want to provide."

Building a Network

Neither Ted Shaw nor others in the outsourcing field can cite one central resource that helps job searchers find out more about outsourcing companies. Instead, Shaw suggests relying on bank associates and others to establish an information network the do-it-yourself way. "The best way to find a job in outsourcing is to link up with people who use outsourcing or with those you know who have started their own businesses providing the services banks need."

"It all starts with your local contacts. If you tie in with those local networks, your contact network will keep expanding," Shaw says. If a former banker with data processing experience is interested in employment with a data processing vendor, contacts within the bank and with the service bureaus the bank uses are good places to start. Human resources directors with outsourcing companies or independent data processing consultants may be willing to spend time with job hunters to discuss the industry and how to apply skills, regardless of their hiring needs.

Bellinger recommends these strategies to former bankers who want to effectively communicate the advantages of their skills to prospective employers: "I'm more interested in track record than I am in title. I want to know how results-oriented they are, and their accomplishments are extremely important. Applicants should come in to an interview confident, able to state what they can do for the company, and present a strong, positive image."

Gary Young emphasizes other qualities that may be particularly meaningful to employers in general service outsourcing who need consultants who are true problem-solving salespeople: "They need to have banking skills — that's a given — but the kind of people I'm looking for also have sales skills, are entrepreneurial, and can see things differently. The fact that a person has an insatiable desire to learn, to do quality work, to sell — those are the skills that I'm looking for. I believe that's what other employers providing this kind of work are looking for. And, in fact, that's what banks need."

"When I interview people, I try to look at their innovativeness, their excitement, their sales skills," he says. Because salesmanship might be an integral part of the job, Young advises people looking for a position in outsourcing to examine "the relationship between your personality and the personality of the job."

You can learn more about outsourcers through contacts with people in the industry (annual) reports, and company press coverage. To discover the location of those companies, Young suggests contacting state or national banking trade associations, many of which may have associate members who provide services to financial institutions. (And don't neglect to consult the directory of outsourcers in the Appendix section of this book.)

Young believes a successful job search begins as an information search. "Learn as much as you can about the business that you're interviewing with," he says. "When job candidates have to ask me a lot of questions about what we do during an interview, that's my signal that I don't want this person in my organization. I want someone who meets with clients to be well prepared and to have done their homework."

The ingredients it takes to make up a good job search in the outsourcing field turn out to be the same as those used for finding a job in banking or any other industry: close self-examination has to come first, followed by fact-finding. Finding a job in outsourcing depends upon whether the position you apply for requires skills that you already possess and whether you can actively demonstrate to the hiring outsourcer that you have them.

■ RESOURCES

Other bankers and outsourcing vendors are the best sources of information about outsourcing job possibilities. An alphabetic directory of U.S. companies that sell products and services to banks is included in the Appendix section of this book. The other sources listed below may be helpful in identifying outsourcers in specific job markets:

The business reference section of your local library (for financial business directories)

Community or state banking trade associations

American Bankers Association, 1120 Connecticut Avenue, NW, Washington, DC 20036; 202/663-5000; www.aba.bom/aba

Independent Bankers Association of America, 1 Thomas Circle, NW, Ste. 950, Washington, DC 20005; 202/659-8111; www.ibaa.org

Thomson's Blue Book: The Banker's Guide to Product and Service Providers, Thomson Financial Publishing, 4709 West Golf Road, Skokie, IL 60076-1253, 800/321-3373, 847/676-9600

Business and financial trade publications including *American Banker, Information Week, The Wall Street Journal, Forbes, Fortune, Barron's, Business Week, Bank Management, Jobs for Bankers*

7

Jobs In The Financial Services Industry

■ ■ ■

Accounting and Auditing ■ *Financial Analysis* ■ *Investment Management* ■ *Securities* ■ *Financial Planning* ■ *Treasury Management* ■ *Credit Specialists*

Bankers with experience in these areas may be qualified to move to jobs in the financial services industry:

ACCOUNTING AND AUDITING
BRANCH MANAGEMENT
COMMERCIAL LENDING
CONSUMER LOANS
CREDIT
FINANCE MANAGEMENT
MARKETING AND
   PRODUCT MANAGEMENT

OPERATIONS
RELATIONSHIP MANAGEMENT
SYSTEMS DESIGN AND
   INTEGRATION
TREASURY CONSULTING
TRUST AND ESTATE
   PLANNING

A banker doesn't need a springboard to jump into a job in the financial services industry. In fact, such a move can be better described as a slide, because the skills honed in banking are particularly adaptable to related jobs in the financial services industry.

Bankers use analytical skills and cultivate bank-client relationships on a daily basis. These skills and others required in the rapidly evolving banking environment qualify career changers for jobs in the financial services industry. Further, many of the trends that have created job opportunities in the financial services industry mimic changes long under way in banking — globalization, restructuring, accelerated competition, rapidly changing financial products, expanding fee-based services, and rocketing systems technology.

Consequently, the lines between banking jobs and some of the jobs described in this chapter are fuzzy. The job transition of former banker Daniel Perkins is a good example of how bankers may be able to continue to perform the jobs they always have by the simple expedient of switching industries; Perkins went straight to work for Arthur Andersen from his job at a Chicago bank.

A Jump to the Big Six

"While I was with the bank I was a vice president and manager, specializing in full-time treasury management consulting," Perkins says. "I generated revenue from fee-based consulting work done on the premises of clients, spending time analyzing their problems."

"When I was told that the bank was going to phase out the consulting division, I was aware that Arthur Andersen had entered this market. As it turned out, I was able to develop the business for them. The key was that Arthur Andersen wanted to expand this segment of their market. I presented a skill and a reputation that they found desirable; and there was support from my management at the bank and senior management here to actually bring me in."

"I looked around, and this is where I felt my skills would best be used. I would have the system support I wanted, and I wanted to work for a worldwide network. I'm involved in cash management, foreign exchange, and treasury organization consulting, generally for multinational and medium-sized corporations and financial institutions."

"I have a bachelor of science degree in finance and an M.B.A. in marketing, and I am definitely not an accountant by training. I do not have a C.P.A. or an audit background. Although Arthur Andersen does have other business advisory consulting specialties and a few other consultants like me who came from other industries, my transition was atypical. I am an exception, but the job was the right fit."

Perkins literally crossed the street to manage a group in treasury consulting, the same job he had filled at the bank. His client base at Arthur Andersen is similar to the one he had with the bank, but he savors some of the differences between the jobs and being part of a new business culture. "I like the high level of professionalism here and the real enthusiasm of some of the younger people who are assisting with these projects. I find that the talent and the ability, and the credentials of the firm are impeccable," he says. "It's excellent to have that."

Perkins's career move into a Big Six accounting firm may be unusual, but the trait that landed him there is one many experienced bankers share: an expertise that can generate profits. High marks on the bottom line in banking can often translate into resumes that are marketable to accounting and other financial service firms.

Former bank vice president and credit officer Mac Smith employed another useful tool for career transfer — personal contacts — to facilitate his move to a job in securities at the regional brokerage firm Robinson-Humphrey in Augusta, Georgia. Although his new career does use some of the skills he acquired as a banker, he is, for the most part, a banker in a strange land. Smith says what made his new job a natural fit was his long-term sideline interest in investing.

Why Not Do What You Like Full-Time?

"I had worked in banks all my life," Smith says. "I worked as credit officer for a statewide bank that was subsequently bought out — that happened in 1985 — so I've been through this before. I did consulting work for about a year. I was a registered investment advisor with the SEC and monitored small companies as well as individuals. Then Bankers First Corporation, a firm I worked for on a consulting basis, made me an offer to come and be their credit officer."

"I was there six and a half years and spent most of my time working out problem loans. Then the bank decided to let me go. So the question became, *What do you do now?* I wanted to write a book, so I wrote one. It's on changes in the banking industry in the last twenty years."

"I spent six months working on that — I was also doing some consulting work valuing an S&L portfolio — then one day I got a call from an associate who told me that Robinson-Humphrey was looking for a few new brokers. He wanted to know if he could recommend me. Then someone else called to say he had recommended me for the same position."

"I had never really thought about going into securities prior to that. I had always dabbled in stocks, and I had been fairly successful at it. So a light went on, and I said to myself, *I've done that for thirty years. Why not do it full-time?* I went through the interview process at Robinson-Humphrey. I was honest with the manager, and he was honest with me. I'm not exactly a spring chicken, but I don't start from zero because I've had fairly good investment experience for the last thirty years. And I do know a number of people all over the Southeast."

"I did the testing in December, and I was told I had the job in February. There is a two-month training program to prepare me for the Series 7 examination, which covers twenty-two different topics on various types of securities and regulations. It definitely helped to have actively invested for some time. I'm looking for all the training they will offer me because I think it will be useful and profitable for me."

"There's really not a lot from the banking side that's transferable — looking at companies and making decisions about leverage and income and that type of thing — other than personal contacts."

"My advice to others leaving banking is to do something that you like and have always wanted to do."

■ **THE SKILLS BANKERS BRING TO THE**
   FINANCIAL SERVICES INDUSTRY

Terry L. Blum, director of transition services and a principal at
Arthur Andersen, agrees with Daniel Perkins that moving from a
bank to the accounting firm is very unusual. In fact, more than 95
percent of the firm's personnel were hired at entry level. "The firm
puts over 10 percent of its gross revenues back into training,"
Blum says. "It is part of the culture of Arthur Andersen."
The hiring policies of other Big Six and regional accounting firms
may differ, however. Blum is quick to point out that there are opportunities for bankers in the field. "Their skills are transferable if they are
functionally skilled in accounting and external reporting, regulatory
reporting like the SEC, certainly bank and other loan covenant reporting requirements, and maybe even venture capital requirements."
Blum explains that in any accounting position today, "people have to
be more knowledgeable about the technical aspects of accounting. Accounting technical knowledge has just ballooned."
Besides the crossover potential of functional skills, changes in the
character of accounting firms make it easier for bankers to move into
accounting. Blum says that most large public accounting firms today
are evolving into financial consulting firms, so the products those
firms offer have grown far beyond traditional auditing functions and
have become increasingly similar to those available from other financial services companies.
Bank managers with a systems specialization may find their skills
also in demand in the financial services industry. Andersen Consulting, the largest accounting consulting practice in the world, is primarily involved in consulting on issues of information technology in all industries. Information systems technology has exploded in many
financial services firms just as it has in banking, and information systems expertise can provide a bridge to careers outside banking.
Bankers not only possess knowledge of the banking industry, but
also of functional areas like accounting, systems, capital markets, and

specialized business analysis. For example, loan workout and management skills are in demand because of recent banking industry mergers,
acquisitions, and insolvencies. A financial consultant in asset management who travels the country assisting financial institutions says,
"There are opportunities for bankers if they've had experience in special asset management or in commercial loans. And there are some
wonderful opportunities out there for thrift industry experts who've
spent time in investor servicing, the servicing phase of the mortgage
business."

Bank human resources professionals interviewed identified the
skills mentioned above as well as many others as valuable in moving
from banking to other financial services jobs.

Accounting was named as one of the most easily transferred skills
— it is a "universal role," according to Larry DeMeyers, chief operating officer of Bankers First Savings Bank in Augusta, Georgia. De-
Meyers, whose own background includes human resources management and methods analysis for personnel restructuring, cited
accounting, auditing, and financial controlling as areas into which
bankers moved smoothly.

Nancy Seever, vice president with First Chicago and the manager
of that bank's career counseling center, says that while accounting
know-how is valued across the financial services industry, she recommends that bankers explore opportunities with smaller accounting
consulting firms, since they are "popping up everywhere," she says.

"Credit workout is clearly the best placement we see for bankers,"
says John Durkin, human resources director for Heritage Federal Savings Bank in Richmond, Virginia. Durkin named this skill area as particularly promising for transfers to other banks and to financial services firms and suggests that a banker "look for a position with an
institution that has a similar asset portfolio." Durkin also says that the
analytical skills developed in credit analysis can be applied to securities and other investment environments.

Retail branch management, relationship management, and com-

mercial lending, which develop the ability to sell and retain accounts, may be translated into several sorts of sales careers in the financial services industry. "Bankers with these backgrounds know how to close a deal," asserts DeMeyers.

Trust and investment professionals who have been involved in mergers, consolidations, and acquisitions have many valuable skills, personnel managers say. Their expertise "can be transferred to any service industry that's consolidating — or to any consulting firm that is consulting on acquisitions," says Robin McNeil, manager of employee relations and staffing at Great Western Bank in Northridge, California. According to First Chicago's Seever, some of the trust and investment bankers leaving that bank have gone to foreign banks.

The finance and financial planning savvy possessed by many experienced bankers is absolutely transferable to many other areas. However, further education or certification may be desirable or necessary for bankers who want to remain in finance.

Consumer lenders may discover new career possibilities in various places in the financial services industry. "The consumer guy can go anywhere," says DeMeyers. Consumer lenders are particularly likely to find new jobs in finance or credit card companies or within the credit departments of other sorts of companies.

■   **LANDING IN THE RIGHT**
    FINANCIAL SERVICES JOB

Despite the toll of shakeouts and restructuring in the financial services industry, it still may be a great place to look for a job. The outlook for careers in financial services is promising because, across the board, financial services jobs are growing more complex. With this increasing complexity comes heightened demand for expertise. Successful job seekers are able to respond to the avalanche of technology with a broad perspective on the business world and a knowledge of computerized analysis.

Bankers may be unusually attractive to employers because the need for specialized business financial information is increasing. Experience working as part of a team also enhances a banker's value because assigning a collection of specialists to a financial problem in business is an increasingly common approach.

Accounting

Lots of current career handbooks maintain that management consulting is the biggest growth area in accounting. Opportunities are more numerous and pay is higher for financial planning and analysis positions than for pure accounting and auditing jobs. This trend may reflect employment trends, since management analysis and consulting occupations are expected to grow rapidly in the 1990s, earning a ranking in the 1995 edition of *America's 50 Fastest Growing Jobs* and scoring high in the U.S. Department of Labor's *Occupational Outlook Handbook* predictions. Although it is unusual to see accounting professionals move from the management and corporate areas of accounting to public accounting, the move from public to corporate accounting is much more common.

Because constantly changing tax laws and business regulations continually complicate the accountant's job, the capacity for learning is an important factor in success as an accountant. And the nearly one million accountants in the United States perform many more tasks than the traditional tax and audit functions. Their work includes actuarial functions, advising regarding mergers and acquisitions, and systems design. An increasing number of people in accounting choose to work for themselves. According to *Career Choices For the '90s*, there are 100,000 self-employed accountants in the United States, not counting those who are small-business proprietors — in short, accounting may be a good fit for entrepreneurs.

Securities

In securities, a field many displaced bankers consider, banking experience may be meaningful at both the entry and experienced-hire levels because many securities firms have expanded to offer more bank-like products.

Because there is more knowledge to market in the investment supermarkets, there may be more specialty niches available for skilled bankers. For instance, the financial analyst's job is one position available to many bankers that offers superior growth and earnings potential. The skills financial analysts need clearly overlap those used in banking and securities; the book *Top Professions* reports that 21 percent of financial analysts are employed in brokerage houses and 16 percent in banks.

Treasury and Investment Consulting

Treasury consulting jobs like the one Daniel Perkins landed at Arthur Andersen can offer a close match for former bankers who have domestic or international treasury experience.

Jobs in treasury consulting and investment consulting may combine several areas of concentration, and bankers with wide-ranging backgrounds may find that they can use all their experience in these jobs. For example, a former employee of an independent bank in California who had experience in branch management, cash management, commercial lending, and marketing was able to employ his skills in an investment management company.

Credit Specialists

Credit unions are one of the most aggressive and fastest-growing segments of the financial services industry. Consequently, credit unions may offer opportunities to former bankers.

Consumer lending institutions have profited from the current consumer enthusiasm for refinancing. Bank human resources managers report that, as a result, bankers are going to work for these institutions. Career counselors suggest that bank credit managers can often apply their talents to work with credit card companies. Investment bankers may also profit from the growing demand for their skills in consumer credit organizations.

■ DO YOU NEED MORE EDUCATION OR CERTIFICATION?

Further education may be necessary, especially for bankers seeking re-employment in the financial services industry. M.B.A.'s are increasingly common at large accounting consulting firms, and the broader perspective afforded by many master's programs is a useful complement to bankers' solid business experience in areas traditionally related to banking.

Securities firms are enrolling more M.B.A.'s for sales, research, and analyst positions, too, but hiring preferences vary. A master's degree in financial planning, or a diploma from an academic center for financial planning, such as the College of Financial Planning in Denver, Colorado, definitely enhances the chance for advancement in this specialized field.

Certain certifications are standard within accountancy and can ease the transition from banking to a career within the financial services industry. Some pertinent facts emphasize the value of several kinds of certification:

■ According to the U.S. Department of Labor, one-third of accountants are C.P.A.'s. Entrepreneurial accounting ventures benefit from certification, and certified accountants earn 10 percent more than those who are not certified, according to the book *Career Choices*.

■ The guidebook *Jobs '96* reports that more than 40 percent of all accountants and auditors possess certification.

■ Numerous career guides suggest that further education in financial planning or membership in the Financial Analysts Federation may be required to advance in these specialties.

■ Besides having more stringent certification requirements, more financial jobs now require a working knowledge of financial software programs.

To learn more about the C.P.A., C.M.A., or C.I.A. certifications, contact your state board of accountancy, the American Institute of Certified Public Accountants, the Institute of Management Accountants, or the Institute of Internal Auditors at the addresses listed below.

■ LEARNING MORE ABOUT BREAKING IN

Who you know may be as critical as what you know in the financial services industry; knowing the right people can be an experienced banker's only way into many firms.

The largest national accounting firms still recruit mostly at business schools, which is, of course, not where most experienced bankers find themselves. But, as Terry Blum says, companies like Arthur Andersen "never say never." Revenue-generating skills and an established client base or technological knowledge of systems specific to an industry can ensure that a banker seeking re-employment is hired.

Regional and local financial services firms may recruit through personal referrals and newspaper advertisements but, as with any job search, the best response is the one tailored to the need. The edge in a job application or in pursuing a personal contact in any organization can come from learning more about the job you think you can fill.

Reliable sources for learning more include your local library, professional publications and associations, and organization insiders. Library business reference sections typically house a mountain of industry-specific reference materials, and reference librarians are the curators of all that information. Don't hesitate to describe the information you're seeking and request a librarian's help.

Your inquiries into banking-related or new fields should be fueled by your curiosity. Which financial services or products do prospective employers sell that parallel your banking experience? How has the firm expanded? Has the press reported any plans for expansion or restructuring that might require new employees with your expertise? Cutbacks in one area can spawn opportunities in another.

Some professional organizations offer publications and job service listings that can assist bankers looking for new jobs. Some, like the National Association of Credit Managers, run employment referral services.

A former banker with a specialty could mean a new profit center within an organization. In short, if you can tell them how you can help their bottom line, you're hired.

■ RESOURCES

Moody's Bank and Finance Manual (Moody's Investors Service) (annual)

Standard and Poor's Security Dealers of North America, (semiannual with supplements published every six weeks)

Journal of Accountancy and other technical and professional journals published by the American Institute of Certified Public Accountants

Accounting Today magazine

Business publications, including *The Wall Street Journal*, *Forbes*, *Fortune*, *Barron's*, *Business Week*

National Business Employment Weekly, Jobs for Bankers

Professional Associations

American Institute of Certified Public Accountants, 1211 Avenue of the Americas, New York, NY 10036-8775; 800/862-4272 or 212/596-6200 in New York

Institute of Management Accountants, 10 Paragon Drive, Montvale, NJ 07645-1760; 800/638-4427; www.rutgers.edu/accountng/raw/ima

Institute of Internal Auditors, Inc., 249 Maitland Avenue, Altamonte Springs, FL 32701-4201; 407/830-7600

International Board of Standards and Practices for Certified Financial Planners, 1660 Lincoln, Ste. 3050, Denver, CO 80111; 303/830-7543

Association for Investment Management and Research (formerly Institute of Chartered Financial Analysts and Financial Analysts Federation), P.O. Box 3668, Charlottesville, VA 22903; 804/977-6600; www.aimr.com/aimr.html

Financial Management Association, International University of South Florida College of Business, Ste. 3331, Tampa, FL 33620; 813/974-2084; www.aglover@bsn01.bsn.usf.edu

National Association of Security Dealers, 1735 K St., NW, Washington, DC 20006; 202/728-8000

8

JOBS IN EDUCATION

■ ■ ■

*Teaching ■ Administration ■ Financial Management ■
Human Resources ■ Development*

*Bankers with experience in these areas may be qualified to move to
jobs in education:*

ACCOUNTING AND AUDITING	FINANCIAL ANALYST
SUPERVISION	INTERNATIONAL
CERTIFIED APPRAISER	HUMAN RESOURCES
CONTROLLER	MARKETING
CORPORATE MANAGEMENT	OPERATIONS
CORPORATE PLANNING	SYSTEMS
CREDIT MANAGEMENT	TRUSTS AND INVESTMENTS

One former banker describes his new job in education this
way: "There's a learning curve that seems to rejuvenate me." Like the
other former bankers now in education discussed in this chapter, that
rejuvenated banker possesses traits that made a job in education interesting to him in unanticipated ways.

From VP/Corporate Planner to Classroom Business Strategist

Like most bankers-turned-educators, Dr. Ray Grubbs, professor of
management at the Else School of Management at Millsaps College,

didn't wait until he left banking to begin his postgraduate studies. His interest in continued education actually prepared him for the job change he didn't know he would make. After leaving banking during the 1970s to get a master's degree in management, Dr. Grubbs returned to banking and worked his way up to vice president and director of corporate planning and marketing at a statewide Mississippi bank.

Dr. Grubbs earned his doctorate while working full-time at the bank, teaching two or three nights a week. He left banking again to write his doctoral dissertation on management. When he returned to banking the second time, he felt ambivalent about banking.

"As director of corporate planning and marketing, my primary responsibilities were to try to apply a more systematic approach to planning, to run and manage the marketing function, and to make an attempt to interface marketing with planning," Dr. Grubbs says.

"My decision to leave banking for good, which was not at all easy, was helped by an associate. Together we wrote a book called *New Product Development in Banking, A Manager's Guide*, published by Prentice Hall. I could see in him a lot of the other things that I could be doing. I realized I could still stay active in banking through writing and research and through consulting. I also realized that I could be supported in those activities if I could get into an academic situation."

"One of the things that teaching has given me is the opportunity to write. I've now written four books that have all been directed toward the banking industry. I share the experience that made those books possible with my students and with groups with which I consult. Some teachers don't have the first-hand, practical experience I have."

"You don't make the decision to go into teaching for money. You do it for other reasons — for your own satisfaction, for your own enjoyment, for the lifestyle."

Dr. Grubbs's present career is truly a hybrid. He teaches several courses, including an introductory management course, a senior business strategy class, and the school's graduate-level capstone M.B.A. course. He also works on long-term consulting projects. Dr. Grubbs's book writing has fueled his consulting, primarily in the human resources field. This consulting work often consists of complex tasks that are not being performed by the banks that hire him, such as designing salary administration programs, analyzing the structure and classification of jobs, and defining the quality of services offered.

The Best of Both Worlds for a Finance Educator

A teaching career can offer job diversity and the opportunity to work in areas of special interest. Those are some of the reasons that Dr. Hazel Johnson, assistant professor of finance at the University of Louisville, switched from banking to education. She worked as a C.P.A., then as a bank financial analyst and accounting supervisor. Along the way she found out that she enjoyed teaching others, and she found the autonomy possible in teaching appealing.

"I received a lot of satisfaction from supervising the employees for whom I was responsible," Dr. Johnson says. While completing my master's program I saw that my professors seemed to enjoy the best of both worlds — they were able to train *and* teach, apparently receiving a lot of satisfaction from that. At the same time they were able to pursue their individual interests. They had a great deal of autonomy and could research those questions that intrigued them.

"I made a direct move to education, forgoing a respectable salary and becoming a student. The transition would not require as much risk-taking if you were already displaced. Education at this level is very much self-driven. The lifestyle is very good if you can manage your own time and if you are a self-starter. Anyone considering education should understand this."

Although Dr. Johnson had worked while earning her master's degree earlier in her career, her only support during her doctoral studies was from a teaching assistantship and a grant. She chose the University of Florida for her doctorate because it gave her the chance to work with a finance professor who was a leader in the field. She continues to shape her academic activities with similar purposefulness, writing books and delving deeper into international activities as associate director of the University of Louisville's International Business Unit.

Robert I. Spengler, a former bank president and chief operating officer, also left banking for education. However, instead of getting a master's degree or doctorate, he chose a new career as senior development officer for gift and estate planning at the University of Colorado Foundation in Boulder, a career involving an altogether different set of responsibilities.

Looking for a Change in Education

"My experience really spanned the administrative side and concentrated on general management, including investments and operations as well as all other facets of the bank," Spengler says. "I turned fifty at the same time I completed twenty years with the organization, so it was in that framework that I looked at ways that I could leave."

"I left the bank without any clear picture of where I wanted to be. Part of the excitement to me was having the chance to step back from a successful career and explore other ideas — going back to school, getting into academics, maybe getting involved in a small business arrangement, or joining the corporate environment from a different angle. I took three months and looked at a really wide spectrum of opportunities."

"I was looking for a change, so when I looked at my options, I asked, *What are the things that are similar? What are the things that are different? Where do I get different challenges?* The job I accepted combined the new with the familiar. It provided an affiliation with the university and a chance to improve the academic environment and further the opportunities for young people to receive a superior education, something that's always been very important to me. And it provided me with a different kind of role; here, I'm not running an organization with 250 people and $350 million in assets."

"My job is completely the opposite of that. This time around, I'm part of a staff, and I'm focused as a technical person. I am involved in any type of giving that might come to the university, but my focus is on trust and estate planning. The correlation with banking comes from my financial background, dealing with businesspeople in large businesses and individual donors."

"I have the opportunity to explore completely new horizons and enter a professional terrain that is unfamiliar and filled with new challenges. There's a learning curve that rejuvenates me."

■ THE SKILLS BANKERS BRING TO EDUCATION

Bankers bring to education their business acumen, their practical problem-solving orientation, and the application of academic economic principles to everyday challenges. Former bank vice president Dr. Grubbs insists that his years in banking have had a significant effect on his teaching: "Graduate and undergraduate students tell me they really appreciate the practical applications of course material I take into my classes."

Knowledge, Technical Expertise, and Contacts

"I think bankers can be very successful in teaching because they have perspective," Dr. Grubbs says. "Having worked within an organization, they are able to translate that experience into something that students can relate to better than they can relate to a textbook."

Bankers who have been involved in training, human resources or other departments, or who have financial certifications and supervisory experience, may bring marketable talents to a career as an educator. Dr. Johnson teaches corporate finance, but she makes direct use of her years as a banker both in another course she teaches and in writing her books. "My focus on bank management and financial institutions is a very strong part of my professional life today. The banking experience has been very helpful."

Many business students today study finance and credit basics and much more — including integrated information and manufacturing systems courses, financial planning licensing courses, and entrepreneurship courses — in classroom environments very different from those at traditional four-year colleges. The variety of disciplines that today's bankers must master make them valuable as teachers. Dr. Michael Homer, dean of the School of Business and Technology at Salt Lake Community College in Salt Lake City, Utah, explains that business studies increasingly involve the integration of multiple disciplines emphasizing cross-training in a variety of functional areas. The characteristics necessary to this teaching approach — "teamwork, human relations skills, a solid understanding of the economy, and respect for the profit motive and the work ethic" — are traits many bankers have.

Yet teaching is just one of many skill applications in education. Some banking-to-education job moves are, like many opportunities in business and industry, direct transfers of skills, especially for bankers with accounting, administration, and human resources experience. Robert Spengler, the former banker who is now senior development officer at the University of Colorado, believes that bankers bring a broad range of skills to education.

"The philosophy and the background bankers have serve them very well in the educational environment. By and large, most of them are thoughtful and analytical. In most cases, if they've been successful in banking, they also have people skills. These attributes transfer over into many academic areas, including management roles in university administration, financial roles in the treasurer's office, or people roles in alumni relations or development work," he says.

■ LANDING IN THE RIGHT JOB IN EDUCATION

Switching from banking to education may take considerable time and creativity, whatever the education job. For teaching, time may be required for retraining to acquire the necessary credentials; in other areas of education employment, candidates may need to carefully examine their skills and convince prospective employers that those skills can be useful in new jobs.

Patience is important. "My best advice is to invest your time as carefully as you invest your money. Every investment won't necessarily pay off immediately and the transition may not be immediate, but you're really planning the rest of your career," Dr. Hazel Johnson says.

Job descriptions in teaching vary greatly. Opportunities may be best in part-time adjunct teaching and corporate training jobs; such jobs can allow former bankers to create hybrid careers by combining teaching with consulting or other activities.

Occupational openings in education are expected to rise in the nineties, mainly because of retiring professors and the introduction of new courses. The key to finding employment in education is taking the long view in looking for an education job and knowing where to look.

Teaching in a Four-year College or University

Sharon Barber, director of communications for the American Assembly of Collegiate Schools of Business, reports that, largely because of hiring freezes resulting from budget crunches at state schools, faculty hiring is down in business studies, the academic area in which most former bankers may be qualified. Yet this trend appears to contradict enrollment figures and a perceived shortage of business school faculty. Barber attributes these conflicting trends to increased interest in business degrees: "Over one-fourth of all students in this country, both undergraduates and graduate students, are getting their degrees in business. As a result, many business schools have had to limit enrollment."

Retrenchments in academic hiring, however, are expected to give way to the pressure for more instructors, resulting in a shortage of teachers.

Teaching in a Community College

Because the number of job openings is high, teaching in community colleges may be the most promising area for re-employment for former bankers who are interested in educational positions. "Community college enrollments are the fastest growing segment of higher education in the United States," Dr. Homer says. He anticipates growth in the number of teaching positions available at community colleges, despite state budget cuts, and says that opportunities may be greatest for experienced minority job seekers.

Teaching professionals agree that the more broad-based educational mission at many community colleges allows greater room for accommodating the wide range of business experience some bankers possess. Specialty courses with practical or certification goals are common at community colleges, as are fundamental courses in economics. Teaching such courses may be the perfect niche for an experienced banker. Dr. Joe Kinzer, president of Northern Oklahoma College and of the Association of Collegiate Business Schools and Programs, says, "There are some really nice opportunities for middle and upper level bankers to make a contribution in higher education, particularly at the junior college level." These opportunities may require a less traditional approach to employment, however.

Dr. Kinzer relates the flexible approach of a former Oklahoma bank president who wanted to teach at Northern Oklahoma College. "He has an undergraduate business degree, an M.B.A., and twenty years of banking experience — the best credentials you could ask for," Dr. Kinzer says. Because budget constraints made it impossible for Dr.

Kinzer to offer him a full-time job, the former banker agreed to join the college faculty as a part-time member, teaching one class.

Secondary School Teaching

Secondary school teaching may be a rare second career for bankers, but it is attracting many nontraditional candidates across the country in the wake of a renewed emphasis on teaching as a career. The job satisfaction and personal fulfillment that can accompany a career in secondary education may overshadow perceived drawbacks to make teaching attractive to former bankers.

A recent survey by the American Association of Colleges for Teacher Education reported that alternative teacher certification programs in thirty states make the job change easier for professionals with undergraduate degrees. Some new model certification programs put experienced businesspeople into the classroom immediately after they pass basic examinations and allow them to fulfill extra course requirements for licensing while they're on the job.

Corporate Training and Noncredit Executive Education

Whereas some college faculty positions teaching business courses require "terminal degrees" (degrees considered by the college to be the final step in training for the field), hiring decisions for noncredit teaching positions typically are based on a candidate's experience and personality. Dr. Russell Nelson, dean of the College of Business and Administration at the University of Colorado in Boulder, believes that noncredit teaching positions are a promising field for former bankers. "Since it is a nondegree job improvement or perspective-shifting activity," Nelson says, "the requirements are simply that you be good at it. People with highly developed job skills and the ability to make presentations and interact well with executive audiences may find some great opportunities in this field."

Demand is increasing for remedial and economic development

training. (One business school dean reports that the industrial contract training component of his enrollment, classes that teach skills specific to an industry, is growing four times faster than general business enrollment.) Kathryn and Ross Petras write in their guidebook that corporations are training and retraining as many as ten million workers a year, and the book *Top Professions* predicts that the number of corporate training specialist positions will grow dramatically. Increasingly, basic business skills will be taught to employees by American businesses. Often, university-based programs are the source for this training.

■ DO YOU NEED MORE EDUCATION OR CERTIFICATION?

More education can be a ticket to advancement in jobs in the financial services industries, but in the teaching field, most former bankers will need to possess advanced degrees to be considered at all for many available positions. Gaining even the basic credentials for teaching at the four-year college level may require years of study.

Four-year business school deans asked about these qualifications said unanimously that a doctorate is necessary for employment. According to the American Association of Collegiate Schools of Business, faculty hiring at the nation's business schools is down and competition for available positions is up. "Having a master's degree under your belt shortens the amount of time it takes to terminally qualify yourself," Dr. Grubbs says, "but if college teaching is what you want to do, you've got to be prepared to get your doctorate and get that stamp of validation."

Earning a doctorate to teach in a business school requires more than focus and direction; in most cases, doctoral-program students must be full-time, residential students. Assistantships or grants can help, as they did in the case of Dr. Johnson.

One exception to the rule that a doctorate is required is in teaching accounting. Dr. Nelson explains, "In many schools the accounting program is oriented toward professional accountancy. A C.P.A. and an M.B.A. may be sufficient for certain types of teaching, but there are a goodly number of highly qualified accountants who are available for such work." It's one of the "facts of life" that bankers considering education as a second career should know, Dr. Nelson believes.

Credentials requirements may be more flexible at the community college or secondary education level. Yet business educators agree that a master's degree is "strongly preferred" for business teachers at community colleges and in high schools. Dr. Homer recalls filling a finance and credit faculty position in 1991. Of the screened applicants, 80 percent had master's degrees — yet, he states, "We're not locked into that. If they had one or more certifications with a good, rich experiential background and a bachelor's degree in the field, they would be competitive with an individual who had a master's degree." At Salt Lake Community College, the dean weighs the number of courses an applicant has taken in accounting and finance and the applicant's valid work experience and certifications when evaluating candidates for vacant faculty positions.

■ LEARNING MORE AND BREAKING IN

Certifications and educational requirements, many of which are dictated by state law, vary greatly from institution to institution. So the best way to get the information you need to assess the sufficiency of your qualifications is to ask the schools in your area and your state department of education what qualifications they require.

Taking a teaching job on an adjunct basis can accomplish two things; such part-time teaching can open the door to full-time employment and can allow the adjunct teacher to test the waters in education. Dr. Homer says, "One of the best ways to become a candidate for a job opening that appears full-time at a community college is to first teach part-time and develop a reputation as a good teacher. Not every practitioner in the business community can teach, nor can all teachers successfully practice in specific professional settings." In Salt Lake Community College's business program, approximately twice as many part-time as full-time teachers are employed.

"Most community colleges do not hire through national searches or national advertising," says Bill Reinhard, assistant vice president for communications for the American Association of Community and Junior Colleges. "Most of them hire locally, especially when it comes to the part-time continuing education classes." Nevertheless, Dr. Homer says he does advertise in the *Chronicle of Higher Education, Community College Week*, and *Community, Technical and Junior College Times*. The *Chronicle* now posts copies of their publication at their Web site, along with job listings that are posted and updated monthly.

■ RESOURCES

Peterson's Guide to Four Year Colleges, Peterson's Guide to Two Year Colleges, Peterson's regional educational directories

Peterson's American Education (Educational Directories) (annual)

Chronicle of Higher Education (weekly newspaper)

Requirements for Certification of Teachers, Counselors, Librarians, Administrators for Elementary and Secondary Schools by John Tryneski (University of Chicago) (annual)

Community, Technical and Junior College Times, published by the American Association of Community and Junior Colleges

Jobs in Education (Career/Consultants in Education) (monthly job listings)

Professional Associations

National Education Association, 1201 Sixteenth St., NW, Washington, DC 20036; 202/833-4000; www.nea.org

American Federation of Teachers, 555 New Jersey Ave., NW, Washington, DC 20001; 202/879-4400; www.aft.org

American Assembly of Collegiate Schools of Business, 600 Emerson Rd., Ste. 300, St. Louis, MO 63141-6762; 314/872-8481; www.aacsb.edu

American Association of Community and Junior Colleges, 1 Dupont Circle, NW, Ste. 410, Washington, DC 20036; 202/728-0200; www.aac.ncag.edu

Association of Collegiate Business Schools and Programs (accredits associate-level and smaller four-year college business programs), 7007 College Blvd., 420, Overland Park, KS 66211; 913/339-9356; www.admin1.athens.tec.ga.un/acbsp.html

American Society for Training and Development, 1640 King St., Box 1443, Alexandria, VA 22313; 703/683-8100; www.astd.org.

9

JOBS IN GOVERNMENT

■ ■ ■

Bankers with experience in these areas may be especially likely to be hired by municipal, county, state, and federal governments and government agencies and government contractors:

ACCOUNTING AND AUDITING   FINANCE
ADMINISTRATION   HUMAN RESOURCES
COMMERCIAL LENDING   REAL ESTATE
CONSUMER LENDING   RETAIL BANKING
CREDIT   SYSTEMS TECHNOLOGY

Many public-sector jobs, from small town tax assessor to U.S. Treasury Commissioner, require, to some extent, the skills of a banker. Jobs with the federal government generally reflect the occupational diversity of public jobs. The listings in the *Federal Career Directory* make it clear that if a position exists in private business, its twin can be found in one or another department of the federal government. There are about 900 occupations listed in the *Directory*, but openings change and jobs evolve as new laws and regulations are implemented.

It's easier to target a federal job than to figure out how to land it. Even experienced professionals may find entering government service difficult. The former bankers interviewed for this chapter were hired for their government jobs by departments that needed their particular skills and talents.

A New RTC Job Transfers Lending and Administration Expertise

Former bank executive vice president Jay Thrash, Jr., had done everything in a bank; now he does everything in banks all over the country for the Resolution Trust Corporation (RTC) as a managing agent. His career change demonstrates the often tight fit between banking administration and public jobs.

"It frankly got to the point that it wasn't any fun to go to work anymore, and I had the opportunity to bail out of the situation. I didn't do anything for ninety days," Thrash says. "I looked around and had some other opportunities. I just made the decision that I didn't want to move. I looked at all kinds of banks and savings and loans and all sorts of financial industry firms because that's what I had always done."

"I was a commercial banker for almost thirty years. My dad was a commercial banker. I'm fifty-two years old — I've lived around banking ever since I can remember and I never really thought of doing anything other than banking. It just happened that this fellow who was a headhunter had been talking to me. He said one day, 'Look, why don't you go to work for me? You know everybody in the banks all over the South.' I did that for about a year."

"Then the opportunity with the RTC came along and I took it. With the RTC, we're essentially operating two different companies at the same time. You're operating the conservatorship, which still has branches open taking deposits, and the receivership, which you're trying to liquidate. I fill both of those jobs. Basically the function is to replace the board of directors in the association. So you're wearing — well, it isn't two hats, it's probably more like 100 hats."

"I still think like a banker rather than a regulator. My expertise is oriented toward both retail and commercial lending, and toward the

overall administration of the bank. One of my real strengths is working with people. So I don't have any problem with this job."

"This is the ninth bank dissolution I've helped manage. I've had
two banks from the day that they were taken over, what the RTC refers
to as the 'date of conservatorship,' to the date of resolution. I've also
worked with seven banks that I've taken over at some point in the conservatorship process. I've seen banks continue operations after
takeover for four or five months. I've seen others go for two years —
everywhere from $250 million to in excess of $1 billion. I've been involved with banks that had two or three branches, and others which
had thirty or forty. In this job, I leave my house Monday mornings to
catch a plane out; then I catch another plane back home on Friday af-
ternoons."

Thrash's RTC job required highly developed skills, and such positions are rare. But, in general, government finance agencies present as
many opportunities for former bankers as business and industry. Even
bankers from specialized areas like lending can find jobs in government — one former vice president of lending interviewed took a new
post as director of the home ownership mortgage division in a state
housing development agency.

■ THE SKILLS BANKERS BRING TO GOVERNMENT SERVICE

Bankers' experience may serve them well in public work,
where the potential for applying banking skills is nearly limitless.

Accounting and Financial Analysis

Budget management skills are in demand in federal, state, county,
and municipal government agencies. Bankers with accounting or au-

diting experience can apply their skills to jobs as financial examiners or analysts for government agencies; in fact, the IRS is the single largest employer of accountants in the United States. Training opportunities, job security, and good benefits contribute to the appeal of working in accounting for either a federal or state agency.

Bank liquidation requires the expertise of operating a continuing institution. This private-sector expertise, as demonstrated by Jay Thrash, can be turned into a job with the RTC. While federal job watchers and personnel directors say competition for managing agent positions is fierce, the need for loan workout and assets disposition skills in government foreclosures and other merger and acquisition situations across the country is growing.

Private-sector lending savvy is needed at the Office of the Comptroller of the Currency (OCC), according to DeeDee Tostanoski, the OCC's national recruitment coordinator. It is a "very new trend," she adds, but credit examiners are coming out of bank credit, lending, asset-based lending, and consumer loan and services departments. Some consumer examiners hired recently by the OCC are former bankers who focus on bank compliance with home mortgage disclosure and truth-in-lending laws and other consumer-protection statutes, Tostanoski says. Hired at the precommissioned level (before completing the Uniform Commission Examination), many bankers with experience in lending and operations who have joined the OCC have gone on to become bank examiners.

Information Systems

Information technology has transformed many public jobs as well as private-sector jobs. The federal government is the single biggest user of computers in the world, and this increased computerization of records and processes may present opportunities to former bankers. The pace of computerization may be even more rapid in some state and local governments, as single-function systems combine with larger systems.

The guidebook *Jobs '96* calls the prospect for employment in federal government information management positions "bright," as an increasing demand for government efficiency and accountability leads to greater reliance on today's most innovative systems technologies. Responding to the demand, federal agencies are offering salaries comparable to those in business and industry for employees who have solid systems experience. Many of the systems challenges confronting business and industry are the same as those faced by government — including the need to effectively manage new storage technologies and databases; to establish and manage presence and services on the Internet; and to ensure hardware, software, and networking capabilities keep pace with emerging technologies.

In addition to general skills in information management, former bankers who possess information transfer expertise may find compatible jobs in agencies like the Federal Reserve Bank.

■ LANDING THE RIGHT GOVERNMENT JOB

Private-sector professionals may now find federal salaries more competitive with those in business and industry. In 1992, Congress authorized pay increases for federal professional positions in an effort to make them compare more favorably with private-sector salaries, but there's more than money to consider.

Along with its specified mission, each public agency also has its own culture. This fact, coupled with the diversity of bankers' skills, means that there is no one best place for a banker to seek government employment. Bankers interested in government employment will need to evaluate their individual skills and geographic preferences to find the agency whose needs may best match the skills they have to offer. Still, some areas of government are more promising than others for former bankers:

Federal

The demand for accounting and finance workers remains fairly consistent throughout government. Those with human resources, data processing, marketing, and operations experience may also find many government agencies seeking their skills. The analytical bent and experience of some bankers can be useful in many government agencies, including the IRS and F.B.I.

The demand for knowledge specific to banking in some departments of government has now cooled. Peter Ognibene, editor of *Federal Jobs Digest*, says, "The RTC and the FDIC are the two best places to look for a job, but they are inundated with applicants. Probably only the better, more highly qualified people can get in at this point."

A 1992 issue of *Federal Jobs Digest* reports that, despite this, 5,000 banking professionals are hired annually to fill financial openings. The newspaper identified the principal regulatory agencies hiring bankers:

Federal Deposit Insurance Corporation
Office of Comptroller of the Currency
Federal Reserve Board
Export/Import Bank of the United States
Farm Credit Administration
Overseas Private Investment Corporation
Securities and Exchange Commission
Department of Housing and Urban Development
Small Business Administration
National Credit Union Administration
Financial Management Service
Office of Thrift Supervision

Titles for financial jobs in these agencies range from financial institution examiner to realty specialist to computer specialist. While the titles for many government jobs may differ from those found in banking, the transfer of banking-related skills can be, in some cases, direct. Job seekers may want to consider field employment with a regulatory agency as a temporary career change. A recruitment and placement official with the FDIC reports that field positions may be the best entry option, and he says that temporary hires can enter agencies at high levels.

State and Municipal

One former bank accountant interviewed for this chapter is now a certified information system analyst with a state comptroller's office. There are a myriad of job possibilities for former bankers because state, city, and town governments need the skills of financial professionals from all areas of banking.

In fact, although the growth of federal jobs in the late 1990s is expected to be small, the outlook for growth in government jobs at the state and local level will continue at an average pace, according to *Jobs '96*. Cutbacks at the federal level and privatization measures throughout government do not always mean jobs disappear; they may just relocate to the private sector. The authors of *Jobs '96* emphasize that some private companies expect government service contracts to increase their staff size by 10 percent in the next decade. At all levels of government, the job outlook varies greatly by specialty area. Political appointee jobs routinely turn over every two to four years, and information management positions in government will be increasingly essential to mobilizing staff downsizing efforts.

Connecting to Government Contracting

The "right" government job may not be in government at all these days — increasingly, it may be with a private-sector firm contracting to supply loan workout or other financial services to a government department or agency. Contracting could be the wave of the future that meets the demand for banking experts in government receiverships and provides the skill for loan workouts.

Independent finance-related contracting projects are on the increase; many merge credit experience with a government undertaking. The new SAMDA (standard asset management and disposition agreement) contractors working with the RTC, for example, may be former bank executives with substantial credit experience.

■ DO YOU NEED MORE EDUCATION OR CERTIFICATION?

Job criteria for public positions may be more inflexible than for private-sector jobs. Many state and federal employers are required to evaluate applicants based on the applicant's education and the certificates he or she has earned, to consider whether the applicant is a veteran or a member of a minority group, and to consider the results of any required testing.

In government work, job advancement and pay are also dependent upon the educational level the employee has attained. Experience may be the natural trump card for landing specialized banking regulatory agency positions, but overall, many former bankers may find financial certifications and a master's degree carry even greater weight.

According to *Federal Jobs Digest*, federal banking agencies have many jobs for experienced candidates at the GS-11 to GS-15 levels that require considerable banking experience or a graduate degree. *The Digest* reports that at the level of positions such as senior financial analyst, job prerequisites "become more varied and job-specific, and may include a Ph.D. and/or extensive administrative experience."

As elsewhere, the need for additional certification for local government jobs varies with the field of specialty and the governmental agency.

■ LEARNING MORE AND BREAKING IN

Former bankers interested in public-sector jobs should first recognize that there are opportunities everywhere. In addition to jobs with local and state governments, federal positions are found in all fifty states. Although the *Federal Career Directory* states that only 14 percent of federal workers are employed in Washington, D.C., willingness to relocate may be a critical factor in securing a suitable position.

Federal Positions

Some highly specialized jobs within federal departments are not easily filled. A successful job hunter will define his or her area of expertise and research government jobs to make the connection between his or her skills and vacant jobs in which those skills may be employed. This research may also provide a crash course in "governmentese," in which acronyms and abbreviations for government departments and job classifications abound. Research into federal jobs may be relatively easy, since some or most of the sources listed below are probably available in the reference section of your local library.

After you have targeted a job, you must, of course, then follow the appropriate employment procedures, but this is not a set of ropes bankers should have any difficulty handling. In most professional positions in government, the application is far from the most decisive factor in the hiring process. One FDIC regulator applied the term "black hole" to the applications process and told a funny and enlightening tale: he landed his job quickly, after having completed the standard FDIC employment application. Thirteen months after he went to work for the agency, he got a form in the mail from the regional personnel office for his division, telling him, "Thank you for your application for employment. Because of the number of applications we have received, you have not been chosen . . . ."

This former banker and many other professional government employees discovered that personal contact at the field level is the surest route for securing a public job. One federal employee says, "If you don't have some sort of contact with a real human, you're probably going to have no chance of getting a job."

Many of the finance-related positions in government are not filled by the Office of Personnel Management; instead agencies with "direct-hire authority" are authorized to fill these positions independently. Federal job hunters are advised to stay in contact with both the OPM and the agencies in which they're interested.

State and Municipal Positions

An assistant director in the office of a state comptroller of the treasury offers the tip that state and local governments may look outside the organization for experienced hires while larger state or federal agencies would tend to fill vacancies from pools of existing employees. Again, gaining a foothold requires investigation and time spent getting to know the organization you're interested in. State and city applications must be completed and inquiries made at state and municipal personnel offices. Your local library's periodicals section may be an invaluable resource in locating vacant state and city positions, since many such jobs are advertised in local and regional newspapers. Many local and state governments now have Web sites on the Internet where jobs and job descriptions may be posted.

State and local chapters of national professional organizations may also be helpful in learning more about vacancies.

Job Hot Lines and Listings

Numerous publications, hot lines, and Web sites provide job seekers with information about job opportunities. The *Federal Jobs Digest*, for example, publishes information about as many as 30,000 federal jobs twice a month.

Libraries often subscribe to periodicals that list federal jobs. Call your local, state, and university libraries to find out which institutions are government document repositories. These libraries are required by law to carry such federal publications. However, depending on the local availability of such publications and how convenient access to them is, one or more personal subscriptions may provide more timely leads. Publishers and professional organizations run many government job banks. And many of the job listing publications or fee-based job banks run by professional associations offer services to nonmembers. The federal government's presence on the Internet has grown dramatically in the last few years. In many cases, the most timely information available regarding federal job openings will be found on Web sites maintained by government agencies.

■ RESOURCES

FEDERAL

U. S. Office of Personnel Management's federal job information centers, or Job Information Center, U.S. Office of Personnel Management, 1900 E St., NW, Washington, DC 20451; 202/632-7484

Federal Jobs Digest, 310 N. Highland Avenue, Ossining, NY 10562; 800/824-5000

Federal Career Directory, U.S. Office of Personnel Management (U.S. Government Printing Office), 202/783-3238

The Complete Guide to Public Employment by Ronald and Caryl Krannich (Impact Publications)

The principal federal financial agencies identified by *Federal Jobs Digest* can provide general information and contacts for regional personnel offices:

Federal Deposit Insurance Corporation, Office of Personnel, 550 Seventeenth St., NW, Washington, DC 20429;
202/898-3853 or 3854; job information: 800/898-8890

Office of the Comptroller of the Currency, Human Resources Division, National Recruitment Coordinator, 250 E St., SW, Washington, DC 20219; 202/874-4490

Export-Import Bank of the U.S., Personnel Director, 811 Vermont Avenue, NW, Room 1005, Washington, DC 20571; 202/566-8834

Federal Reserve System Board of Governors, Division of Human Resources Management, 20th and Constitution Avenue, NW, Washington, DC 20551; 202/452-3880

Department of Housing and Urban Development, Office of Personnel and Training, Room 2258, 451 Seventh St., SW, Washington, DC 20410; 202/708-2000; vacancy hot line: 202/708-3203

Overseas Private Investment Corporation, Human Resources, 1615 M St., NW, Washington, DC 20527; 202/457-7075; job line: 202/457-7013

Small Business Administration, Central Personnel Office, 409 Third St., SW, Washington, DC 20416; 202/205-6780

Farm Credit Administration, Human Resources Division, 1501 Farm Credit Drive, McLean, VA 22102-5090; 703/883-4135

National Credit Union Administration, Personnel Office, 1776 G St., NW, Washington, DC 20456; 202/682-9720

Department of Treasury Financial Management Service, Recruitment Coordinator, Personnel Operations Branch, 401 Fourteenth St., SW, Room 120, Washington, DC 20227; 202/874-7090

Office of Thrift Supervision, Office of Human Resources, 1700 G St., NW, Washington, DC 20552; 202/906-6060

STATE AND LOCAL

IMCA Newsletter, International City-County Management Association, 1120 G St., NW, Washington, DC 20005; 202/289-4262

City-County Recruiter and the *State Recruiter*, biweekly subscription newspapers, P.O. Box 2400, Station B, Lincoln, NE 68502

The Municipal Yearbook (annual)

The National Directory of State Agencies (annual)

Careers in State and Local Government by John Zehring (Garrett Park Press)

Professional Associations

American Society for Public Administration, 1120 G St., NW, Ste. 700, Washington, DC 20005; 202/393-7878

Association of Government Accountants, 2200 Mount Vernon Avenue, Alexandria, VA 22301; 703/684-6931

American Federation of Government Employees, 80 F St., NW, Washington, DC 20001; 202/737-8700

(The professional associations listed in other chapters may offer job listings or referral services that include job opportunities in government.)

10

JOBS IN BUSINESS AND INDUSTRY

■ ■ ■

Teaching ■ Administration ■ Financial Management ■ Human Resources ■ Development ■ Service Industries ■ Retail ■ Manufacturing

---

Bankers with experience in these areas may qualified to move to jobs in business and industry:

ACCOUNTING AND FINANCE	MARKETING
CORPORATE STAFFING	OPERATIONS
CREDIT	REAL ESTATE
DATA PROCESSING	RETAIL BANKING
FACILITIES	STRATEGIC MANAGEMENT
HUMAN RESOURCES	PLANNING
SYSTEMS ANALYSIS	INTERNATIONAL

Business and industry are a wide-open employment market for bankers. In fact, the challenge is not finding a job opening, because jobs in business and industry are plentiful. Rather, the challenge is figuring out which job best suits your skills and communicating that suitability to a prospective employer. Bankers who make successful transitions to jobs in business and industry focus on their own skills in targeting jobs and remain flexible about which field in business or industry they will work in. Because the opportunities for employment in business and industry are numerous and diverse, job seekers need to investigate available openings carefully in order to find a good match for their skills.

Today, any banker seeking a job in business or industry must keep in mind two important principles that guide most successful companies. First, in every type of business or industry, the bottom line rules. Any prospective employee who demonstrates that he or she can measurably reduce the costs of getting products and services to market has an edge over anyone else applying for the same job. Second, technology developments, particularly those related to software, personal computers, and the Internet, now influence and inform virtually every trend and innovation in American commerce.

At a minimum, job candidates for positions in business and industry will be expected to be familiar with the critical technological and economic factors driving recent developments in the information revolution. The candidate who can demonstrate the ability to apply this knowledge to improve service delivery or expand market share may achieve a critical advantage over other job seekers. To the right employer, candidates with proven skills in developing or managing information systems may seem indispensable new hires. Because bankers are typically experienced in either money management or information management or both, they are well equipped for jobs in business and industry.

Often there is a very direct transfer of skills from banking to a new job in business. Former banker Francisco Sanchez, now a treasury manager for S.C. Johnson and Son in Racine, Wisconsin, found that his banking experience created the opportunity for his present job.

Crossing the Desk to a Career with a Former Customer

"I was vice president and head of marketing at First Chicago," says Francisco Sanchez, "in charge of relationship management and selling banking products to the customer base the bank had in Australia and New Zealand. I was part of the international banking group."

"I came back from Australia in July of 1991. I had been with the bank overseas a total of eight years and wanted to come back to the head office. When I got back to Chicago, though, the bank was going through a lot of changes — I felt that the fit between First Chicago as an employer and my own career aspirations in international banking was no longer good. I began to look elsewhere. I had been calling on the treasurers of multinational companies overseas and on the U.S. subsidiaries of many American multinationals. When I called on these companies, I was trying to address many of the concerns that somebody working in the international treasury area of the parent company would have."

"Anyone who has had a lot of experience calling on customers domestically or overseas should realize that the products that banks try to provide are the same kinds of products that you look for when you are on the other side of the desk. I knew the other side and I knew the banking scenery. I said to myself, *I can work for multinationals.*"

"I made a list of about 100 multinationals. I got the names of each of the treasurers in those companies and their telephone numbers and began calling them directly and talking with them about my background and whether or not they were doing any hiring. The finance manager for Latin America in one of these companies said to me, 'We're not hiring at this point, but the kind of skills you describe and the sort of experience you've had fit a job that a headhunter I know is trying to fill.'"

"That's how it happened. I called the headhunter and explained who I was, and he told me to send him a resume. The company had been looking for some time. It had proven difficult to identify the right candidate, and I think I was able to emphasize the skills they were looking for. It was a good fit."

"My job as a treasury manager involves working with those areas within the corporation that have dealings with Latin America or the

Asia-Pacific region. I am a financial advisor in those markets. My responsibilities include cash management, foreign exchange, and tax planning. And my responsibility is to make sure that in the regions I cover, these areas are working efficiently. As a treasury manager, I have a number of issues to deal with that are similar in nature to the concerns I was trying to resolve as a banker."

Sanchez knew his skills and saw the advantage his knowledge of banking gave him. Not every banker has the sort of international experience that Sanchez used to turn his client base into a springboard to a new job. Fortunately, however, most of the other functions in a bank can also be marketed by former bankers to new employers. For example, as marketing director with the bank where he was formerly employed, Mark Bennett sold the bank's services to its customers. Now, as president of MemberServ, a division of Demco in Madison, Wisconsin, Bennett sells training and reference materials and supplies to bankers.

Empathy for Bankers Puts Marketing Skills To Use

"The bank holding company I worked for was fairly small, so I had a lot of different responsibilities," Mark Bennett says. "When we acquired a new bank, I would work with them to help them train their staff in the procedures that we had in place at the main bank. We also developed new products and marketed them to customers and the public. I was a loan officer before working in the marketing area."

"When I left the bank I went to work as vice president of Financial Education and Development in Madison, Wisconsin, a company that was started by another banker who left banking. I wrote and conducted training seminars throughout the country. When I started with the company, they were primarily in the seminar business and really did not have individual products to offer the financial industry. Our first product, a videotape, was on the Bank Secrecy Act. Working with state banking associations, we marketed the tape nationally. From there, we decided that we would put together a catalog of training and reference materials, basically a source that bankers could go to for many of their training needs."

"MemberServ was started in 1988 as an offshoot of the training company, and our first catalog was developed."

MemberServ's first direct mail catalog contained twenty-four pages. The next year its size doubled. By 1992 there were two catalogs, one for training products and another for supplies and equipment. Bennett feels that he has a special viewpoint on the needs of his customers, a "real understanding of the pressures bankers are under on a day-to-day basis." This empathy and the product development and marketing skills he developed as a banker have contributed to his success in his present position.

■ THE SKILLS BANKERS BRING TO BUSINESS AND INDUSTRY

The categories of employment in business and industry that former bankers enter are too numerous to list. Interviews with bank human resources professionals and business and industry executives confirm that some strong transfer areas can be identified, however.

Accounting and Finance

Accounting and finance are probably the most valuable and marketable functions that bankers bring to business and industry. According to Larry DeMeyers, chief operating officer at Banker's First Savings Bank in Augusta, Georgia, "A banker could work in a golf cart company and he would still be doing accounts payable, accounts receivable, general ledger, inventory control — a great many of the same things you'd do in a bank."

When defining their marketable financial skills, bankers should remember this business truism: the smaller the company, the more compressed the roles. Treasurer, CEO, comptroller, finance director — all are jobs that may overlap or be combined in some companies. In other words, small companies are just as likely to be able to use bankers' skills as large ones. Nancy Seever, human resources vice president at First Chicago, says that, for this reason, "Many people are looking at smaller companies."

Lending and Real Estate

In today's economy, bankers with consumer lending experience have an edge over those who have only commercial experience, because consumer lending experience is transferable to various businesses where consumer credit services are offered, such as retail stores, automobile dealers, and other businesses that sell to consumers, and these businesses are numerous. If a commercial loan officer looks beyond job titles to analyze the nuts-and-bolts functions involved in commercial lending, it becomes clear that commercial lending experience can be transferred to sales, investment, management, and facilities expansion jobs that involve commercial property. One healthcare industry headhunter suggests that commercial lending or real estate expertise can be used to land jobs with healthcare companies that own facilities in more than one state.

Administration and Retail Management

Human resources director John Durkin of Heritage Federal Savings Bank in Richmond, Virginia, describes how a retail banking administrator moved to a regional sales position in the medical industry. "He had managed a very customer service-oriented branch system. He took his skills in promoting the products of the bank, which were essentially loans and service, and moved to a regional sales management position with a company that sells medical products to doctors and hospitals."

Larry DeMeyers confirms that retail branch managers usually have skills that are useful to other businesses. "They possess not just financial management, accounting or finance skills, but a basic sense about good business. There are a lot of companies that have dispersed locations, from gas stations to convenience stores. A retail manager can move into an operations job with almost any company that has multiple locations."

"I think if you can manage a bank well, you can probably manage a lot of businesses well," DeMeyers says. The analytical, financial, organizational, and personal skills cultivated in banking are applicable in many business settings. Trish Benninger, human resources vice president at Great Western Bank in Northridge, California, says that the high degree of public contact required of branch managers can even be put to use in public relations jobs.

Relationship Sales and Marketing

Personnel directors name marketing time after time as one of the "most transferable" of bankers' skills. Former bank marketing managers now sell data processing services, marketing software, conduct market research, and develop consumer products.

And, like Francisco Sanchez, a great many former bankers look to their former clients for bridges to other careers. Sanchez suggests, "For those people who have been in the area of managing relationships, it is necessary not only to look at their own skills from a technical standpoint, but to actually assess the job that they've been doing and the customer base they have been in contact with for a number of years."

First Chicago's Nancy Seever described another job searcher's use of his contacts: "We had a banker here who called on bottling companies. He looked at all the industries that service bottling companies to see where he could fit in. It was a good lesson for me to watch him operate, because he really pushed those walls out." The knowledge bankers accumulate about other industries can be used to great advantage during a job search. "It may not show up on your resume as a skill," Sanchez pointed out, "but the fact of the matter is that it is a skill."

"Because you have been selling to that industry from a banking perspective," Sanchez adds, "you become a part of that industry. You have an advantage, an edge over people who have been in that industry all their lives but have never looked at it from the outside." For example, if a banker has extensive experience doing cash management studies for a particular industry, that experience can be turned into a job in that same industry.

"They were never really bankers," a New York City bank personnel director said of some displaced bank marketing professionals. "We saw someone go to Pepsi-Cola, one to a mail order house, someone to Procter and Gamble . . . all in marketing." In some industries, such as the computer industry, sales and marketing positions are the most lucrative jobs. Former bankers may have the qualities necessary for success with these firms — knowledge, confidence, and excellent people skills.

Human Resources

Despite the seemingly wide differences between managing bank personnel and, say, factory workers, experienced bank human resources people are often able to successfully transfer their skills to the human resources departments of other sorts of organizations. Bernard Ford, a principal at Ford and Ford Search Consultants in Needham, Massachusetts, says that former bankers with human resources experience, "especially middle managers who can undertake higher level positions," can easily make the transition. "In human resources, the skills that are in demand are in the benefits area and in the healthcare area, because these areas are under great cost pressures in most companies. If someone is a good compensation person or benefits person in banking, their skills are transferable."

With an expected growth rate of 22 percent in the next decade, human resources made the cut in the career handbook *Top Professions'* list of the most promising careers. The reasons for the field's promise include the bottom-line impact that employee satisfaction and training can have on productivity. Tremendous growth is expected in the area of corporate training, with corporations currently spending about $30 million annually on executive training alone. Those seeking human resources positions may also want to acquaint themselves with training and recruiting resources on the World Wide Web, a forum in which an increasing number of employers are participating, since Internet-based recruiting efforts are far cheaper than more traditional methods.

Information Systems and Operations

Information systems and operations skills may be the most marketable of bankers' talents; *Top Professions* estimates that computer and information processing jobs will continue to grow rapidly, by as much as 48 percent by the year 2000. Personnel directors report that technical experience in a bank can be transferred to many other jobs, with data processing capabilities being especially in demand. One New York human resources director reports that former bank systems professionals in that city are moving to jobs in manufacturing companies and computer firms.

Computer skills are even more valuable when combined with more general experience. For example, many employers want computer programmers who are capable of understanding the business problems that can be solved with technology and who are capable of communicating with nontechnical managers and employees about those problems and their solutions.

Employers in business and industry seem to value specific computer skills and experience over general familiarity with technology. Interoperability expertise, electronic data interchange, local area networks, and remote processing are among the kinds of highly developed systems experience touted by occupational professionals. Expertise in electronic financial transactions, and the software platforms that enable this commerce, will be especially valuable to employers who want to bring their products and services to customers on-line.

The experience of any former banker whose job emphasized making information technology more responsive to the bottom line will be especially valued. Corporations are increasingly seeking those whose information management experience includes developing platforms that manage data exchange, sales, and inventory for both large and small accounts or businesses.

■ LANDING THE RIGHT JOB IN BUSINESS AND INDUSTRY

"For small business, the 1980s are going to be a tough act to follow," according to an editorial column in *USA Today*. For the first time, the newspaper adds, small business is creating two out of three new jobs.

Jobs '96 advises that in many industries "the bottom line, of course, is to have the right specialty . . . and those who want jobs should keep abreast of the latest technologies." Fewer recent small business failures contribute to the rosy picture in small business. Corporate personnel directors and others confirm the trend: smaller companies may be perfect for bankers who must look for work outside of banking. If the skills match is there, small business may be the place to use them.

What are the most promising areas of employment in business and industry? Predictions vary, but some fields, like the healthcare, pharmaceuticals, food processing, chemicals, household products, and computer software industries, turn up on everybody's list.

Sales

Sales and management talents can land a former banker in a retail job, but so can other banking skills.

"The retail companies are conglomerating," advises Bernard Ford, whose specialties include recruiting for retail sales and healthcare positions. "This means that they have to become more structured in the systems area and in the operations area, similar to banking." Systems skills are clearly transferable to retail applications, he says. He believes that retail bank managers who "bring some technology with them" are in the best position.

Service Industries

"By the year 2000, projections indicate that nearly four out of five jobs will be in industries that provide services," predicts *America's 50 Fastest Growing Jobs*. This giant and growing segment of the economy is a promising area for bankers. In interviews across the country, the healthcare field was named repeatedly as a service business with great potential for former bankers. Banking administrative, accounting, personnel, and marketing skills may be directly transferable to similar service industry jobs. Former bankers whose jobs entailed outside sales may find that their talents and experience are in demand in service companies. Ford predicts, "The relationship people should do well when they are dealing with either marketing intangibles or marketing corporate products."

Manufacturing

The push toward increased automation, systems integration, and greater efficiency in banking that has eliminated many banking jobs may create jobs for former bankers in manufacturing companies. Following the same path as banks, these companies will increasingly merge electronic functions. Banking professionals from systems or operations backgrounds with heavy EDP experience can seize opportunities in manufacturing companies. Bank finance managers may also be able to find jobs in manufacturing companies, since financial statements, general and cost accounting, internal auditing, forecasts, analysis, and planning are all functions of the finance area in these companies.

The handbook *Career Choices for the '90s* identifies industrial relations/human relations and industrial marketing as two growing occupational areas in manufacturing to which former bankers from other departments may bring expertise.

Because so many positions in manufacturing companies require a knowledge of the particular industry, bankers who have experience specifically relevant to the manufacturer often have better luck landing jobs.

■ DO YOU NEED MORE EDUCATION OR CERTIFICATION?

Certain degrees and certifications are desirable and may be necessary for some corporate finance and treasury positions, but in other business and industry job areas a former banker's professional experience may be more valuable than an M.B.A.

Human resources professionals vary in their assessment of the value of an M.B.A., depending on the job area. Many feel that the corporate job market is overcrowded with people who have earned M.B.A.'s; this can mean either that the degree has lost the cachet it once had or that job hunters must possess one to complete. Other human resources professionals feel that the M.B.A. is the preferred credential for bankers seeking jobs in business and industry — "the most bang for the buck."

Francisco Sanchez feels that his M.B.A. is important to his international corporate treasury work. "My master's concentration was in finance," he says. "It is not a must, but I do feel that if you don't have it, you're at a disadvantage."

Certification can be more critical in corporate systems and managerial technical positions than it is in finance. Systems analysis and EDP auditing, skills that span job titles in computer products and services, accounting, and general industry, require advanced technical knowledge, but the track for advancement in these specialties varies with the industry.

■ LEARNING MORE AND BREAKING IN

Francisco Sanchez had to gather information and make a lot of cold calls before he was hired as a corporate treasury manager.

"I had to do a bit of research to identify those companies that might want to hire me," he says. "Then I had to call and tell them about myself. You can be proactive if you know something about the company's plans to expand in areas where you have a particular expertise. In some cases I said, 'I just read in the paper that you are going to be expanding your operations in Latin America. I happen to have a background in Latin America.'"

"I think people are afraid to bring things up for fear of being too up-front, but the fact of the matter is that if you don't tell people that you have expertise in that particular market or area, you may miss the opportunity."

Sanchez's experience points up the fact that, to be hired, a job seeker must be able to demonstrate to a prospective employer that he or she has some knowledge of the job. Fortunately, such information is relatively easy to gather. Some of the resources listed at the end of this chapter can help you learn what you need to know about a corporation for which you want to work. The best strategy is to research the company in directories and in newspapers and other periodicals in the business reference section of your local library and call or write the company for a copy of its most recent annual report. Sometimes exploratory phone calls to friends and business associates are informative — "a who-do-you-know-who-knows-somebody, second-level type of thing," as one career counselor phrased it.

Once you have identified a company where you can apply your skills, it's critically important to heed the advice of Bernard Ford: "Be flexible. Market what you have that is of use to that particular company, and that means marketing accomplishments or functions, not marketing a job title."

Former bankers looking for jobs in business and industry can be encouraged by a trend in corporate America — industry-swapping. A recent article in *The Wall Street Journal* heralds a dramatic increase in the number of industry outsiders recruited for top executive slots, including positions at Goodyear Tire and Rubber Company, AT&T, and Eastern Enterprises. It appears that corporate America believes that, just as people are refreshed by new horizons, some jobs can be enriched by new perspectives. The Journal article suggests that some corporations may now care more about hiring the best managerial know-how available than they do about industry expertise.

■ RESOURCES

Corporate Financial Bluebook (National Register Publishing Company) (annual)

Trade publications, including *Sales and Marketing Management, Marketing Times,* and *The Marketing News and Agency Sales Magazine*

MacRaes' Blue Book, Moody's Industrial Manual, and *Thomas Register of American Manufacturers* (annual)

Standard and Poor's Register of Corporations, Directors and Executives (Standard and Poor's) (annual)

Corporate Technology Directory (Corporate Technology Information Services) (annual)

Publications including *The Wall Street Journal, Forbes, Fortune, Barron's, Business Week, Nation's Business,* and *National Business Employment Weekly, Jobs for Bankers*

Journal of Systems Management (monthly), *JobLink and Job Seeker* (membership notices) published by Association for Systems Management

Professional Associations

FINANCE

(The national associations listed in Chapter 7 may also be of assistance.)

International Board of Standards and Practices for Certified Financial Planners, 5445 DTC Parkway, Ste. P-1, Englewood, CO 80111; 303/830-7543

Healthcare Financial Management Association, 2 Westbrook
Corporate Center, Ste. 700, Westchester, IL 60154; 708/531-9600

SALES AND MARKETING

American Marketing Association, 250 S. Wacker Drive, Chicago, IL
60606; 312/648-0536

National Network of Women in Sales, P.O. Box 116, Arlington
Heights, IL 60006; 708/253-2661

Manufacturers' Agents National Association, P.O. Box 3467, Laguna
Hills, CA 92654; 714/859-4040

HUMAN RESOURCES AND RECRUITING

American Association for Counseling and Development, 5999
Stevenson Avenue, Alexandria, VA 22304; 703/823-9800

Association of Outplacement Consulting Firms, Inc., 364 Parsippany
Road, Parsippany, NJ 07054; 201/887-6667

Association of Executive Search Consultants, 230 Park Avenue, Ste.
1549, New York, NY 10169; 212/949-9556

American Guidance Association, 6231 Leesburg Pike, Ste. 305, Falls
Church, VA 22044; 703/533-1464

Employment Management Association, 1100 Raleigh Building,
5 West Hargett St., Raleigh, NC 27601; 919/828-6614

INFORMATION SYSTEMS

Institute for Certification of Computer Professionals, 2200 E. Devon
Avenue, Ste. 268, Des Plaines, IL 60018; 708/299-4227

Association for Systems Management, P.O. Box 38370, Cleveland,
OH 44138; 216/243-6900

Data Processing Management Association, 505 Busse Highway, Park
Ridge, IL 60068; 312/693-5070

11

JOBS IN CONSULTING

■ ■ ■

Asset Management ■ Finance and Accounting ■ Training ■ Marketing ■ Real Estat e ■ Systems

Bankers with experience in these areas may be qualified to move to jobs in consulting:

ACCOUNTING AND FINANCE	FINANCE
APPRAISAL	HUMAN RESOURCES
ASSET/LIABILITY MANAGEMENT	INTERNATIONAL
BRANCH OPERATIONS	LOAN ANALYSIS
COMMERCIAL LENDING	MARKETING
CORPORATE STAFFING	MORTGAGE LENDING
CREDIT CARD OPERATIONS	OPERATIONS
DATA PROCESSING	SYSTEMS TECHNOLOGY
FACILITIES MANAGEMENT	TRUST AND INVESTMENT
MANAGEMENT	

With the right skills, former bankers can successfully apply their financial knowledge and managerial experience to careers as management consultants. Although professional associations and consulting handbooks often consider management consulting a single profession, the field is really comprised of many careers rolled into one, and former bankers may find numerous opportunities for applying their banking skills. Management consultants serve diverse clients in an expanding array of capacities. The 1995 edition of *America's 50 Fastest Growing Jobs* calls management consulting an area of "much faster than average employment growth," as companies increasingly turn to outside vendors to satisfy internal operations needs.

Two economic trends continue to work in the consultant's favor: corporate downsizing and the demand for increased organizational efficiency. U.S. Bureau of Labor Statistics data on the occupational group comprising management analysts and consultants indicates a rising demand for their services and predicts a faster-than-average growth of 35 percent for the field during the 1990s. Michael Farr, in *America's 50 Fastest Growing Jobs*, emphasizes that the demand for management consultants will be driven in the future "by the need for firms to improve performance, expand markets, incorporate new technologies, cope with government regulations, and adapt to a changing labor force." Individuals entering this field will face keen competition in spite of its rapid growth, Farr predicts.

Many of the largest U.S. consulting firms are members of the Association of Management Consulting Firms, known as ACME. A survey of association members reported in the association newsletter *ACME News* indicates that although member management consulting firms experienced annual revenue increases as great as 20 percent during the consulting boom of the 1980s, consulting revenues for 1991 and 1992 were expected to increase only by 10 percent and 13 percent, respectively, indicating that although the boom may have slowed, consulting is still growing at a healthy rate.

Some consultants are employed for the objectivity that an outsider can bring to complex problems in business and industry. Other, single-function, consultants simply fill a specific expertise gap in the client's organization. *Top Professions* describes the efficiency consultants offer clients: "Decisions about pay scales, operating efficiency, growth, training, marketing, and many other things can be made by an internal staff, once it has the appropriate training and enough time to study the issue. Alternatively, management can hire a consultant, or consultants, already experienced in the topic of interest and in a few weeks or months have detailed answers to its questions. With greater frequency, organizations are opting for the latter course."

Any former banker who considers consulting as a new career should not let the promising outlook for the field as a whole obscure the drawbacks of working as a consultant. The failure rate for solo consultants who launch their own businesses can be as high as 90 percent in the first two years, according to the trade newsletter *Consultants News*. "The outlook for consulting is good for those who can handle it," *Consultants News* managing editor David Lord observes.

Establishing a consulting niche seems to be the key to survival, along with the ability to market the services offered. Experience in bank human resources or marketing departments seems to produce the communications ability necessary to succeed as a consultant, as shown by Clifford Rutz's experience. Formerly director of human resources at First Federal Association in Orlando, Rutz has started a consulting business that he believes is promising.

Launching a Solo Practice with Expertise Honed in Banking

"I worked with the First Federal Association for almost ten years," Clifford Rutz says. "I had been a consultant prior to joining them, for approximately two-and-a-half years, mainly in the training area — in leadership training, more effective supervision, performance reviews, and selection interviews. In fact, I was doing a sales training program for managers and customer relations staff for the First F.A. when I got an entree there."

"My position as human resources director enabled me to expand my area in consulting to not only a heavy concentration on training but also on the whole human resources area — from compensation to benefits to employment to terminations — all areas that I wasn't well acquainted with prior to joining the First F.A."

"I believe that organizations that have between forty-five and 250 employees and don't have a human resources department really need my services. They may have a person who is responsible for four or five things and, unfortunately, human resources is number five. So what I do is call on organizations of that size to impress upon them the importance of having good sound human resources policies and procedures in hiring and terminations, affirmative action, equal employment opportunity, compensation benefits, and so forth. I would like to find eight to twelve firms for whom I would work on a retainer basis and function as their human resources department."

"I am looking at banks, certainly, because of my experience with them, but a lot of other businesses are also potential clients. Depending on your company size, why pay a human resources director $30,000 to $50,000 when I can do as much for less money? I think there is an extremely strong market for my services. I believe that there's a tremendous need out there even in large companies that aren't maintaining a large training staff, or they're using a lot of people from the outside to do some extra work for them when they need it instead of having to pay those salaries throughout the year."

"Apart from years of experience in the human resources function and previous success in training, I don't have any particular certification. I do have an undergraduate degree in economics and an M.B.A. in human resources. But the rest of it is simply having some good experience and being able to convince people that the services I can provide are worthwhile."

Many consultants are sole practitioners. The solo consultant needs a wider array of skills than the consultant who works for a large firm, but enjoys more independence and control. Whether a banker goes to work for a big consulting firm or decides to fly solo, however, some ingredients for success are the same. Rutz believes success requires salesmanship and confidence and rules out individuals who lack experience.

"Successful consultants have a certain confidence that their business will be a success," Rutz says. "But they also have to do some initial research to determine that there is a need for what they're offering. How do you do that? You do that by bouncing your idea off everybody you run into regardless of what kind of business they're in."

"Number one, you had better have credentials, because first of all you have to get in and convince somebody that they need a consultant and that they need you. Once you convince them of that then you have to be able to produce. The other part of being an effective consultant is being able to sit down with somebody and share your experience with them. It's almost like an interview when you think about it. You're convincing them that you have the skills to make their organization a better organization in the specific field."

"I'm going to continue to consult for different firms, and I might come across a firm and say to myself, I wouldn't mind working for them. I haven't ruled that out. But I think the world has changed dramatically in that job security and stability are no longer part of any organization. So my approach is, I'd rather be my own boss and be in control of what I can do to create business instead of working for an organization where who knows when a merger or cutback might occur. I want to be in control of my own destiny. Being a consultant is my long-term plan."

■ THE SKILLS BANKERS BRING TO CONSULTING

Just as analytical abilities are of prime importance in consulting work, the job search for an aspiring management consultant is largely cerebral. Former bankers exploring consulting must ask themselves exactly what knowledge they can offer potential clients.

"I guess there are two dimensions to consulting," Rutz says. "One dimension is the knowledge that you've gained from different areas in banking, and the other dimension is the communications and decision-making and analytical skills that you have." Rutz could have added that without good communications skills, a consultant's other abilities are almost immaterial.

The Prime Prerequisite: Communications

Management consultants may be accountants or financial advisors or automated manufacturing specialists, but one thing is certain: a consultant is first and foremost a communicator.

It's not enough to be able to communicate, however; consultants must also have the ability to persuade. Edward Hendricks, president of ACME and spokesman for the Council of Consulting Organizations, advises, "You have to be able to sell, and what you're selling is you. You're selling your expertise, your knowledge, and your capabilities. It doesn't matter that all the people you talked with around the water cooler told you you'd make a great consultant. If you can't sell yourself to other people, no one is going to know about it." Rutz suggests that former bankers from many departments may possess this elemental consulting skill. "Bankers are selling themselves constantly, no matter what they do, and if you're a good communicator, whether one-on-one or with a group, then you will probably be relatively successful going into consulting," he says.

Relationship Marketing of Financial Services

A banker skilled in relationship marketing already has two of the prerequisites for consulting. One prerequisite is the relationship sales skills necessary for success in any area of concentration in consulting; the other prerequisite is the sharp financial skills required of many bank relationship managers.

Many financial services companies provide consulting services to clients in areas such as treasury, finance, and accounting. Bankers in these jobs can transfer their skills directly to consulting careers.

Hendricks points out the growing demand for a particular expertise: "The entire financial services area is growing in international consulting, particularly in the insurance field, as U.S. companies attempt to practice in a 'borderless Europe.' Bankers who have some international skills might have a leg up on marketing themselves to some of the larger consulting firms and also to potential clients, small- to mid-sized firms that are interested in cracking the European market."

Lending and Appraisal

Bankers experienced in mortgage or commercial lending can apply their skills to consulting, and even a bleak real estate market may hold promise for a job seeker with expertise in certain areas.

Appraisal skills are in demand in both real estate firms and consulting firms, Hendricks says. Many skills lenders possess, such as loan workout, commercial acquisitions and assets disposition capabilities, form the hub of many consulting practices. The key to applying banking skills in a way that maximizes employment prospects is to evaluate skills from a strictly functional viewpoint.

"Many financial service skills can be transferred into other types of consulting. For instance, in the manufacturing field, a former banker with asset and liability management skills might be able to work in conjunction with an industrial engineer on how to cut costs in a manufacturing operation and how to manage present assets," Hendricks says.

Fiscal Accountability

Consulting assignments often merge a technical or operational challenge with its fiscal consequences. What the former banker brings to the consulting equation is the financial side. "Some consulting firms are functionally based; some firms are industry-oriented. So the skills bankers bring to consulting are not limited to, and they should not perceive themselves as being limited to, financial institutions," maintains Hendricks.

Regardless of the focus of their previous jobs, bank managers may enjoy certain advantages in consulting, because banking experience often creates a keen sensitivity to the impact all business decisions have on the bottom line.

■ LANDING THE RIGHT JOB IN CONSULTING

Your ability to affect the bottom line can be decisive in securing a consulting job. "Any type of profitability approach is a good choice for consulting. Somebody who was heavily involved in bank operations who came up with a plan to make branches more profitable, that's a good area," Clifford Rutz observes.

Hendricks offers another tip: as consulting grows more competitive, more consulting firms will offer complete departmental functions formerly handled inside a client's company; this is referred to as "implementation." "Everyone in consulting is recognizing a trend toward implementation of the project or the product of the consulting assignment," Hendricks says. "Where several years ago a consultant might have given the client a recommendation on how to manage assets and liabilities, the client is now saying, 'We don't have the people to do it. Can you help us implement your recommendations?'" Hendricks believes this trend opens up opportunities for, among others, experienced bankers and other financial services executives.

David Lord at *Consultants News* observes that there are three current consulting growth areas that may have potential for former bankers: information systems, human resources, and what Lord calls "time-based competition." Lord says that others have different names for "time-based competition," but in general the term describes a focus on cost-effectiveness and efficiency of operations.

Several specialties in consulting may offer opportunities for former bankers:

Systems Consulting

Consultants News, ACME News, and other publications for professional consultants agree that information systems remains a hot area in consulting. Lord says that the demand for service, systems change, and systems management is growing at a faster pace than many other consulting specialties. Hendricks says, "That means a former banker who has experience in information technology and financial services has a good background for consulting right now. It's an area where a number of people have started up smaller firms and have done quite well for themselves where they've been able to carve out a particular market niche."

Consultants News confirms that systems consulting is growing even more rapidly than consulting in general. Clifford Rutz reports, "There is still a tremendous need for software programs in different areas, not only in banking, but in very specific applications." Nancy Seever, vice president and director of the career counseling center at First Chicago, reports that former bankers are using their expertise in setting up data processing systems to go to work for consulting firms or to launch their own businesses.

Marketing

Bankers from marketing and from customer service-based management positions may have both the credentials and the bent needed to succeed in consulting, because jobs in both bank departments require service/product development skills and the ability to communicate.

"Bankers often have skills in assessing customers' needs," Hendricks says. "Many bankers have done a good job of marketing their services. One of the primary components of a total quality management program, a whole new emphasis in a number of consulting firms now, is understanding customers' needs."

Human Resources and Training

David Lord is not the only consultant watcher who believes that human resources is an expanding area. Bank human resources professionals still working for banks identify the field as one in which know-how in banking can easily transfer to other sorts of businesses.

Rutz identified compensation, benefits, affirmative action, and equal employment opportunity policies as increasingly important to the organizations he is targeting in his consulting practice. Personnel change management is another skill area in demand as downsizing continues in the financial services industry and other industries. Many functions of human resources departments can be easily assumed by an outside management consultant, including conducting human resources audits, establishing programs, and producing procedure manuals and audit reports.

Asset Management

Former bankers can also forge valuable consulting specializations from backgrounds in commercial lending, loan workout, and asset/liability management. Ken Davis, formerly a bank chief lending officer, is now a financial consultant in asset management who travels from one bankrupt financial institution to another working on asset disposition. "They bring me in, for lack of a better term, as a 'fast gun' who knows the drill," he says.

Davis's talent for managing commercial assets, loans and special assets was a natural lead-in to his new career. After living through two bank mergers and losing his job after the second, Davis began consulting. He took on an assignment as part of a team to restructure a failing bank and ended up being referred to other conservatorship managing agents who were eager for his expertise. Because they are temporary jobs, the projects Davis undertakes for financial institutions are really not consulting assignments in the usual sense, but his experience demonstrates how the same economic forces that deprive bankers of their jobs can also give them new opportunities to employ their experience and abilities.

Consulting Practice Areas for Former Bankers

Almost every area of management in business and industry is mirrored by an area of concentration in consulting. There are, consequently, far more consulting specialties than can be enumerated here. However, the following list of consulting specialties, selected from a list of the practice areas of ACME-member consulting firms, identifies areas in which former bankers may apply their skills. (Opportunities for experienced-hire positions may be more available at smaller consulting firms, since many large consulting firms often hire their personnel at entry level and train them extensively.)

- Services — general management, diversification, mergers, acquisitions and joint ventures, general business surveys, management reports and controls, operations research, profit improvement programs, and strategic business planning and long-range objectives
- Information systems
- Benefits and compensation
- Human resources
- Marketing
- Finance and accounting
- Administration
- International operations
- Insurance
- Real estate
- Recruiting
- Relocation services

■ DO YOU NEED MORE EDUCATION OR CERTIFICATION?

In management consulting, professional designations and education beyond a bachelor's degree are significant advantages both in solo consulting practices and larger firms.

America's 50 Fastest Growing Jobs observes that opportunities in the consulting field are best for those who have graduate degrees or experience in the relevant industry. Often an individual's consulting specialization is determined by his or her professional degrees or certifications. Designations within professional disciplines carry the greatest weight, but the Certified Management Consultant designation conferred by the Institute of Management Consultants can also give a boost to a consultant's career.

"The C.M.C. designation is available to full-time management consultants who have had about five years of experience in consulting," explains ACME's Edward Hendricks. Like ACME, the Institute of Management Consultants (IMC) is an affiliate of the Council of Consulting Organizations. The C.M.C. designation is "not designed for those who are entering the field," Hendricks says, and in addition to experience requires participation in the three-day IMC course in consulting and written and oral examinations.

Bankers who want to learn more about consulting service opportunities can easily educate themselves. In addition to the books on consulting available in bookstores and libraries, the specialty publisher that produces *Consultants News*, Kennedy Publications, has a selection of titles aimed specifically at consultants. How-to manuals on topics from general consulting processes to setting fees to writing proposals to competing for clients are available.

■ LEARNING MORE AND BREAKING IN

The first consideration for anyone starting a consulting business sounds simple, but it is too basic to overlook: know yourself. "If you're going into consulting on your own, first identify what makes you different — what you have to offer that someone is going to be willing to buy that they may not be able to get, or get in a similar manner, from someone else," Hendricks says. "Then really concentrate on making that niche your niche. That includes maintaining memberships in the trade and professional organizations in the field in which you have expertise."

Networking and visibility are essential to launching a consulting career and ensuring that it thrives. A solo consultant can avoid feeling isolated by maintaining membership in trade and professional organizations or, even more economically, by attending local chapter meetings of such organizations, which are often open to nonmembers. Affiliations with professional organizations also are conducive to the steady marketing effort consultants say is necessary for success. Hendricks suggests, "Get yourself on the speaker's platform as often as possible to develop name recognition for yourself. Write articles for magazines in the field so people come to recognize you."

Many consultants will tell you that your former employer may be the most likely source for your first consulting job. This advice is validated by the number of bankers who are now performing contract work for the banks that let them go. Robin McNeil, manager of employee relations and staffing at Great Western Bank, advises, "Particularly in specialized areas, bankers with long tenure who have a lot of experience and knowledge with a company may still be needed. Their background is still valuable even though their function has been eliminated."

Not burning your bridges may pay off in ways other than consulting assignments after you are terminated. The contacts and networking possibilities available through your former employer can produce real advantages when you apply for positions in consulting, according to Hendricks. He says, "One of the things that a consulting firm is going to look for is, 'Who do you know, who can you put us in touch with, and who might you be able to sell an assignment to?'"

A new consultant whose first client is his or her former employer should not believe that new business will always come so easily, according to James Kennedy, publisher of *Consultants News*. "One danger is luxuriating in the false sense of security that can come from getting your first client, and then falling off the shelf when the first contract ends," he says. "Marketing must start on day one and be continuous; one rule of thumb is one day a week."

Consultants who form teams with other consultants to secure contracts are increasingly common, according to a recent article in *Consultants News*. An association of this sort can help consultants build their specialties and may smooth the rough spots inherent in an entrepreneurial consulting venture.

Directories of consulting firms available in many libraries or directly from their publishers, like the *ACME Directory of Members* and Kennedy Publications' *Directory of Management Consultants*, list firms and their areas of practice. Other publications that may be helpful to job hunters exploring the consulting field are the ACME *Survey of Key Management Information*, a compilation of statistics on consulting, and ACME's *Professional Profile of Management Consultants*, which describes the consulting process in depth.

While revenues continue to grow at established, larger, consulting firms, many of consulting's current success stories are small, flexible, start-up firms. "We're seeing a lot of smaller start-up companies that have identified niches," says ACME's Edward Hendricks. "They can respond more quickly than the big firms, and they're doing very well."

For former bankers who have the right experience, enough energy to go after clients, and, more often than not, the ability to travel extensively, consulting merits consideration.

■ RESOURCES

Consulting to Management by Larry E. Greiner and Robert O. Metzger (Prentice-Hall)

Handbook of Management Consulting Service, edited by Samuel W. Barcus and Joseph W. Wilkinson (McGraw-Hill)

The Consultant's Guide to Winning Clients, by Herman Holtz (John Wiley)

The Contract and Fee-Setting for Consultants and Professionals, by
  Howard L. Shenson (John Wiley)
ACME Directory of Members
Directory of Management Consultants (Kennedy Publications)
ACME *U.S. Survey of Key Management Information*
ACME *Professional Profile of Management Consultants*
Consultants News, monthly newsletter published by Kennedy Publi-
  cations

Professional Associations

IMC, Institute of Management Consultants, a division of the Council
  of Consulting Organizations, 521 Fifth Avenue, 35th Floor, New
  York, NY 10175-3598; 212/697-9693
ACME, Association of Management Consulting Firms, a division of
  the Council of Consulting Organizations, 521 Fifth Avenue, 35th
  Floor, New York, NY 10175-3598; 212/697-9693

12

JOBS IN REAL ESTATE

■ ■ ■

Agent ■ Broker ■ Investment Broker ■ Appraiser ■ Property Manager ■ Developer ■ Mortgage Broker ■ Asset Manager

---

Bankers with experience in these areas may be qualified to move to jobs in real estate

---

APPRAISAL
ASSET/LIABILITY
   MANAGEMENT
BRANCH MANAGEMENT
CONSUMER LOANS
COMMERCIAL LENDING
CORPORATE STAFFING
CUSTOMER SERVICE
FACILITIES MANAGEMENT

HUMAN RESOURCES
LOAN ANALYSIS
MARKETING
MORTGAGE LENDING
SECURITIES
TRUST AND INVESTMENTS

The fields of banking and real estate are linked in many ways. Professionals in both areas of employment work together in mortgage and commercial property financing, and bank lending departments are the launching pads for many bankers who make a move into real estate specialties.

This linkage means that former bankers may find considerable potential for skill transfers into real estate. The two fields share more than occupational crossover, however — real estate, like banking, has had its share of problems in recent years. As a result of the excesses that were common in the American real estate industry of the 1980s, the industry has spent much of the 1990s recovering from the hangover. Industry watchers predict only modest gains in the home real estate market and flat if not declining commercial sales as the industry recovers from soaring prices.

The career handbook *Jobs '96* calls the jobs outlook in real estate "good" in the long term and "bumpy" in the short term, as the industry continues to undergo significant restructuring. "Companies are shedding real estate to cut costs — reducing the number of offices, the size of offices and the duration of leases." Telecommuting and "hoteling" in the business community, an arrangement in which multiple employees share the same space at different times, could negatively impact the industry. "Should these alternate forms of work really catch on," the book warns, "watch office demand drop — and commercial real estate feel the resulting pinch."

Jobs '96 points to another strong trend in the industry that should be closely watched by career changers, the consolidation of the real estate industry into two tiers. "The top tier will be the larger, well-financed firms that were best able to weather the recent slump and can take the downturns in the cyclical industry best. The other tier will consist of smaller developers that are attuned to local markets and can be more flexible because of their size." So who will be casualties of this realignment in real estate? Mid-sized firms and developers. Bankers seeking long-term stability in a new real estate career may wish to focus their sights on smaller firms specializing in local markets within high-growth communities, or on larger, national firms with the geographic coverage, size, and access to capital that predicts long-term survival in turbulent markets.

Many trends may work in favor of former bankers making a move to real estate — including the boom in home refinancing, vigorous activity in trade-up sales in certain markets, the increased demand for expertise in the management and disposition of real estate assets, and foreign investment in U.S. property.

And another factor that can make real estate a promising career for former bankers is the fact that property sales, management, and appraisal firms employ professionals in positions other than the traditional agent or broker roles — in marketing, human resources, and management, for example. Because many bankers have cultivated skills in these other areas, real estate employers can make use of their rich business experience in ways that do not require specific real estate knowledge or training.

The two job-change stories that follow illustrate the potential for new careers in real estate that do apply real estate experience acquired in banking: one banker went to work as a commission-based investment broker and the other has become a self-employed appraiser.

Banking Is a Great Training Ground for Investment Broker

Gary Weiss, who was a commercial lender for a middle market bank in Chicago when he chose to move to real estate, is convinced the experience he gained from the rotational management trainee positions he held at that bank now serve him well in his new career as a sales associate for Corporate Realty Advisors in Des Plaines, Illinois. He was promoted to credit associate with the bank before he changed careers.

"The opportunity to go into the bank, when it presented itself right out of school, was too good an opportunity to pass up — the position offered the chance to get educated about the industry, and to develop street — smarts, business acumen, and relationship skills. But my degree was in finance with a concentration in real estate, and my family had always been in real estate," Weiss says.

"Banking turned out to be a great training ground. In fact, one of my lending accounts when I was a credit analyst at the bank connected me with someone who helped catapult me out of banking and into real estate."

"As an investment sales broker, my clients are developers, institutions, pension funds, and pension fund advisors. It involves much more than pure brokerage when you're marrying property to user. We're also underwriting the investment potential of the properties. Working with financial analysts, we examine leases, review the credit information on tenants, the income levels and expense levels, and then we forecast the value of the property over time given the market. We're really telling a story for the prospective investor."

"I find the process to be a lot more rewarding, a lot more analytical and challenging, than user brokerage. The deals are definitely larger. Our typical transactions are in the tens of millions of dollars. I had to get licensed by the state to sell real estate; and subsequently I obtained the Certified Commercial Investment Member designation. In addition to understanding real estate, I also have to understand the tenant's business and the tenant's market niche."

Unlike Weiss, who knew his professional preference lay in real estate rather than banking before he made his career move, Jim Rachwitz was a twenty-five year S&L veteran when he found himself suddenly out of a job. Although he initially chose a job in another field, Rachwitz eventually returned to the same area in which he had concentrated as senior vice president/chief appraiser for Mutual Savings Bank in Bay City, Michigan, but this time as a self-employed, certified real estate appraiser.

Applying Concentration in Banking to Independent Appraisal

"I started with the bank as a residential appraiser and eventually became chief appraiser and manager of real estate. I had always been in the real estate end of banking," Rachwitz says.

"I wanted to try something different. I figured that if they fire you after putting in twenty-five years, you should be trying something else. So I gave insurance a try. There probably could have been good income in it, but sales was an altogether different business than anything I had in the past. I was not happy there."

"Then I decided to do appraisals. I took the appraisal exam. In the state of Michigan, a real estate broker's license used to be all you needed to perform appraisals. But under the new law — and other states have now passed similar laws — you have to be a licensed appraiser. It was sort of a natural way for me to go, and it was probably the way I should have gone right from the beginning."

"My work is different now because when I was a chief appraiser, I was completely managerial. Now I receive the appraisal requests and perform the appraisals."

"This was a good time for me to get into the field, because there will probably be a two- or three-year door during which there will be a lack of licensed appraisers. Most of my clients will be institutional; the projects I'm doing right now are with the S&L that I left. Most of the calls for appraisals are from banks, S&Ls, credit unions, and mortgage companies that require appraisals for their loans. Another market I haven't experienced yet is that of refinancing."

Rachwitz channeled his specific know-how in banking into his new profession; his alternative career is a good example of how easily experience in bank real estate departments can transfer to a new job.

■ THE SKILLS BANKERS BRING TO REAL ESTATE

Other professional opportunities in real estate are not as obvious as the paths taken by Rachwitz or Weiss. The story of Thomas Markovich's move out of banking, for instance, shows how a branch manager's options could include employment with a real estate association or council.

Markovich, now a policy analyst for the National Association of Realtors, was in banking for fourteen years. He managed a branch with about $50 million in deposits. Markovich was trained in commercial and mortgage lending, installment portfolios, and operations, and demonstrated strong customer-service capabilities along the way.

In banking, Markovich excelled when implementing new policies and new product ideas. The challenges of his new career, Markovich says, are not so different from those of his old one: "The relationships that we have with the associations and the services that we provide members are crucial, so it's a very good place to start for someone with my skills level. My job requires a great deal of thinking and writing and customer service, dealing with people who run the boards of realtors out in the field. As branch manager at the bank, I had to get out there in the community and become involved in organizations. You need strong communication skills in this job."

"Those aspects of my training and background, coupled with the fact that I had a master's degree in business and could apply my administrative experience managing people, all fit in very nicely," Markovich says. Service and communications expertise are not the only skills developed in a bank managerial position that can be applied to real estate. One of the most direct banking experience applications to real estate — sales skills — tops this list of the professional tools bankers can employ in real estate jobs.

Relationship Sales

The business-relationship savvy honed in banking positions such as branch management and outside sales of financial service products are essential for success in many brokerage positions in real estate, from selling homes to putting together multimillion-dollar commercial property transactions.

Because sales skills are paramount, the real estate agent's job does not necessarily make use of specific lending experience. Instead, the business contacts and well-developed people skills of many former bankers are reported to be the transferable talents most highly valued in real estate. And whether a banker enjoyed the sales aspects of his or her former bank job can be a telling indicator of whether a job in real estate sales will be a good match. "The outside sales skills are a natural. I think I already had some of the personality traits that put a person in an interface-with-clients type of position, but those skills were certainly refined at the bank," Weiss believes.

In addition to pure selling experience, relationship sales jobs in banking often require financial analysis skills that are critical to many real estate undertakings. Weiss says that the skills he developed at the bank, including analyzing businesses from an operational as well as a financial perspective, have been extremely valuable in his position as an investment broker. "I think it has helped me to be a productive and successful broker faster."

Mortgage Lending

The financial, regulatory and relationship skills cultivated by former bankers in mortgage lending present opportunities for direct applications not only within agencies but also in other finance, government, construction, and development organizations.

"A knowledge of mortgages would allow someone to make a transition into real estate policy formulation just like I'm doing," Markovich says. But he believes that his job is but one example of the numerous career paths former lenders can take.

Commercial Lending

Perhaps more than other former bankers, commercial lenders are trained in skills that may prepare them for an easy transfer out of banking into promising areas of real estate. Trish Benninger, human resources vice president at Great Western Bank, says real estate is the obvious choice for a banker with a background in commercial lending, adding that real estate management is "probably your best bet for getting a job." She suggests that lenders who have picked up special knowledge along the way may be equipped to explore particular fields, such as construction.

"Those who have developed good relationships with the real estate community in their lending operations are destined for success," says Steven Pope, executive vice president of the Commercial Investment Real Estate Institute. "If bankers understand the needs of the buyers, sellers, and brokers, then they are particularly well suited to move into the business."

Pope also points out that commercial lending as well as other banking positions nurture skills in client relationship-building that apply to real estate brokerage. "If you sell from a property standpoint, you're not developing any continuing business opportunity. But a banker who understands that he has to develop a relationship with his client is going to be better served in a brokerage operation because he'll go prospecting for business on a client-relationship basis and earn and win clients before he wins any brokerage fees."

■ LANDING THE RIGHT JOB IN REAL ESTATE

The real estate industry employs approximately 422,000 people in the agent, broker, and appraiser fields, according to the U.S. Bureau of Labor Statistics, with another 72,000 expected to join the ranks by the year 2000. Yet membership in the National Association of Realtors numbers 750,000, and that estimate does not include many specialists whose focus may not be in the brokerage side. These figures indicate that there may easily be more than a million professionals employed in the industry.

The Bureau of Labor Statistics anticipates an average employment growth in the sales and appraiser fields of 17 percent. In property and real estate management, where the Bureau estimates that more than 225,000 people are employed, growth is predicted to be slightly higher. Overall, an upturn in the prospect for real estate is expected in the last part of the decade.

"There are more challenging and rewarding opportunities for those who uncover specialized areas that are in demand," according to *Top*

Professions. "These areas include dealing in commercial property and real estate investing."

Real estate agents represent the largest group of workers employed in the field and experience the greatest turnover rate and uncertainty in earnings. All agents must be licensed, but acquiring certification can be a simple step for experienced former bankers. Because brokerage is a commission-based business, agents set their own hours and must be highly self-motivated.

A job in sales also offers the opportunity for a hybrid career that merges real estate with another endeavor. Gary Weiss wants to teach in addition to being a broker, so he is exploring becoming a C.C.I.M.-curriculum investment real estate instructor at a community college.

Residential Sales Agent or Broker

After sagging market levels and the recent slight upturn in many locations, the nature of residential sales continues to evolve. "The real estate market will be changing from one where there are many first-time home buyers and many new-home sales to one where buyers are trading up existing properties for bigger or better ones," according to *Top Professions*.

The qualifications for a broker who manages a real estate office usually include extensive real estate sales experience and a certain number of years' work as an agent under another broker. Brokers' duties also include managerial skills that former bankers may possess — such as supervising sales efforts, securing listings, handling promotion and coordinating office administration.

Commercial or Industrial Brokerage

The jobs in commercial and industrial property sales are not limited to real estate firms; corporations, insurance companies, and financial services firms also employ professionals trained in the acquisition and disposition of commercial property.

A promising area for many former lenders, specialization in commercial and industrial brokerage often makes more use of finance expertise and investment evaluation than do other sales jobs in real estate. Selling income-producing property typically involves far higher prices, as well as the application of the economics of different businesses and industries. Especially in industrial brokerage, a former banker may be required to have industry-specific knowledge of transportation variables, materials and energy sources, labor availability, and local zoning and tax laws.

Securities Broker

Like commercial brokerage, property investment brokerage positions are not limited to real estate companies. Insurance companies, corporations, and the gamut of financial services and consulting firms are active in property investment.

Real estate securities and syndication, a relatively new specialty, is described as "increasingly important" by the National Association of Realtors. Syndicators develop and market real estate limited partnerships, and for bankers whose experience includes finance, lending, or investments, the field could make strong use of existing skills.

Former bankers interested in real estate syndication may need experience in real estate sales or property management, and they should possess solid persuasive skills.

Appraiser

The appraisal field is being shaken up by the federal Institutions Reform, Recovery and Enforcement Act of 1989, which requires the licensing of all appraisers working for federally chartered or insured financial institutions. The original deadline for compliance was July 1, 1991, but enforcement has been extended while states scramble to enact compliance legislation.

The National Association of Realtors' "Careers In Real Estate" guide suggests that opportunities for appraisers are best in large real estate firms, insurance companies, specialist appraisal firms, government agencies, and tax assessment firms.

Jim Rachwitz reports that there is an increasing amount of fee appraising being done. "There are more people going into fee work because, with mergers and acquisitions, S&Ls and banks can cut their operating and their overhead costs considerably just by cutting out the appraisal department and going to fee appraisals."

Developer

Strong financial skills may serve a former banker well in real estate development, a field in which a knowledge of lending institutions can be a critical factor for success. Other skills are required of developers, however — including know-how in market research, construction cost management, and sales. Former bankers who possess heavy experience in residential, commercial, or industrial development financing may be on a natural career track for land development jobs, because many high-finance developers merge a background in business administration and finance with knowledge of real estate.

The National Association of Realtors' guidebook identifies these key skills for land development: "executive ability; substantial experience in real estate; knowledge of financing; knowledge of all the major real estate specialties; knowledge of the community and awareness of its growth trends; and knowledge of zoning and other laws."

"Two trends have propelled real estate development in recent years," *Top Professions* advises: "the demographics of the U.S. population and the deregulation of financial markets." Declining demand for housing in the nineties, as the number of twenty-five- to thirty-four-year-olds decline, combined with the chill on financing as the S&L bailout continues, has resulted in a continued competitive and lean development industry.

Property Manager

Former bankers can transfer job functions directly from within a bank's real estate department to becoming property managers for real estate firms. Related managerial and financial skills can also be applied to a new career in property management, a field in which attributes possessed by many bankers — including finely tuned relationship skills and marketing know-how — are in demand.

Maintenance and reconstruction costing, property operation, rent collection, and financial record keeping are of course among a property manager's responsibilities, as well as a supervisory role for maintenance. But property managers must also keep tenants. For this reason, the National Association of Realtors suggests that successful job candidates must be able to demonstrate that they have problem-solving skills.

The Bureau of Labor Statistics predicts that there will be 267,000 property managers by the year 2000. Some property managers may also be real estate developers or brokers, and there is considerable crossover of functions between the specialties.

"The rise in property values over the past ten years or so has made property management a more prestigious occupation with higher stakes," according to *Top Professions*. "In addition, the business trends that are clouding the outlook for real estate development translate into offering better building services as a bargaining chip to entice tenants into a development. Both of these factors auger well for building managers and their job outlook." Thomas Markovich confirms this view: "If someone has gotten additional schooling in property management, that seems to be a hot field now."

Mortgage Financing Specialist

As liaisons between buyers and sellers who specialize in knowing both the real estate and mortgage markets, mortgage brokers and mortgage bankers work in banking and other financial services industries as well as in insurance and real estate firms.

Mortgage financing positions require considerable experience and preferred candidates have master's degrees, yet the background requirements are similar to many former bankers' lending or accounting concentrations. The National Association of Realtors' "Careers in Real Estate" guide outlines some ingredients for success: "a bachelor's or master's degree in business, finance or related fields; broad business experience; an understanding of all the other real estate specialties; accurate, up-to-date knowledge of financing; and knowledge of federal and state laws that regulate mortgage financing."

Asset Manager

Corresponding to the increased demand for asset management and loan workout expertise both in financial institutions and the economy at large, real estate asset manager is a specialty cited as a prime area for employment in real estate for former bankers. Steven Pope at the Commercial Investment Real Estate Institute asserts, "The hot area right now is asset management. It's doing the same things that a corporate real estate executive would do, for a private group. A lot of Certified Commercial Investment Members are asset managers; they're real estate portfolio managers for insurance companies; or they may work for the government doing the same kind of asset management. The job requires understanding all the aspects of a real estate portfolio and then making the decisions as to whether there should be a redevelopment or disposition, for example."

The wave of S&L dispositions and financial institution acquisitions is fueling demand for asset disposition services, and different kinds of firms are rushing to meet the need, including accounting firms contracting with the RTC, property management firms, and real estate companies specializing in niches like hotel/motel and apartment properties.

■ DO YOU NEED MORE CERTIFICATION OR EDUCATION?

Not only is more education a profitable complement to just about any new job in real estate; some training is necessary for employment in licensed agent positions. According to the National Association of Realtors, more than half of the state license commissions specify education, experience, or equivalents in their licensing requirements. Licensing courses are widely available.

Acquiring additional education is the most popular method for entering real estate. In the opinion of Thomas Markovich, "Skills enhancement is probably the best thing you can do, the first step. Go for a master's degree or enhance your skills level — something that would allow you to bridge the gap."

Fortunately, most real estate certification programs are not as time- and cost-intensive as earning a master's degree, and many of the professional designations can pay off nicely. A study conducted by the Institute of Real Estate Management in 1986 compared the earnings of Certified Property Managers with non-C.P.M.-designated property managers and illustrates the weight certain professional certifications can carry in the real estate field. The average compensation reported for the approximately 8,500 C.P.M.'s was $64,500, while those who were C.P.M. candidates earned an average of $42,600.

Gary Weiss, the former banker whose investment brokerage position was built on securing the C.C.I.M. designation, points out another key benefit of joining professional associations and institutes: more business. "There are a limited number of C.C.I.M.'s, and it's a great group from the standpoint of networking. I can make contacts when there is an opportunity in another city, and I know the broker I'm associating with has at least the education that I possess through the C.C.I.M. program."

An affiliate of the National Association of Realtors, the Commercial Investment Real Estate Institute has been conferring the C.C.I.M. designation for twenty years. According to Steven Pope, there are currently 3,300 active C.C.I.M.'s. "Bankers are particularly well suited to get into commercial real estate through our organization because so much of what we teach in our courses is financial analysis and decision analysis, which most bankers will probably have had some grounding in, making the translation of those concepts into real estate easier for them to understand."

"The skills you get from the C.C.I.M. education prepare you for commercial brokerage, mortgage banking or brokerage, and corporate real estate," says Pope, "and I think the C.C.I.M. would be particularly valuable to a banker making the transition to corporate real estate."

"I would also strongly encourage bankers — if they're headed toward asset management — to take the Institute of Real Estate Management courses," Pope adds. "Their courses have traditionally been property management — based but they are also very sensitive to the growing need for property managers to truly be asset managers. The institute has some excellent courses leading to the C.P.M. designation, and those asset management courses would further fill out their education and understanding of the real estate aspects of this career."

Speaking from his job-search experience, Markovich suggests that former bankers entering real estate, or any field, may benefit from other professional self-improvement. "Enhance your speaking and writing skills and computer knowledge. In every position I had at the bank, I always had secretaries doing everything for me, and I learned that I had lost most of my computer skills. I've got a PC in my office now, and I'm making sure that my skills are fine-tuned because it is something every employer seems to desire right now."

■ LEARNING MORE AND BREAKING IN

A real estate board is a career resource for anyone entering the field, as are many of the national trade associations. Because so many real estate courses are introductory and the ones focused within a discipline are continually updated due to changes in laws or regulations, becoming a member or participating in the educational programs sponsored by local boards and national organizations can be beneficial for anyone who plans to enter the field.

Using banking contacts to explore promising areas is another route for learning more, especially because bank real estate departments have ties to many segments of the field. Business contacts in other financial institutions, as well as acquaintances in real estate firms, development companies, and management firms, can help to introduce former bankers to new areas. State real estate associations can also be information sources, as well as real estate directories in library business reference sections.

Former bank managers and others from positions not closely aligned to real estate functions will find it challenging to apply their broad-based experience to the field, but by carefully examining their skills, they too can connect to many jobs in real estate. "I really have a toolkit of knowledge and experience, and I've pulled out what I need to do and what I want to do," says former branch manager Thomas Markovich.

What skills do you highlight on your resume? Where do you look? After closely examining what experience you have that you can apply to the real estate field and exploring what skill enhancements might serve you well, it is advisable to learn as much as you can about the employment area you choose and about companies targeted in your job search.

Dallas-based Trammell Crow Company, a real estate services firm ranked the largest management and development company in the United States, employs 2,600 nationwide. Like other large real estate companies, Trammell Crow is changing in response to a changing market. Steve Laver, chief administrative officer, states that the company's activities, once focused on development, today emphasize management, leasing and marketing, project construction management, and financial services. "Today about half our business comes from third-party service customers," Laver says.

Real estate is increasingly complex and competitive, and many employers in the field are changing fast to accommodate evolving markets. Former bankers must learn the waters before they can successfully identify the abilities they can bring to the job.

■ RESOURCES

State real estate commissions
Local boards of realtors
State associations of realtors

Publications include *Real Estate News, National Real Estate Investor, Skylines: News of the Office Building Industry* (all usually available in libraries), *Journal of Property Management* (published by Institute of Real Estate Management), and *Commercial Investment Real Estate Journal* (published by Commercial Investment Real Estate Institute)

Professional Associations

National Association of Realtors, 430 N. Michigan Avenue, Chicago, IL 60611-4087; 312/329-8261
Institute of Real Estate Management, 430 N. Michigan Avenue, Chicago, IL 60611; 312/661-1930
Commercial Investment Real Estate Institute, 430 N. Michigan

Avenue, Chicago, IL 60611-4092; 312/321-4471

Appraisal Institute, 875 N. Michigan Avenue, Ste. 2400, Chicago, IL 60611-1980; 312/335-4476

American Society of Appraisers, P.O. Box 17265, Washington, DC 20041; 703/478-2228

American Association of Certified Appraisers, 800 Compton Road, Ste. 10, Cincinnati, OH 45231; 800/543-2222

National Association of Independent Fee Appraisers, Inc., 7501 Murdoch Avenue, St. Louis, MO 63119; 314/781-6688

Institute of Real Estate Management, National Association of Realtors, P.O. Box 109025, Chicago, IL 60611; 312/661-0004

National Association of Home Builders, Fifteenth and M Sts., NW, Washington, DC 20005; 202/822-0200

Building Owners and Managers Institute International, 1521 Ritchie Highway, Arnold, MD 21012; 410/974-1410

13

JOBS IN INSURANCE

■ ■ ■

Sales ■ Brokerage ■ Financial Planning ■ Management ■ Underwriting ■ Actuary ■ Asset Management ■ Human Resources ■ Information Systems

Bankers with experience in these areas may be qualified to move to jobs in insurance:

ACCOUNTING AND FINANCE   HUMAN RESOURCES
APPRAISAL   INFORMATION SYSTEMS
ASSET/LIABILITY MANAGEMENT LOAN ANALYSIS
BRANCH MANAGEMENT   MARKETING
COMMERCIAL LENDING   MORTGAGE BANKING
CONSUMER LOANS   SECURITIES
CORPORATE STAFF   TRUST AND
CUSTOMER SERVICE   INVESTMENT
FACILITIES

Former bankers may find the insurance field ripe for growing a new career. Several factors make it so. First, there are many similarities in the skills demanded by the two fields' financial/operational/investment emphases. Secondly, the direct sales and personal contact skills banking positions often develop also allow for job crossovers. Thirdly, the general business disciplines common to both industries —

for example, information systems, training, and human resources —
further enable successful transfers of experience from banking to insurance.

Knowing which economic trends affect insurance can help job
searchers tailor the marketing of their skills to prospective employers.
Industry publications and career handbooks report that new regulations, shifting market demand and increased competition are bringing
changes to the industry. Many insurance companies are streamlining
and consolidating. There is a new focus on smaller niches, rather than
multi-line insurance products.

Jobs '96 calls the overall outlook for the industry "fairly good,"
with substantial growth occurring in the healthcare lines of business as
enrollments in HMOs and other managed care hybrids steadily rise.
Property and casualty insurers continue to consolidate into larger,
stronger companies, some even shedding loss leader lines of business
like workers compensation and automobile insurance. Along with
their counterparts in the life insurance lines, property and casualty insurers will likely see tremendous growth in their international business, including expansion into overseas markets where claims processing, actuarial, and information services will be offered to these new
markets. Life insurance companies, predicts *Jobs '96*, will need to di-
versify their offerings to offset the penetration of non-insurance companies like banks and other financial institutions into their traditional
markets. Former bankers may want to pay close attention to developments in life insurance, since these companies may increasingly turn
to banking, real estate, securities, and other investment products to sta-
bilize their revenue base.

Although certain types of insurance coverage may be scaled back
through regulatory intervention and consolidation, agents and
providers will aggressively concentrate on specialized retirement planning, or property and casualty for a targeted type of commercial account such as midsize manufacturers. As the industry begins to rely on
overseas markets for growth, career changers with a background in in-

ternational banking, investments, transportation, or regional politics, may be especially well positioned for a move into insurance.

While many job seekers with a banking background may find themselves qualified for positions as insurance agents, the key to making a successful career change that "fits" usually lies in the nature of the job changer and the process of self-evaluation. *Top Professions* notes a high fallout rate among agents (90 percent turnover within two years) and identifies the following factors as critical for success in insurance sales: a "winning personality, a businesslike appearance, and a gritty determination to succeed."

One former banker who believes that he is in an agent's job to stay is Carl Boroff, former vice president/loan originator for Mutual Savings and Loan in Bay City, Michigan. Boroff chose to go to work for Farm Bureau Insurance because he perceived insurance to offer more security than other financial services fields, and the challenge of a change appealed to him. What the former lender says, after his twenty-plus years in banking, was that he had contacts to put to work in a career in insurance sales.

Contacts Profit Former Lender in New Insurance Position

"I felt my background in banking, especially with my business contacts, would be an advantage in getting into either investments or insurance," Carl Boroff says. "I did look at the investment field. I really didn't have my mind made up at first. Then the opportunity came up with Farm Bureau."

"I decided my future would be more secure in insurance. I've been here six months. My training included passing a licensing exam for the state of Michigan. I got some training in property and casualty and life and health, and also attended a week of intensive training at the home office of Farm Bureau. The professional training is ongoing, even after you're licensed. The philosophy of Farm Bureau, a multi-line company that can offer any type of insurance, appealed to me.

When I left the bank it was multi-line as well, offering savings, checking and so forth."

"At the bank I learned skills in cross-selling other accounts. That's really beneficial for me here, because I utilize the background to cross-sell other insurance products. This city has a population of about 12,000, and I know a lot of those people because I worked with them on mortgage loans. Because I am active in the community, everybody more or less knows me. Probably the number of contacts I had led me to choose insurance, although the skills that I picked up at Mutual Savings and Loan were not all lost."

"What I like most of all about my new job is the people. I've always related well to people and really like to help them. They come back because they appreciate that."

An insurance sales position such as Boroff's is usually all-commission, after a training period during which a base salary is provided. Most independent agents selling insurance are self-employed. The switch to such a sales-dependent income, requiring great self-motivation for success, is ideal for some people and very unsuitable for others. For Boroff, sales is the right fit:

"The key difference is that at the bank I got a paycheck, whether or not I was producing, and here I'm really self-employed. I enjoyed managing in banking, but I'm finding myself enjoying being self-employed more because my time is my own. I don't have to worry about what somebody else is doing. I'm my own boss. If I don't work, I don't have a job."

"I think insurance is a great field. Plan on a lot of hard work and longer hours than you had in banking. But if you like people and you like your own time and your own hours, you're going to like insurance."

In a field as large as insurance, which by some estimates employs three million people, there are myriad job descriptions. Many are independent positions in sales but most are jobs with insurance companies. To find the one job that might be right for you, you must first identify the skills you bring to the field.

■ The Skills Bankers Bring To Insurance

Various backgrounds, ranging from the experience gained in front-line customer service positions to commercial lending to assets disposition to systems design, can serve a banker well in a new career in insurance. But the fact that the two industries are both grounded in accounting and finance makes it likely that anyone who switches from banking to insurance will find his or her background quite useful.

A former banker entering the insurance industry will find that it is guided by a familiar goal: using money to make money. The jobs listed below all share purposes common to both banking and insurance: managing financial assets and marketing financial products to individuals and businesses.

Accounting and Finance

Jeff Hamilton, insurance manager for Dunhill Professional Service, a Columbus, Ohio, recruiting firm which specializes in placements in the insurance industry, believes the strong applications of banking skills to the insurance field begin in accounting and finance. Former banker Dr. Hazel Johnson, a college finance professor who tells in chapter 8 how she changed from banking to education, demonstrates how accounting functions overlap in these industries. She began her career in the insurance field after graduate school, becoming a manager of internal audit with a national insurance company; she was then a bank financial analyst and accounting supervisor before accepting her present position at the University of Louisville.

Rapport with Individual and Commercial Customers

The contacts and account relationship experience possessed by some former bankers can be put to immediate use in a career in agency or brokerage sales or in representing a carrier. "I see a lot of former bankers go to the brokerage side in insurance sales because of their outside contacts and also because of their people skills," says Hamilton.

John Durkin, human resources director of Heritage Federal Savings Bank in Richmond, Virginia, confirms that Carl Boroff is not the only former banker utilizing communications skills and sales polish in insurance. "We found that insurance companies approached several former branch managers, those very oriented toward producing loans, because they had a network of contacts."

In commercial account relationships, bankers usually develop skills in another key area in insurance — financial accountability. "For field management positions in insurance, companies are looking for people who can manage an account, keep an eye on the bottom line, and make a branch more profitable. Bankers are very used to doing that," Hamilton says.

Retail Branch and Bank Department Management

Boroff suggests that bank management positions produce experience that is an advantage in insurance. "For someone coming into the managerial part of an insurance company, I think there are some definite advantages; you're going to have some people skills, some marketing skills and so forth that would be applicable to insurance companies." It's a former banker's eye for the bottom line, however, that may make a job candidate for an insurance management position stand out.

Asset Management

The asset management abilities that many bankers in real estate departments or commercial lending have developed can be transferred across industries and applied to real estate portfolio management for insurance companies. Talents in asset acquisition and disposition, as noted in earlier chapters on jobs in other occupational fields, are increasingly in demand.

Securing a professional designation or further education may be a valuable aid in marketing asset management skills to insurance companies. "A lot of Certified Commercial Investment Members are real estate portfolio managers for insurance companies," says Steven Pope, executive vice president of the Commercial Investment Real Estate Institute, the organization that confers the C.C.I.M. designation.

■ LANDING THE RIGHT JOB IN INSURANCE

Jobs as insurance agents are accessible to many job seekers, regardless of specifically applicable business experience; yet other opportunities in insurance, including finance and management positions, may be particularly suitable for some former bankers.

Bankers with financial planning expertise, or with the desire to work toward advising clients on special financial options, such as annuities or mutual funds, may be ready to capitalize on the continuing trend in insurance toward more comprehensive financial planning services. *Top Professions* says that more insurance agents are securing additional training and marketing themselves to clients as financial planners. The U.S. Bureau of Labor Statistics predicts average growth in the near future for insurance sales jobs, and the volume of some insurance lines has grown so tremendously that agents remain in demand. Since 1985, the volume of life insurance premiums has jumped from $160 billion to more than $250 billion.

This list of insurance jobs for which former bankers may be qualified is just a starting point for bankers who want to identify where they can sell their skills. Employment opportunities are not limited to sales, accounting, and management; for example, some bankers can count themselves equipped to tackle information systems and human resources jobs in the insurance field as well.

Agency, Brokerage, and Carrier Sales

Bankers may have the right tools to land field positions in insurance and prosper. Representatives are employed in all sectors of the insurance industry. According to the Bureau of Labor Statistics' 1992 estimates, there are about 652,000 agents and brokers, and about 221,000 new jobs will be added to the field by the year 2005.

The duties sales positions entail vary greatly, but in many cases, former bankers are at an advantage. A life insurance agent's client could be a former lender's mortgage customer. Field jobs that focus on selling commercial coverage to businesses can make good use of some former bankers' commercial account contacts. "A lot of job seekers are afraid to talk with insurance companies if they don't already have a background in insurance. In reality, what insurance companies look for is someone who is people-focused and has the ability to talk to and work with commercial accounts," advises recruiter Jeff Hamilton.

Larry DeMeyers, the chief operating officer at Bankers First Savings Bank in Augusta, Georgia, says his experience leads him to believe that former bankers from trust and investment departments can easily apply their skills to insurance sales jobs, especially annuity sales positions that increasingly make use of financial planning services.

Finance and Accounting

Certain finance positions in insurance may make more use of functional skills than actual insurance experience, suggests Hamilton. The orientation in insurance on bottom-line profits, he adds, means bankers who recognize the industry's revenue imperatives and present their career experience in that light may be more attractive to potential employers.

"I've seen a few former bankers who go into the financial operational end in insurance — the analysts," Hamilton adds. This experienced-hire career switch requires heavy financial analyst qualifications that some former bankers from accounting and corporate bank departments possess. However, many other accounting professionals in banking could make moves to other insurance jobs with an eventual goal of landing jobs as financial analysts.

Underwriting

Although most former bankers would be required to study for professional certification and gain additional training in order to enter the field of insurance underwriting, many individuals in banking may have skills that are compatible with the underwriting specialties. There are approximately 100,000 underwriters working in various areas — including disability, health, and property and casualty — analyzing the financial impact of insurance product risks. The career guidebook *Jobs '96* reports that on average, an estimated 14,000 jobs will open each year in the underwriting profession because of industry growth and replacement needs. Insurance companies, brokers, and independent agencies employ underwriters.

The Bureau of Labor Statistics expects the number of jobs available in underwriting to increase faster than even insurance sales jobs, growing by 29 percent by the year 2000. Former bankers with commercial account experience may find they possess skills that are valuable to the commercial account underwriter's job, where business operation analysis and financial evaluation experience are crucial. In fact, general underwriting skills involving financial data may also make use of backgrounds in credit analysis, auditing, appraisal, and other banking areas.

Actuary

The approximately 15,000 U.S. actuaries who calculate the probability of loss for insurance companies generally have few counterparts in the banking industry, and advancement in the insurance industry as an actuary requires extensive study and professional certification. Yet many jobs in banking share the analytical bent that is required for actuarial positions, and former bankers without actuarial designations may nevertheless be able to make a career change to insurance that will allow them to work toward actuarial jobs.

Insurance actuaries may specialize in health, casualty, benefits management, or other types of insurance. Their numbers will be increasing rapidly through the year 2000, according to the Bureau of Labor Statistics prediction of a 54 percent growth rate. Like those who consider moving into insurance sales, career changers thinking about the actuarial field should evaluate carefully whether they possess the occupational determination, interests, and personality to succeed as an actuary.

Unlike many other career placements that may require additional training or certification, the actuarial field demands that candidates meet exacting performance standards that are measured by a series of ten increasingly sophisticated and challenging exams in the theory and mathematics of actuarial study. Most full-fledged actuaries or "fellows" in the Society of Actuaries take from six to ten years to complete all exams (employers of actuaries traditionally allocate structured time at work each year to prepare for the next exam). While there is pressure to take — and pass — the exams regularly, there are also significant financial incentives for completing each exam successfully. For this reason, the successful actuarial student enjoys much higher than average annual salary increases tied to exam completion.

Former bankers interested in the actuarial field will also benefit from computer programming and systems experience, since the field in the last fifteen years has increasingly used mainframe computers to process complex actuarial functions and tables. Bankers without programming experience who are interested in the security and financial rewards of the actuarial profession may improve their opportunities in the field by enrolling in intermediate and advanced computer programming courses.

Branch or Territory Manager

Bankers from several bank departments may find a close skills fit in insurance management positions. Unlike underwriting and loss-control positions, an insurance branch manager or regional manager needs less experience specific to the insurance industry. Prospective employers have more of a bottom-line orientation to filling these positions, reports Jeff Hamilton. "If the position available is a regional manager, the insurance company is not looking so much at banking or insurance industry background. They will look at how good the person's profit and loss responsibilities have been, how well they can manage a budget, and how well they can actually take over a branch and put the dollars on the bottom line where they count." Supervising personnel, accounting functions, image processing, record retrieval, and knowledge of SEC guidelines and tax laws may all be aspects of an insurance branch or territory manager's job.

Information Systems

Many of the same advances in data transfer and computer technology that are transforming the world of banking are similarly impacting the insurance industry. As the consolidation trends in the industry continue to favor the economies of scale achieved in larger insurance companies, technological innovations will be increasingly critical to sustaining growth and competitiveness.

Now that policies, underwriting, and premium payments have been automated, larger insurance companies are positioned to adopt new information platforms. *Jobs '96* spotlights the industry's need for technology experts, as many companies are shifting from the use of traditional mainframe systems to the use of LANs, CASE tools, and open, client/server environments. Openings for candidates with experience in these areas will dramatically increase in the next ten years, especially for those whose experience includes integrating old systems with newer technology platforms.

■ DO YOU NEED MORE CERTIFICATION OR EDUCATION?

Carl Boroff says the best advice he can give former bankers is "expect to learn." Especially in the insurance field, employment and advancement opportunities are linked to further education and certification. Bankers may bring sound financial experience and perhaps valuable specialized knowledge to insurance from their years in banking, but in many employment areas in insurance, they will be required to learn more. Fortunately, professional associations, institutes, and long-standing company training programs in the insurance industry enable career changers to enter the field with no specific insurance knowledge. Sales positions require state licensing, a step which will not be difficult for most former bankers, and usually entail on-the-job training as well. Other insurance careers necessitate continuing study, and certain positions, like those in the actuarial field, are dependent upon securing professional designations.

Professional associations, academic institutions, and colleges offer the various professional accreditations for advancement in the insurance field, including the Certified Life Underwriter (C.L.U.), Certified Property and Casualty Underwriter (C.P.C.U.), and Chartered Financial Planner (Ch.F.P.) designations. These are good sources for more information about the professional educational track required.

The *Business and Finance Career Directory* includes a partial list of opportunities for certification in the insurance field:

C.P.C.U. — CHARTERED PROPERTY AND CASUALTY UNDERWRITER
A.I.C. — ASSOCIATE IN CLAIMS
A.A.I. — ACCREDITED ADVISOR IN INSURANCE
C.L.U. — CHARTERED LIFE UNDERWRITER
F.L.M.I. — FELLOW OF THE LIFE MANAGEMENT INSTITUTE
C.F.P. — CERTIFIED FINANCIAL PLANNER
C.E.B.S. — CERTIFIED EMPLOYEE BENEFITS SPECIALIST

(The Insurance Institute of America also offers Associate certifications in Risk Management, Management, Underwriting, Loss Control Management, Premium Auditing, Research and Planning, Insurance Accounting and Finance, Marine Insurance Management and Automation Management).

More extended study is required for professional certification as an actuary than for other designations common in the field usually five to ten years to complete the examinations and become a fellow in the Society of Actuaries or the Casualty Actuarial Society. Prerequisites for successfully completing the actuary examinations include advanced mathematical aptitude, disciplined study habits, and a keen desire to use advanced mathematical and computer programming models in daily work. Business administration and computer systems knowledge also may be valuable in the discipline.

Both in jobs with insurance companies and with agencies, computer skills and a basic knowledge of data base technologies are increasingly indispensable as the insurance industry becomes more automated. According to the book *America's 50 Fastest Growing Jobs*, computer skills are becoming a necessity for advancement in insurance sales and management as well as in underwriting and actuarial positions.

■ LEARNING MORE AND BREAKING IN

By reviewing some of the publications listed below, along with similar materials found in the business reference section of your local library, you can quickly gain additional information about insurance careers. Many of the professional associations listed below also provide general information and some offer introductory courses of study. (A career handbook is available from the Insurance Information Institute, a property and casualty company membership organization.)

Jobs '96 reports that about 240,000 new jobs will be created over the next twelve years at insurance carriers, bringing the total number of jobs in the field to 1.7 million. The book cautions that automation in the industry may result in fewer jobs for claims processors than for others in the industry, however, while new positions for insurance agents and brokers are expected to rise sharply. The book recommends that those entering the insurance job market "keep abreast of industry developments; target companies that show strength in specific niches; [and] check A.M. Best's, Standard and Poor's, and Moody's ratings of insurance companies for insight."

Some entrees into insurance, especially in the sales and brokerage side of the business, are heavily dependent on personal contacts. If you have good personal skills and experience in lending or branch management, for example, and a job in commercial property and casualty insurance sales appeals to you, think of your former contact base in terms of a prospective employer's market. After finding out as much as possible about an available job and about the company you are targeting in your search, communicate the advantages you would bring to the job clearly and specifically to the prospective employer.

And when applying for management positions in insurance, job changers may benefit from Jeff Hamilton's advice: "There are a lot of changes in recruiting over the last five years. The process has become more focused on the person's accomplishments, what they have done to help save the company money or make money, rather than just, 'We want someone who has five years of this and five years of that.' Now insurance companies are getting past the old titles, duties, and money aspects and looking for a dollar-minded person, a person who knows how to effectively manage time and manage cash flow. Whether the background industry is banking or financial doesn't seem to be quite as important."

■ RESOURCES

State government departments of insurance

State independent insurance agents associations

Insurance Almanac (Underwriting Printing and Publishing Company) (annual)

Best's Agents Guide to Life Insurance Companies (A.M. Best Company) (annual)

Best's Insurance Reports, Property and Casualty (A.M. Best Company) (annual)

Business Insurance Reports, Life and Health (A.M. Best Company) (annual)

Best's Insurance (Crain Communications) (weekly)

Insurance Information Institute, 110 William St., New York, NY 10038; 212/669-9200

The College of Insurance, 101 Murray St., New York, NY 10007; 212/962-4111

Insurance Institute of America, 720 Providence Road, Malvern, PA 19355-0770; 215/644-2100

Professional Associations

National Association of Life Underwriters, 1922 F St., NW, Washington, DC 20006; 202/393-5240

American Council on Life Insurance, Ste. 500, 1001 Pennsylvania Avenue, NW, Washington, DC 20004-2599; 202/624-2000

American Institute for Property and Liability Underwriters, 720 Providence Road, Malvern, PA 19355-0770; 215/644-2100

Independent Insurance Agents of America, 127 S. Peyton St., Alexandria, VA 22314; 703/683-4422

American Council of Life Insurance, 1001 Pennsylvania Avenue, NW, Washington, DC 20004-2599; 202/624-2000

Risk and Insurance Management Society, Ste. 1504, 205 E. 42nd St., New York, NY 10017; 212/286-9364

Society of Actuaries, 475 N. Martingale Road, Ste. 800, Schaumburg, IL 60173-2226; 708/773-3010

Casualty Actuarial Society, 1100 N. Glebe Road, Ste. 600, Arlington, VA 22201; 703/276-3100

Society of Chartered Property and Casualty Underwriters, Kahler Hall, CB9, 720 Providence Road, Malvern, PA 19355; 215/251-2728

Health Insurance Association of America, 1025 Connecticut Avenue, NW, Ste. 1200, Washington, DC 20036-3998; 202/223-7780

Underwriters Management Association, 95 White Bridge Road, Ste. 216, Nashville, TN 37205; 615/356-7272

Life Office Management Association, 5770 Powers Ferry Road, Atlanta, GA 30327-4308; 404/951-1770

14

CREATING A JOB FOR YOURSELF

■ ■ ■

Entrepreneurship ■ *Franchise Operation*

> *Almost any sort of banking experience can be helpful to an entrepreneur — but an entrepreneur's personality traits are at least as important to success as his or her banking experience.*

Where the ability to follow directions and to perform one well-defined function may be esteemed in a corporate banking environment, in the world of self-employment, ingenuity shines and rebelliousness may pay off. Independence — that exciting and frightening condition many job searchers yearn to end by attaining the security of working for someone else — is a permanent state of mind for the self-employed.

The differences between banking and working for yourself are perhaps more pronounced than those between banking and any of the other careers discussed in this book. Other chapters examine occupations in which a former banker may be self-employed (jobs in the financial services industry, consulting, real estate, and insurance). This chapter is devoted to examining the challenge of fashioning your own career regardless of the service specialty or product you have to offer.

The number of self-employed people is growing fast. The job changer's handbook *Shifting Gears* reports that the number of entrepreneurs in America has grown tenfold since the 1970s. As staff reductions and restructuring change the way many firms do business, thousands of professionals are choosing to become their own bosses, electing to shape their own livelihoods in a time when corporate job security has become corporate job insecurity. The career guide book *Jobs '96* confirms that the number of out-of-work executives choosing to work for themselves is on the rise, climbing to 12 percent in 1992. And by the year 2005, the number of self-employed executives is expected to rise by 37 percent.

In addition to the former lending director profiled below, several other former bankers contacted in the course of research for this book have chosen to work for themselves. These former bankers include a marketing manager, a human resources vice president, and a real estate appraiser. "Inventiveness, gut instinct, the entrepreneurial spirit, and personal values are more than ever assets in a world that allows a greater range of individual choice than before," according to *Shifting Gears*. Some economic factors weigh in the favor of those who choose to be self-employed. Among them are the increasing market segment dominated by service industries, advances in home office technology, and the capabilities of modern computers and telecommunications. These factors explain in part why so many people are choosing self-employment. But launching and sustaining an entrepreneurial undertaking is impossible without the core ingredient: the right individual. The late nineties may be ripe for entrepreneurial endeavor; but at the end of the day, there is nothing but you standing between success and failure. Creating a job for yourself can be a lonely challenge.

Former banker Don Taylor was a senior vice president and director of lending at Mutual Savings and Loan in Bay City, Michigan, when he lost his job. He served briefly as executive vice president at the Bank of Lakeview before choosing to create a job for himself. Like many entrepreneurs, Taylor began looking for an existing business to buy. He and his wife elected to purchase a Wild Birds Unlimited franchise, and Taylor believes the decision has made the self-employment alternative easier for him.

Former Lender Applies Business and People Skills to Franchise

"I was in banking for over twenty-two years," Don Taylor says. "My experience was split about equally between commercial banks and savings and loans. The reason I went with Mutual Savings and Loan was that they were diversifying their interests, getting away from just the mortgage lending side and into commercial and consumer lending. Eventually I worked my way up to director of lending."

"I liked working with people. My dad was self-employed, so I grew up in an environment of entrepreneurship. I think that's one of the big reasons I decided to explore opening my own business. Although I went back to the commercial banking industry at Lakeview Bank, I could tell that it was just not a good fit. It led me to believe that there was something I could do for myself and be a lot happier. I said to myself, *If I buy my own business I'm controlling my own destiny, and if it's taken over it's going to be strictly up to my wife and me. We're in this together; there's the two of us, not a twelve-member board.*"

"I had been investigating business opportunities, and I was working with a business brokerage in Grand Rapids. All they deal in is businesses. I went there initially looking for a hardware store or a convenience store, something of that nature. Then I learned about a Wild Birds Unlimited business for sale that was established ten years ago, part of a ninety-seven store franchise. The franchise is also about ten years old, one of the top 100 franchises in the United States. It's not quite like starting your own business."

"Despite the name Wild Birds Unlimited, we do not sell birds. It is a backyard bird-feeding, nature type of store. We sell bird seed, bird houses, bird feeders, gift items and sweatshirts. The retail nature of the job recalls my background when I was growing up and in college — I worked my way through college in the retail business. As a banker, I was always working with individuals, small mom-and-pop operations. I always felt that if I found the right business and the right location I could make a go of a retail business."

"I had not considered a franchise when I started looking for a business. But once I saw this business, I immediately became interested in it. It's nicely merchandised, and it's related to a hardware store. There are a lot of things I can do; I repair feeders and so on. The business broker showed me the financial statements for the last four years. With my background it was easy for me to sit down and do some of the analytical work, look at the ratios, determine whether expenses were in line, and where there was room to cut. So that part of determining whether a business was a good investment was probably simpler for me than it would be for a lot of other people who want to buy or start a business."

"If I had not had the banking background, I could not have moved as quickly and probably would not have been able to get the business."

"Now that I've gotten started and I've worked with the franchise and other store owners, I realize there are a lot of pluses to a franchise. There is a support group out there of ninety-seven other stores; there is a franchise office I can call for help; and the franchise office does a good job of product analysis. You do pay a franchise fee, but I have to say that my first six months tell me that the franchise fee was well worth it. There are things we are trying to do in the franchise organization to establish identity, but I still feel very much like an independent. For example, if I want to sell everything this afternoon at 50 percent off, I can. There are some limitations and contractual restrictions to franchising, but I really don't feel hampered by that. I look forward to going to regional franchise meetings just like I used to look forward to going to the banking conventions and exchanging ideas with fellow bankers."

"My plan is to buy more stores. There are a lot of opportunities out there and this is a good industry right now, because people are getting back to nature and ecology. I look at self-employment as I once looked at banking when I was a youngster — what I want to put into it is what I can take out of it."

"The bottom line is that going into business for yourself is scary.

It's a big step. There's no weekly paycheck; there are no benefits any longer; you pay for your own health insurance. That's the down side. But the up side for me, and I know anyone who has been in top management will agree, is that the stress level is totally different. I don't know whether anyone is going to walk in tomorrow and buy a bag of bird seed, and if they don't, I don't have a paycheck. But there is still a lot I can do to control my own destiny. There is a peace of mind in knowing that I'm in control."

Former bankers who may have the right stuff for an entrepreneurial career come from all bank departments. Yet, like Don Taylor, they possess common characteristics that contribute to their success.

■ THE SKILLS BANKERS BRING TO ENTREPRENEURIAL VENTURES

Although the professional skills outlined below certainly assist former bankers who want to create jobs for themselves, the personal characteristics required for success as an entrepreneur are perhaps more important. Consequently, determining whether you have the necessary skills and personal bent is important when you are investigating the feasibility of going to work for yourself.

Finance and Other Analytical Abilities

Don Taylor was able to quickly ascertain whether the Wild Birds Unlimited franchise was a profitable venture because he was an experienced lender. Other former lenders, as well as accounting managers, asset managers, corporate staffers, and others, may have the same capability. Analytical ability is a skill in which many entrepreneurs are deficient, so most bankers will enter a new business with a built-in advantage.

Sales and Customer Service Know-how

Taylor feels comfortable facing new challenges as a franchise own-er because he is confident about the finance and people skills he de-veloped in his banking experience. "My background tells me how to cross-sell; it tells me how to go out and look for new business. We're setting up some marketing programs; we're calling on commercial customers."

Every entrepreneur needs sales acumen and relationship skills — for pitching the business, securing financing, and winning and keeping customers and employees. Trish Benninger, first vice president of hu-man resources at Great Western Bank in Northridge, California, iden-tifies strong skills crossover potential for bankers regardless of the en-trepreneurial venture they choose. "Going into business for yourself is a strong possibility, especially in a service industry," she says. "For example, a former marketing person may prefer to start a restaurant or a retail store rather than a marketing business. In any job change like that, all those customer service skills are still very, very important."

Marketing, from the Ground Up

Even if former bankers don't have any experience in marketing, as entrepreneurs they will quickly find that it is a skill all entrepreneurs must develop. Experienced bank marketers are in a good position to create jobs for themselves, and many are doing just that. "We closed up a marketing department in a bank that had six people in it," reports Benninger, "and now they're all self-employed."

Every entrepreneur must market to potential customers, advertise, and promote. Marketing comes into play when a concept is born and the entrepreneur defines how a business will address a need, and it never ceases. Publicity, seminars and speaking engagements, newslet-ters, direct mailings, and trade shows all present opportunities to sell a product or service.

A Manager's Mindset

One of the problems that may confound some entrepreneurs is the need to learn how to manage other people and effectively monitor business performance. Former bank branch and departmental managers are accustomed to such juggling and may find the planning and management inherent in an entrepreneurial venture relatively easy. Because applying effective management skills to business undertakings crosses career borders, former bankers can employ their talents equally well in such diverse businesses as commercial cleaning and wild bird seed sales.

Do You Have the Classic Entrepreneurial Characteristics?

The job-change handbook *Shifting Gears* cautions readers to do a great deal of self-examination before taking the self-employment plunge. It might be wise, the book advises, to evaluate whether you possess the entrepreneurial characteristics identified in a twenty-five-year study conducted by the Harvard Business School. The traits include a high level of personal motivation and drive; great self-confidence; willingness to commit to extensive involvement; viewing money as a measure of success; the ability to solve problems and be persistent; knowledge of how to utilize contacts and resources; tolerance of uncertainty and ambiguity; and the ability to receive either negative or positive feedback and put the experience to good use.

Small business owners encounter challenges daily that many former bankers would find familiar, but there are other issues that bankers would find unfamiliar. If you consider becoming an entrepreneur, you should evaluate your willingness to deal with these new factors on a daily basis. You must learn to accept risk, be willing to be accountable for your decisions, create your own support system and security, set up an efficient office environment, and cope with heavy demands on your time and financial resources. Not the least of these considerations is the impact self-employment can have on a family and lifestyle.

■ PROMISING ROUTES TO ENTREPRENEURIAL SUCCESS

Although circumstance and preparation sometimes land an entrepreneur in a successful venture, a former banker's resume and personal interests will be the biggest influences on the entrepreneurial direction he or she takes. Potential entrepreneurs should ask what they do well, for example whether they possess highly specialized experience that can help them establish a service niche. Many successful businesses are founded on hobbies or avocations.

In *Entrepreneur* magazine's latest annual "Business Opportunity 500" listing of nonfranchise businesses for sale, specific banking skills could apply to six of the top ten fields listed. These fields include: building; business services; computer-related products and services; education and training, financial services; and real estate. The price tags on these sorts of businesses ranged from a $49 laser cartridge recharging service (buyers get a manual and video) to an $80,000-$100,000 retail check cashing service. Credit repair services, investment services, financial education and consulting, and loan brokerage were among financial services business opportunities on the sales block.

From Banker to Baker to Book Writer

The ideal entrepreneur job merges a personal interest and business experience. An example of how a former banker may put ideas to work independently is suggested by Mark Bennett, the former bank marketing director profiled in chapter 10 who is now president of MemberServ in Madison, Wisconsin. MemberServ, a direct mail company that markets training, reference materials, and supplies to banks, is looking for authors with banking backgrounds. "We're always looking for individuals in the industry who are knowledgeable about banking and are interested in sitting down and putting their thoughts together into something that's marketable," Bennett says. Other publishers may be interested in the same expertise.

An entrepreneurial venture can be a manufacturing, retail sales, or service business. The point is to find a need and fill it. A diverse collection of business fields promises dramatic growth by the year 2005, according to *America's 50 Fastest Growing Jobs*. Businesses like child care providers, security services, computer consulting, and commercial janitorial services top the service fields for projected growth. Businesses such as convenience stores and businesses involving food and lodging top the list for entrepreneurial growth areas in the retail sector.

An article on the "ABC's of Business Opportunities" in the magazine *Entrepreneur* explains that business opportunities generally are offered in four ways — by license, distributorship, rack jobbing or wholesaling. These differ from franchises mainly in the manner in which the business is sold and the existence of a Uniform Franchise Offering Circular (UFOC), a seventy-five-to one-hundred-page legal document that details the franchise agreement. According to *Entrepreneur*, business opportunity agreements, now being regulated in many states, generally require much shorter sales contracts, lower legal costs, and less time to complete.

Franchising

Like Don Taylor, many people who turn to self-employment find franchising the safety net that makes going out on a limb a much safer prospect. The International Franchise Association (IFA) reports that the volume of sales in franchising was $800 billion in 1995. By the year 2000, the IFA predicts that more than 50 percent of all retail sales will be processed through a franchise outlet. In 1996, a new franchise business opened every 6.5 minutes.

One franchise category that has enjoyed especially vigorous growth in sales volume is that of business services, a sector of franchising which may offer a strong fit for those with banking skills. Although other high-growth areas in franchising may not use banking experience, the top three — restaurants, retailing, and hotels/motels — are areas in which former bankers may apply their organizational, financial, and marketing business experience. Many franchises are retail-oriented, but some franchises require training or presentation talents instead of retail sales skills.

The International Franchise Association claims that ninety-four percent of franchise business owners are successful. A typical business format franchise offers numerous benefits to a start-up business owner, including assistance with site selection, training, business set-up, existing market research, advertising and marketing, and product supply. (Unlike product and trade name franchises, the business format franchise provides the owner with a complete system of doing business.) A UFOC agreement may guarantee sales. For these services, the franchisee usually pays a franchise fee and continuing royalties. "Someone else has invented the wheel for you," the handbook *Shifting Gears* observes. "If you have the money, or the borrowing power, you can repeat their process."

A drawback to franchising: "When you enter into a franchise agreement, your success is dependent, to one degree or another, on the business skills, determination, financial health, even the ethics and honesty of the franchiser. There are many established, reputable companies offering solid franchise opportunities today, but there are probably even more untested franchise operations looking to establish themselves with your hard-earned funds," advises the book *Parting Company, How To Survive the Loss of a Job and Find Another Successfully*.

Intrapreneurship

A trend closely aligned to entrepreneurship has arisen in the climate of downsizing — "intrapreneurship." The term refers to creating a job for yourself within an organization, using many of the development and management skills needed for an entrepreneurial venture but with the support typically given a subsidiary. Innovation, fresh approaches, new products, or service niches all qualify as ins for intrapreneurs. Yet intrapreneurs must bring highly specialized knowledge and planning abilities to their endeavors, and they must possess the specific industry perspective to structure their intrapreneurial venture according to a company's goals.

Intrapreneurship could provide the opportunity for former bankers' inventiveness to blossom without the risk normally associated with setting up a new business. Salesmanship and communications savvy are necessary to persuade a business or corporation to support the idea. When that persuasion is effective, the track followed by most intrapreneurs is one that keeps them within an organization. If your priority is independence, intrapreneurship may not be the route for you.

Being an intrapreneur takes on an unusual form in the career of former banker Ken Davis, the chief lending officer turned traveling financial consultant to failing financial institutions who is discussed in chapter 11. Davis is on the payroll, temporarily at least, of each financial institution that employs him, so he is not technically self-employed; his task could be considered intrapreneurial. Although he is not offering a subsidiary product or service, he meets an integral demand within an organization.

Seizing a Service Industry Need

The Small Business Administration's Office of Advocacy predictions through the year 2005 give small businesses and service industries a glowing report, forecasting that three-fourths of future jobs in the nation's fastest-growing industries is likely to come from small firms. Based on U.S. Bureau of Labor Statistics data, the report also concludes that the fastest-growing industries in the future will be in two major sectors: health services and business services. This optimism is echoed by the National Federation of Independent Business, which reports that in 1996, small businesses employed almost 60 percent of the U.S. workforce. And small business remains the leading job creator, responsible for creating two-thirds of net new jobs in the last twenty-five years. Choosing an entrepreneurial activity that sells a service can be an easier route than starting a business that requires inventory and delivery. The need does not have to be related to banking, of course, but it can be — including marketing, personal financial services, computer programming or systems analysis, credit services, building inspection or appraisal, loan analysis, loan workout, or expertise in servicing mortgages.

■ THE STEPS: ANALYZE, PLAN WELL, AND PLAN TO PAY FOR IT

The career guidebooks recommend that start-up entrepreneurs first write it all down — regardless of whether acquiring financing will necessitate writing a formal business plan.

The authors of *Parting Company* provide a procedural outline for entrepreneurs to follow that, although ideal, includes steps former bankers should certainly consider in making decisions about self-employment. The steps begin with determining whether you possess the personal qualities that predict successful self-employment and end with the payoff: namely, self-assessment. If self-assessment confirms your prospects for successful self-employment, the authors enumerate several further stages in the process of pursuing self-employment. These are: you review your financial needs and resources; get professional assistance; choose a field and research it; define the market; check the competition; develop a marketing strategy; determine the form of ownership; make a plan; obtain funding; select/train people; develop a P&L statement; determine cash flow; determine the break-even point; and, finally, realize profits.

The analysis process, the authors add, should be "diligent, unbiased, and perhaps somewhat skeptical." They warn: "Unless you have the deep-seated need, relentless determination, and requisite personal and professional qualities to be an entrepreneur, going into business for yourself can turn into a financial and emotional nightmare."

Establishing a Business Plan

The book *250 Home-Based Jobs* calls the business plan a road map for the entrepreneur, a means of self-analysis and idea generation. The book suggests that you include these core sections in your business plan: an overall summary; an organizational description of the company; a market description, including the competition; a product or service description; a marketing strategy; a description of your operations method, including competitive strategies; future organizational goals and needs; and fiscal requirements.

Financing

The importance of adequate financing cannot be underestimated in a successful entrepreneurial venture. One rule of thumb recommended by the editors of the *Entrepreneur Magazine's Complete Guide to Owning A Home-Based Business* is that you set aside reserve capital that equals your expenses for one year. Banks, some of which offer special packages to entrepreneurs, are certainly not the only source of financing. *Small Business Opportunities* magazine suggests that you investigate all borrowing options, including foreign banks and venture capital, and remain persistent with contacts at several financial institutions.

Home-based or Not?

The increase in the number of self-employed people running businesses from their home, in many cases communicating electronically with clients from home-based PCs, is called a "modern day renaissance" by the handbook *Entrepreneur Magazine's Complete Guide to Owning A Home-Based Business*. The handbook estimates that fifteen to twenty-five million people work full-time from their homes, approximately 20 percent of the U.S. workforce.

However, not all home-based businesses operate by telecommunicating via computer or telephone; some involve entrepreneurs who produce a product. But the communications revolution has combined with the advent of the "service age," says the *Entrepreneur's* guide, to create "marvelous new inroads for the home-based entrepreneur." Services, the magazine proclaims, are the "perfect 'products' to sell from home."

Home-based businesses have a downside that is psychological and spatial, the editors add. You are alone. Your family may interrupt you. And the distractions are unlimited. "Working at home requires a great deal of independence and self — discipline, two characteristics that may not be critical when you are working in a corporate environment but that must be present when you are on your own."

Deciding on the Business Form

Sole proprietorships are the most common form of business for self-employed people. But for some, a general partnership, limited partnership, corporation, or other form of doing business may be a better method. You may need the advice of an attorney and an accountant to intelligently weigh the relative advantages of the various business structures available. Having a partner gives you a definite advantage over going it alone, and partnerships are reported to be four times more likely to succeed than solo businesses. Yet the solo self-employed startup company offers incomparable independence and control.

Business filing and permits will be required based on the business form and location chosen, and business owners must set up an adequate financial record-keeping system and establish procedures for filing local, state, and federal taxes.

Survival Tactics

Especially for self-employed people who work at home, concentration and persistence are absolutely necessary to survive a job change. For these people, the *Complete Guide to Owning a Home-Based Business* advises, "The best way to stay motivated and keep your business under control is to get organized and follow a daily routine." Continuous marketing to new clients or customers and a well-maintained network of business contacts are also necessary to success in self-employment. The tendency is to focus on the project at hand and fail to do enough marketing and networking.

■ HOW TO TAKE THE PLUNGE: FIRST, LEARN MORE

Prospective entrepreneurs exploring opportunities will find the available information to be seemingly unlimited. Finding out more about the business or industry in which you're interested may be as simple as talking with established businesspeople in the field, consulting trade publications and books, visiting business reference sections at public and university libraries, and asking government agencies or trade associations for available data.

The Small Business Administration can be a principal source of help in developing, planning, funding, and managing entrepreneurial activities. SBA publications include financial management and analysis handbooks, general management and planning information, and marketing manuals. Other sources of assistance through the SBA are the Service Corps of Retired Business Executives (SCORE); the SBA Surety Bond Guaranty Program; the Small Business Investment Company Program; and educational services through the Small Business Institutes on college campuses and at 600 Small Business Development Centers nationwide. Computer skills, credit and loan guarantees for small businesses, and other opportunities are accessible by contacting one of the regional SBA offices or the administrative office of the SBA in Washington.

The International Franchise Association (IFA) tracks the performance of franchiser companies that are its members and disseminates information about franchising and selecting a franchise. The IFA's Web site on the World Wide Web includes information about member companies and a wide variety of articles and position papers. The IFA sells many publications including the biannual "Franchise Opportunities Guide" that lists 2,600 franchises in sixty business categories. Other organizations such as the Entrepreneurship Institute provide information to assist in entrepreneurial development.

Entrepreneur magazine and other publications publish informative tips, and *Entrepreneur* is also publisher of a selection of software programs, videos, and how-to guides for starting dozens of businesses. Assistance for American entrepreneurs who want to market products or services internationally is available from the World Trade Centers Association, at sixty centers in the United States. Member entrepreneurs receive on-line advertising space and other benefits.

Entrepreneur recommends that individuals setting out to become business owners by purchasing a business opportunity or a franchise investigate the business thoroughly. When researching a business opportunity, look for experience, financial statements, other dealers' references, and contacts. The reputation of the business can be investigated by contacting your state attorney general's office or department of consumer affairs. The magazine also suggests a review of the disclosure agreement and consultation with an attorney and accountant.

Creating a business for yourself may be a long-term career goal that first involves time to develop a concept, to learn new skills on your own or on the job, and to secure financing. Just as you must collect information to explore buying into a business opportunity or franchise, pursuing any form of self-employment will probably involve research. Such a process of discovery has seeded many ingenious new businesses.

"Applying information is the real basis of adaptation in this world," according to *Shifting Gears*. Indeed, the knowledge former bankers can glean from exploring self-employment options may open up their career choices.

■ RESOURCES

The Small Business Administration office in your region (Call the Washington, D.C. office of the SBA at 202/653-7562 for the location of the office in your region.)

The Small Business Administration's *Starting and Managing A Business From Your Home*, P.O. Box 15434, Fort Worth, TX 76119 (ask for their Small Business Directory publication list)

Entrepreneur magazine (*Inc., Success, New Business Opportunities*, and *Franchise World* are other publications that may also be helpful)

Running A One-Person Business (Ten Speed Press)

Entrepreneur Magazine's Complete Guide to Owning A Home-Based Business (Bantam)

Franchise Opportunities Handbook (U.S. Government Printing Office), 202/783-3238

Franchise Buyer's Handbook by Tim Reddon (Scott Foresman and Company)

"Franchise Opportunities Guide," International Franchise Association Publications, P.O. Box 1060, Evans City, PA 16033

Entrepreneur magazine's business guides catalog, 2392 Morse Avenue, P.O. Box 19787, Irvine, CA 92713-9787

Professional Associations

International Franchise Association, 1350 New York Avenue, NW, Ste. 900, Washington, DC 20005-4709; 202/628-8000

American Home Business Association, 397 Post Road, Darien, CT 06820; 203/655-4380

World Trade Centers Association, 1 World Trade Center, Ste. 7701, New York, NY 10048; 212/432-2626

National Association for the Cottage Industry, P.O. Box 14850, Chicago, IL 60614; 312/472-8116

National Association of Home-Based Businesses, 10451 Mill Run Circle, Ste. 400, Owings Mill, MD 21117; 301/363-3698

National Association of Home Business Owners, P.O. Box 423, East Meadow, NY 11554; 516/997-7394

SECTION IV

■■■

Appendix

GEOGRAPHIC DIRECTORY OF THE TOP 500 U.S. BANKS

The following list includes the names, addresses, and phone numbers of the top 500 United States banks. Names and titles of human resources department personnel are given for most banks listed. Every effort has been made to ensure that the information given below is correct; however, you should bear in mind that nothing is more common in today's banking industry than change, and some listings will become outdated. Calling to verify names and addresses before writing or sending resumes could eliminate wasted effort and misdirected inquiries.

Banks are listed geographically and alphabetically by state and city.

Alabama

Birmingham

AmSouth Bank of Alabama
1900 Fifth Ave. N.
Birmingham, AL 35203
205/326-0293

Human Resources Information:
Kathy K. Heard
Senior Vice President/Human Resources Manager
AmSouth Bank of Alabama
P.O. Box 11007
Birmingham, AL 35288
205/801-0582
205/581-7755 (fax)

Compass Bank
15 S. Twentieth St.
Birmingham, AL 35233-2035
205/933-3000

Human Resources Information:
John Faure
Vice President of Staff Recruiting
Compass Bank
15 S. Twentieth St., Twelfth Fl.
Birmingham, AL 35233

SouthTrust Bank of Alabama, N.A.
420 Twentieth St. N.
Birmingham, AL 35290
205/254-5000

Human Resources Information:
Charles D. Whitfield, Jr.
Senior Vice President/Human Resources
SouthTrust Corporation
P.O. Box 2554
Birmingham, AL 35290

Montgomery

Colonial Bank
1 Commerce St.
Montgomery, AL 36101
334/240-5000

Human Resources Information:
Employment Recruiters
Kim Traff and Cynthia Thomas
Colonial Bank
P.O. Box 1108
Montgomery, AL 36101
334/240-5188 (fax)

Regions Financial Corporation (Regions Bank and Affiliates)
P.O. Box 511
Montgomery, AL 36101
334/832-8011

Human Resources Information:
Wanda Lambert, Employment/Employee Relations Manager
Nikki Copeland, Regional Personnel Officer

Beth Rhegness, Regional Personnel Officer
Regions Financial Corporation
P.O. Box 5070
Montgomery, AL 36103-5070
334/832-8314
334/240-2840 (fax)
personnel@regionsbank.com
http://www.regionsbank.com

Alaska

Anchorage

First National Bank of Anchorage
646 W. Fourth Ave.
Anchorage, AK 99501
907/276-6300

Human Resources Information:
Cassandra Anderson
Senior Personnel Officer/Central Support Division
First National Bank of Anchorage
425 G St., Ste. 840
Anchorage, AK 99501

Key Bank of Alaska
101 W. Benson Ave.
Anchorage, AK 99503
907/562-6100

Human Resources Information:
Susan Girvan
Assistant Vice President/Human Resources Manager
Key Bank of Alaska
P.O. Box 100420
Anchorage, AK 99510-0420

National Bank of Alaska
301 W. Northern Lights Blvd.
Anchorage, AK 99503
907/276-1132

Human Resources Information:
Kathy Richter
Vice President and Manager/Human
Resources
National Bank of Alaska
P.O. Box 196127
Anchorage, AK 99519-6127

Arizona

Phoenix

Bank of America Arizona
101 N. First Ave.
Phoenix, AZ 85003
602/597-5000

Human Resources Information:
Ron Clark
Managing, Staffing/Recruiting Ser-
vices Vice President
Bank of America Arizona
2600 N. Central Ave., Ste. 800
Phoenix, AZ 85004
602/248-2505

Bank One, Arizona, N.A.
241 N. Central Ave.
Phoenix, AZ 85004
602/221-2900

Human Resources Information:
Attn: Hiring Center
Bank One, Arizona, N.A.
201 N. Central Ave.
Phoenix, AZ 85001

Norwest Bank Arizona, N.A.
3300 N. Central Ave.
Phoenix, AZ 85012
602/248-2223

Human Resources Information:
Phyllis Winters
Director of Human Resources
Norwest Bank Arizona, N.A.
3300 N. Central Ave.
Phoenix, AZ 85012
Attn: 9014
602/248-3612

Wells Fargo Bank (Arizona), N.A.
4832 E. McDowell Rd.
Phoenix, AZ 85008
602/302-7701

Human Resources Information:
Renee Belisle
Human Resources Consultant
Wells Fargo Bank (Arizona), N.A.
4832 E. McDowell Rd.
Phoenix, AZ 85008

Wells Fargo Bank of Arizona
100 W. Washington St.
Phoenix, AZ 85003
602/229-4690

Human Resources Information:
Linda Rogers
Vice President and Employment
Manager
Wells Fargo Bank of Arizona
Employment Department, Plaza
Bldg.
100 W. Washington, Lower Level
Phoenix, AZ 85003
M/S: 4101-007
602/528-1185

Tempe

Bank of America, N.A.
2727 S. 48th St.
Tempe, AZ 85282-7620
602/594-6305

Human Resources Information:
Debbie Desmond
Senior Vice President and Manager
Bank of America, N.A.
2600 N. Central Ave., Ste. 800
Phoenix, AZ 85004
602/248-2535

Tucson

National Bank of Arizona
335 N. Wilmot Rd.
Tucson, AZ 85711-2632
520/571-1500

Human Resources Information:
Susan Andrews
Senior Vice President of Human Resources
National Bank of Arizona
3101 N. Central
Phoenix, AZ 85012
602/235-6000

Arkansas

Little Rock

First Commercial Bank, N.A.
400 W. Capital Ave.
Little Rock, AR 72201
501/371-7000

Human Resources Information:
Sandra Stroment, Director/Human Resources
Angela Herron, Employment Coordinator
First Commercial Bank, N.A.
P.O. Box 1471
Little Rock, AR 72203

NationsBank (formerly Boatmen's First National Bank of Arkansas)
200 W. Capitol Ave.
Little Rock, AR 72201-3605
501/378-1000

Human Resources Information:
Paula Laird
Employment Recruiter/Human Resources
NationsBank
200 W. Capital Ave., Eleventh Fl.
Little Rock, AR 72201
501/378-1570

North Little Rock

Mercantile Bank
1 Riverfront Pl.
North Little Rock, AR 72114-5640
501/688-1000

Human Resources Information:
Wayne Dierks
Senior Vice President/Human Resources
Mercantile Bank
P.O. Box 15008
Little Rock, AR 72231-5008

California

Anaheim

Fremont Investment and Loan
175 N. Riverview Drive
Anaheim, CA 92808
714/283-6500

Human Resources Information:
Laura Strange
Vice President/Personnel
Fremont Investment and Loan
175 N. Riverview Drive
Anaheim, CA 92808

Beverly Hills

City National Bank
400 N. Roxbury Drive
Beverly Hills, CA 90210
310/550-5400

Human Resources Information:
Kate Dwyer
Senior Vice President/Human Resources Manager
City National Bank
633 W. Fifth St., Tenth Fl.
Los Angeles, CA 90071
213/553-8272

Fairfield

WestAmerica Bank (formerly ValliWide Bank)
4550 Mangels Blvd.
Fairfield, CA 94585
707/863-6000

Human Resources Information:
Sharon Green, Recruiter
WestAmerica Bank
4550 Mangels Blvd.
Fairfield, CA 94585
707/863-6887 (fax)

Inglewood

Imperial Bank
9920 S. La Cienega Blvd.
Inglewood, CA 90301
310/417-5600

Human Resources Information:
J. Richard Barkley
Senior Vice President/Human Resources
Imperial Bank
9920 S. La Cienega Blvd., Ste. 604
Inglewood, CA 90301

Irwindale

Home Savings of America, FSB
4900 Rivergrade Rd.
Irwindale, CA 91706
818/960-6311

Human Resources Information:
Merrill S. Wall
First Vice President and Director/Human Resources
Home Savings of America, FSB
4900 Rivergrade Rd., Bldg. 515
Irwindale, CA 91706

Long Beach

Comerica Bank, California (formerly Comerica Bank)
333 W. Santa Clara St.
San Jose, CA 95113
408/556-5000

Human Resources Information:
Shirley Cameron
Vice President/Human Resources
Comerica Bank, California
301 E. Ocean Blvd., Ste. 1800
Long Beach, CA 90802
562/590-2525

Farmers and Merchants Bank of Long Beach
302 Pine Ave.
Long Beach, CA 90802
562/437-0011

Human Resources Information:
Sheri Mallon
Vice President/Human Resources
Farmers and Merchants Bank of
Long Beach
302 Pine Ave.
Long Beach, CA 90802

Los Angeles

First Business Bank
601 W. Fifth St.
Los Angeles, CA 90071-2004
213/489-1000

Human Resources Information:
Wes Schaefer
Senior Vice President/Human Resources
First Business Bank
601 W. Fifth St., Ninth Fl.
Los Angeles, CA 90071

California Commerce Bank
2029 Century Park E., 42nd Fl.
Los Angeles, CA 90067
800/222-1234

Human Resources Information:
Dennis Campos
Senior Vice President/Human Resources Director
California Commerce Bank
P.O. Box 30886
Los Angeles, CA 90030

Cathay Bank
777 N. Broadway
Los Angeles, CA 90012
213/625-4700

Human Resources Information:
Marina Wong
Assistant Vice President/Personnel Manager
Cathay Bank
777 N. Broadway
Los Angeles, CA 90012
213/625-4754

General Bank
800 W. Sixth St.
Los Angeles, CA 90017
213/972-4230

Human Resources Information:
Sheree Shih
Vice President/Human Resources
General Bank
4128 Tempo City Blvd.
Rosemead, CA 91770
818/582-7222

Manufacturers Bank
515 S. Figueroa St.
Los Angeles, CA 90071
213/489-6200

Human Resources Information:
Michael Moore
Vice President and Manager/Human
Resources
Manufacturers Bank
515 S. Figueroa St., Second Fl.
Los Angeles, CA 90071

Tokai Bank of California
534 W. Sixth St.
Los Angeles, CA 90014
213/972-0200

Human Resources Information:
John Samp
First Vice President/Human Re-
sources
Tokai Bank of California
300 S. Grand Ave., Fifth Fl.
Los Angeles, CA 90071

Richmond

Mechanics Bank
3170 Hilltop Mall Rd.
Richmond, CA 94806-1921
510/262-7200

Human Resources Information:
Stanley R. Adkins, Jr.
Vice President/Human Resources
Mechanics Bank
3170 Hilltop Mall Rd.
Richmond, CA 94806-1921

Sacramento

U.S. Bank of California
980 Ninth St., Ste. 1200
Sacramento, CA 95814
916/552-1800

Human Resources Information:
Sandy Gomes
Vice President/Human Resources Di-
rector
U.S. Bank of California
980 Ninth St., Ste. 1200
Sacramento, CA 95814

San Francisco

**Bank of America National Trust
and Savings Association**
555 California St.
San Francisco, CA 94104
415/622-3456

Human Resources Information:
Northern California Human Re-
sources Center
Bank of America National Trust and
Savings Association
1 S. Van Ness Ave., Fourth Fl.
San Francisco, CA 94103

Bank of the West
180 Montgomery St.
San Francisco, CA 94104
415/765-4800

Human Resources Information:
Lynn Magi Young
Employment Manager
Bank of the West
1450 Treat Blvd., First Fl.
Walnut Creek, CA 94596

BankAmerica International
555 California St.
San Francisco, CA 94104-1502
415/622-3456

Human Resources Information:
Rick Johnson
Senior Vice President/Human Resources
BankAmerica International
P.O. Box 37000
San Francisco, CA 94137

First Republic Thrift and Loan
388 Market St.
San Francisco, CA 94111
415/392-1400

Human Resources Information:
Scott Struever
Manager of Human Resources/Office Services
First Republic Thrift and Loan
388 Market St., Second Fl.
San Francisco, CA 94111
415/392-1413 (fax)

Sanwa Bank California
444 Market St.
San Francisco, CA 94111
415/597-5300

Human Resources Information:
Debra Lehr
Vice President/Human Resources
Manager
Sanwa Bank California
444 Market St., Eighteenth Fl.
San Francisco, CA 94111
415/597-5008

Sumitomo Bank of California
320 California St.
San Francisco, CA 94104
415/445-8000

Human Resources Information:
Bee Chin
Assistant Vice President/Human Resources
Sumitomo Bank of California
320 California St., Third Fl.
San Francisco, CA 94104
http://www.sumitomobankcal.com

Union Bank of California
400 California St.
San Francisco, CA 94104
415/445-0200

Human Resources Information:
Jan Gall
Corporate Staffing
Union Bank of California
350 California St., Ninth Fl.
San Francisco, CA 94104
Fax resumes to: 415/273-2483

Wells Fargo Bank, N.A.
420 Montgomery St., Eleventh Fl.
San Francisco, CA 94104
415/477-1000

Human Resources Information:
Attn: Recruitment Department
Wells Fargo Bank, N.A.
420 Montgomery St., Eleventh Fl.
San Francisco, CA 94163
415/396-5196

San Jose

Comerica Bank California
55 Almaden Blvd.
San Jose, CA 95113
408/294-8940
408/271-4074 (fax)

Human Resources Information:
Attn: Employment Department
Comerica Bank California
55 Almaden Blvd.
San Jose, CA 95113
408/271-4049 (fax)

San Marino

East-West Bank
415 Huntington Drive
San Marino, CA 91108
213/489-5300

Human Resources Information:
Silvia Ross
First Vice President/Human Resources Director
East-West Bank
P.O. Box 80190

San Marino, CA 91118
818/799-5700

San Rafael

WestAmerica Bank
1108 Fifth Ave.
San Rafael, CA 94901
415/257-8000

Human Resources Information:
Attn: Human Resources Department
WestAmerica Bank
P.O. Box 1200
Suisun, CA 94585-1200

Santa Barbara

Santa Barbara Bank and Trust
1021 Anacapa St.
Santa Barbara, CA 93101
805/564-6300

Human Resources Information:
Catherine Steinke
Senior Vice President/Human Resources
Santa Barbara Bank and Trust
P.O. Box 1119
Santa Barbara, CA 93102-1119

Santa Clara

Silicon Valley Bank
3003 Tasman Drive
Santa Clara, CA 95054
408/654-7400

Human Resources Information:
Attn: Human Resources Department

Silicon Valley Bank
3003 Tasman Drive, Second Fl.
Santa Clara, CA 95054

Colorado

Denver

Bank One, Colorado, N.A.
1125 Seventeenth St.
Denver, CO 80202
303/292-4000

Human Resources Information:
Bert Torres
Employee Relations
Bank One, Colorado, N.A.
7301 N. Federal Blvd., Second Fl.
Westminster, CO 80030
303/430-5721 (fax)

Colorado National Bank
918 Seventeenth St.
Denver, CO 80202
303/585-5000

Human Resources Information:
Becky Cordes
Vice President/Human Resources
Colorado National Bank
950 Seventeenth St., Ste. 800
Denver, CO 80202
Attn: CNDT0811
303/585-5050

First Trust Corporation
717 Seventeenth St.
Denver, CO 80202-3323
303/293-2223

Human Resources Information:
Jackie K. Freudenstein
Senior Vice President/Human Resources Operations
First Trust Corporation
717 Seventeenth St., Ste. 2600
Denver, CO 80202
Jobline: 303/294-5877

Norwest Bank Colorado, N.A.
Sixth and Marquette
Minneapolis, MN 55479-1023
303/861-8811

Human Resources Information:
Joan Van Landingham
Senior Vice President/Human Resources
Norwest Bank Colorado, N.A.
1740 Broadway
Denver, CO 80274-8690

Wells Fargo Bank (Colorado)
633 Seventeenth St.
Denver, CO 80270
800/869-3557

Human Resources Information:
Kevin Sullivan
Executive Vice President/Human Resources
Wells Fargo Bank (Colorado)
420 Montgomery St.
San Francisco, CA 94104
415/396-3053

Ft. Collins

Key Bank of Colorado
300 W. Oak St.

Ft. Collins, CO 80521-2737
800/539-2968

Human Resources Information:
Helen Litle
Human Resources Site Manager
Key Bank of Colorado
3300 E. First. Ave.
Denver, CO 80206
303/329-2271

Connecticut

Bridgeport

People's Bank
850 Main St.
Bridgeport, CT 06604-4913
203/338-7171

Human Resources Information:
Barbara Phillips
First Vice President/Human Resources
People's Bank
Bridgeport Center
850 Main St., Tenth Fl.
Bridgeport, CT 06604-4913
Attn: Barbara Phillips
203/338-2231

Derby

Webster Bank (formerly Derby Savings Bank)
1 Elizabeth St.
Derby, CT 06418
203/755-1422

Human Resources Information:
Renee Seefried
Executive Vice President/Human Resources
Webster Bank
145 Bank St.
Waterbury, CT 06702

Hartford

BankBoston (formerly BankBoston Connecticut)
31 Pratt St.
Hartford, CT 06103
860/727-5000

Human Resources Information:
Denise Brian
Human Resources Director
BankBoston
100 Pearl St.
Hartford, CT 06103

Fleet Bank
777 Main St.
Hartford, CT 06115
860/986-2000

Human Resources Information:
Kathy Kelly
Staffing Manager
Fleet Bank
777 Main St.
Hartford, CT 06115
Attn: CTMO210-6

Manchester

Savings Bank of Manchester

923 Main St.
Manchester, CT 06040
860/646-1700

Human Resources Information:
Julia Lampson
Recruiter/Human Resources
Savings Bank of Manchester
923 Main St.
P.O. Box 231
Manchester, CT 06045-0231

Middletown

Liberty Bank
315 Main St.
Middletown, CT 06457
860/344-7200

Human Resources Information:
Steven Barlow
Senior Vice President/Human Resources
Liberty Bank
315 Main St.
Middletown, CT 06457

New Britain

American Savings Bank
178 Main St.
New Britain, CT 06051
860/225-6431

Human Resources Information:
Richard Furniss
Vice President/Human Resources
American Savings Bank
178 Main St.
New Britain, CT 06051

New Haven

New Haven Savings Bank
195 Church St.
New Haven, CT 06510
203/787-1111

Human Resources Information:
Attn: Human Resources
New Haven Savings Bank
195 Church St.
New Haven, CT 06510

Stamford

First Union National Bank of Connecticut
300 Main St.
Stamford, CT 06904
203/348-6211

Human Resources Information:
William Karmen
Executive Vice President/Human Resources
First Union National Bank
190 River Rd.
Summit, NJ 07901
203/578-8460

Waterbury

First Union National Bank
60 N. Main St.
Waterbury, CT 06702
800/634-3705

Human Resources Information:
Kari Jonikas and Cheryl Samaha

Human Resources Generalists
First Union National Bank
1 Jefferson Square
Waterbury, CT 06702
203/578-8460

Webster Bank
145 Bank St., Webster Plaza
Waterbury, CT 06702
203/755-1422

Human Resources Information:
Renee Seefried
Executive Vice President/Human Resources
Webster Bank
145 Bank St.
Waterbury, CT 06702

Delaware

Claymont

Advanta National Bank
Advanta National Bank USA
650 Naamans Rd.
Claymont, DE 19703
302/791-6262

Human Resources Information:
Renee Booth
Senior Vice President/Human Resources
Advanta National Bank
P.O. Box 844
Spring House, PA 19477-0844

Dover

NationsBank of Delaware, N.A.
655 S. Bay Rd., Rte 113
Dover, DE 19901

Human Resources Information:
Clair McElwee
Personnel Director
NationsBank of Delaware, N.A.
P.O. Box 7028
Dover, DE 19903
800/587-5627 (jobline)

New Castle

Citibank Delaware
1 Penn's Way
New Castle, DE 19720
800/341-4727

Human Resources Information:
Mary Johnson-Park
Staffing and Placement/Human Resources
Citibank Delaware
1 Penn's Way
New Castle, DE 19720
302/323-5180
302/323-5976 (fax)

Greenwood Trust Company
12 Reads Way
New Castle, DE 19720-1601
302/323-7110

Human Resources Information:
Karen Reed
Employment Specialist/Human Resources
Greenwood Trust Company

12 Reads Way
New Castle, DE 19720
302/323-7191

Newark

Bank of New York (Delaware)
400 White Clay Center.
Newark, DE 19711
302/451-2500

Human Resources Information:
William Lewis
Senior Vice President and
Director/Human Resources
Bank of New York (Delaware)
400 White Clay Center
Ogletown Rd.
Newark, DE 19711

MBNA America Bank, N.A.
400 Christiana Rd.
Newark, DE 98101
302/453-9930

Human Resources Information:
Attn: Personnel
MBNA America Bank, N.A.
1100 N. King St.
Wilmington, DE 19884

Wilmington

Banc One (formerly First USA Bank)
3 Christina Center
201 N. Walnut
Wilmington, DE 19801
302/594-4000

Human Resources Information:
Daniel C. Barr
Executive Vice President/Human Resources
Banc One
3 Christina Center
201 N. Walnut
Wilmington, DE 19801

Bankers Trust (Delaware)
1001 Jefferson St.
Wilmington, DE 19801

Human Resources Information:
Lorraine DeMeurisse
Vice President/Human Resources
Bankers Trust (Delaware)
1011 Centre Rd., Ste. 200
Wilmington, DE 19805

Beneficial National Bank USA
1 Christina Center
301 N. Walnut St.
Wilmington, DE 19801
302/425-3500

Human Resources Information:
Attn: Human Resources Department
Beneficial National Bank USA
301 N. Walnut St., Lobby Level
Wilmington, DE 19801

Chase Bank
802 Delaware Ave.
Wilmington, DE 19801-1398
302/575-5000

Human Resources Information:

Bonnie Tsaldaris
Recruiter/Human Resources
Chase Bank
802 Delaware Ave.
Wilmington, DE 19801

FCC National Bank
1 Gateway Center
300 King St.
Wilmington, DE 19801
302/594-8606

Human Resources Information:
Carol Fife
Employment Representative/Human
Resources
FCC National Bank
P.O. Box 15075
Wilmington, DE 19850-5075
302/594-8600

First Union (formerly CoreStates Bank of Delaware)
3 Beaver Valley Rd.
Wilmington, DE 19803
302/477-7000

Human Resources Information:
Attn: Human Resources Department
First Union
3 Beaver Valley Rd.
Wilmington, DE 19803
800/833-3012

Fleet Bank
824 N. Market St.
Wilmington, DE 19801
302/784-5000

Human Resources Information:

Nancy Brill
Human Resources Generalist
Fleet Bank
824 N. Market St., Ste. 300
Wilmington, DE 19801

J. P. Morgan Delaware
902 Market St.
Wilmington, DE 19801-3015
302/651-2323

Human Resources Information:
Attn: Human Resources
J. P. Morgan Services, Inc.
500 Stanton Christiana Rd.
Newark, DE 19713-2107

Mellon Bank (DE), N.A.
Tenth and Market Streets.
Wilmington, DE 19801
302/995-5700

Human Resources Information:
Cindy Barone
Human Resources Manager
Mellon Bank (DE), N.A.
4500 New Linden Hill Rd.
Wilmington, DE 19808
302/992-7709

PNC Bank, Delaware
300 Delaware Ave.
Wilmington, DE 19801
302/429-1011

Human Resources Information:
Peggy Glaser
Vice President/Human Resources
PNC Bank, Delaware
100 S. Broad Street

Philadelphia, PA 19101
302/429-1118

PNC National Bank
Bellevue Corporation Center
103 Bellevue Pkwy.
Wilmington, DE 19809
302/791-1200

Human Resources Information:
Rachel Emrich
Senior Human Resources Officer
PNC National Bank
Bellevue Corporation Center
103 Bellevue Pkwy.
Wilmington, DE 19809
302/429-1118

Wilmington Savings Fund Society, FSB
838 Market St.
Wilmington, DE 19801-4903
302/571-7090

Human Resources Information:
Vicki Myoda
Vice President/Human Resources
Wilmington Savings Fund Society, FSB
838 Market St., First Fl.
Wilmington, DE 19899

Wilmington Trust Company
Rodney Square N.
1100 N. Market St.
Wilmington, DE 19890
302/651-1000

Human Resources Information:

Nancy H. James
Divisional Manager/Human Resources
Wilmington Trust Company
Rodney Square N.
1100 N. Market St.
Wilmington, DE 19890-0001
302/651-1463

District of Columbia

Washington

Crestar Bank, N.A.
1445 New York Ave. NW
Washington, DC 20005
202/879-6000

Human Resources Information:
James Kelley
Senior Vice President/Human Resources
Crestar Bank, N.A.
P.O. Box 26665
Richmond, VA 23261
804/270-8880
804/270-8828 (fax)

First Union National Bank of Washington, DC
1425 K St. NW
Washington, DC 20006
202/624-0417

Human Resources Information:
David H. Furman
Vice President/Human Resources Manager
First Union National Bank of Vir-

ginia
1970 Chain Bridge Rd., Fourth Fl.
McLean, VA 22102
703/760-6737

Riggs Bank
1503 Pennsylvania Ave. NW
Washington, DC 20005
301/887-6000

Human Resources Information:
Patti Yoder
Human Resources Manager
Riggs Bank
800 Seventeenth St. NW
Washington, DC 20006

Florida

Brooksville

SunTrust Bank
1 E. Jefferson
Brooksville, FL 34601-2622
352/796-5151

Human Resources Information:
Linda Chatman
Human Resources Director
SunTrust Bank
P.O. Box 156
Brooksville, FL 34605

Daytona Beach

SunTrust Bank, East Central Florida
120 S. Ridgewood Ave.
Daytona Beach, FL 32114-4322
800/786-8787

Human Resources Information:
Attn: Human Resources
SunTrust Bank, East Central Florida
P.O. Box 2120
Daytona Beach, FL 32115

Ft. Lauderdale

NationsBank (formerly Barnett Bank of Broward County, N.A.)
1 E. Broward Blvd.
Ft. Lauderdale, FL 33301
954/327-5600

Human Resources Information:
Attn: Human Resources
NationsBank
1 E. Broward Blvd., Third Fl.
Ft. Lauderdale, FL 33301

SunTrust Bank/South Florida, N.A.
501 E. Las Olas Blvd.
Ft. Lauderdale, FL 33301
954/765-7500

Human Resources Information:
Attn: Human Resources
SunTrust Bank/South Florida, N.A.
SunTrust Center
501 E. Las Olas Blvd., Fifth Fl.
Ft. Lauderdale, FL 33301

Ft. Myers

SunTrust Bank/Southwest Florida
12730 New Brittany Blvd.
Ft. Myers, FL 33907-3646
941/275-3200

Human Resources Information:
Attn: Human Resources
SunTrust Bank/Southwest Florida
P.O. Box 3454
Ft. Myers, FL 33918-3454

Jacksonville

First Union National Bank of Florida
225 Water St.
Jacksonville, FL 32202
904/489-4000

Human Resources Information:
Shannon McFayden
Senior Vice President/Human Resources
First Union National Bank of Florida
225 Water St.
Jacksonville, FL 32202

NationsBank (formerly Barnett Bank of Jacksonville, N.A.)
50 N. Laura St.
Jacksonville, FL 32202-3609
904/791-7500

Human Resources Information:
Staffing Services, Building 400-1
NationsBank
9000 Southside Blvd.
Jacksonville, FL 32256

SunTrust Bank, North Florida
200 W. Forsyth St.
Jacksonville, FL 32202-5157
904/632-2500

Human Resources Information:

Attn: Human Resources
SunTrust Bank, North Florida
200 W. Forsyth St.
Jacksonville, FL 32202

Maitland

Huntington National Bank of Florida
253 N. Orlando Ave.
Maitland, FL 32751-5510
407/740-6300

Human Resources Information:
Lisa Seabolt
Human Resources Generalist
Huntington National Bank of Florida
253 N. Orlando Ave.
Maitland, FL 32751

Miami

Banco Santander International
1401 Brickell Ave., Ste. 1200
Miami, FL 33131-3009
305/539-5900

Human Resources Information:
Seida Domenech
Human Resources Manager
Banco Santander International
1401 Brickell Ave.
Miami, FL 33131

Capital Bank
1221 Brickell Ave.
Miami, FL 33131-3200
305/536-1500

Human Resources Information:
Andrea Batson

Employment Coordinator/Human
Resources
Capital Bank
8900 SW 107th Ave.
Miami, FL 33176
305/270-3930

City National Bank of Florida
25 W. Flagler St.
Miami, FL 33130
305/577-7333

Human Resources Information:
Attn: Human Resources
City National Bank of Florida
25 W. Flagler St., Ste. 400
Miami, FL 33130
305/577-7680

**NationsBank (formerly Barnett
Bank of South Florida, N.A.)**
701 Brickell Ave.
Miami, FL 33131-2822
305/350-7100

Human Resources Information:
Attn: Human Resources Department
NationsBank
701 Brickell Ave., Fifth Fl.
Miami, FL 33131
305/350-7063

**Northern Trust Bank of Florida,
N.A.**
700 Brickell Ave.
Miami, FL 33131-2804
305/372-1000

Human Resources Information:

Attn: Human Resources
Northern Trust Bank of Florida,
N.A.
700 Brickell Ave.
Miami, FL 33131

Ocean Bank
780 NW 42nd Ave.
Miami, FL 33126-5536
305/442-2660

Human Resources Information:
Betty Santos
Human Resource Specialist
Ocean Bank
780 NW, 42nd Ave.
Miami, FL 33126

SunTrust/Miami, N.A.
777 Brickell Ave.
Miami, FL 33131-2806
305/592-0800

Human Resources Information:
Roberta Kressel
Senior Vice President/Human Re-
sources
SunTrust/Miami, N.A.
777 Brickell Ave., First Fl.
Miami, FL 33131-2806

Miami Lakes

**NationsBank (formerly Barnett
Bank)**
5875 NW 100 63rd St.
Miami Lakes, FL 33014
305/350-7100

Human Resources Information:

Attn: Human Resources Department
NationsBank
701 Brickell Ave.
Miami , FL 33131
305/350-7153 (fax)

Naples

**NationsBank (formerly Barnett
Bank of Naples)**
796 Fifth Ave. S.
Naples, FL 33940-6696
941/643-8200

Human Resources Information:
Marilyn Foley
Human Resources Generalist
NationsBank
4501 Tamiami Trail N.
Naples, FL 34103

Orlando

**NationsBank (formerly Barnett
Bank of Central Florida, N.A.)**
390 N. Orange Ave. Ste. 900
Orlando, FL 32801
407/420-2800

Human Resources Information:
Attn: Human Resources Department
NationsBank
Barnett Valencia Center
707 Mendham Blvd.
Orlando, FL 32825

SunTrust Bank, Central Florida
200 S. Orange Ave.
Orlando, FL 32801-3410
407/237-4141

Human Resources Information:
Therese D. Osborne
Senior Vice President/Human Resources
SunTrust Bank, Central Florida
P.O. Box 3833
Orlando, FL 32802

Pensacola

AmSouth Bank of Florida
70 N. Baylen St.
Pensacola, FL 32501
904/444-1102

Human Resources Information:
Sharon Hensel
Vice President/Human Resources
AmSouth Bank of Florida
P.O. Box 12790
Pensacola, FL 32575

Sarasota

**NationsBank (formerly Barnett
Bank of Southwest Florida)**
240 S. Pineapple Ave.
Sarasota, FL 34236-5622
941/951-4800

Human Resources Information:
Attn: Human Resources Department
NationsBank
240 S. Pineapple Ave.
Sarasota, FL 34230

SunTrust Bank/Gulf Coast
1777 Main St.
Sarasota, FL 34236-6772

813/366-7000

Human Resources Information:
Rudi Thompson
Senior Vice President/Human Resources
SunTrust Bank/Gulf Coast
P.O. Box 2138
Sarasota, FL 34230

St. Petersburg

NationsBank (formerly Barnett Bank of Pinellas County)
200 Central Ave.
St. Petersburg, FL 33701
813/535-0711

Human Resources Information:
Attn: Human Resources Department
NationsBank
4800 140 Ave. N.
Clearwater, FL 34622

Republic Bank
111 Second Ave. NE
St. Petersburg, FL 33701
813/823-7300

Human Resources Information:
Kelly Bilancione
Human Resources Manager
Republic Bank
111 Second Ave. NE, Ste. 503
St. Petersburg, FL 33701

SouthTrust Bank of West Florida
150 Second Ave. N.
St. Petersburg, FL 33701-3316
813/894-1035

Human Resources Information:
Michelle Nix
Vice President/Human Resources
SouthTrust Bank of West Florida
P.O. Box 15708
St. Petersburg, FL 33733

Tampa

NationsBank (formerly Barnett Bank of Tampa)
101 E. Kennedy Blvd.
Tampa, FL 33602-5133
813/225-8111

Human Resources Information:
Anita Teft
Senior Vice President/Human Resources Director
NationsBank
101 E. Kennedy Blvd., Second Fl.
Tampa, FL 33602

NationsBank of Florida, N.A.
400 N. Ashley Drive
Tampa, FL 33602
813/224-5805

Human Resources Information:
Margaret Ralph
Florida Personnel Executive
NationsBank of Florida, N.A.
400 N. Ashley Drive
Tampa, FL 33602

SunTrust Bank of Tampa Bay
315 E. Madison St.
Tampa, FL 33602-4816
813/224-2121

Human Resources Information:

Patricia Meckley
Senior Vice President/Human Resources
SunTrust Bank of Tampa Bay
P.O. Box 3303
Tampa, FL 33601

West Palm Beach

NationsBank (formerly Barnett Bank of Palm Beach County)
625 N. Flagler Drive
West Palm Beach, FL 33401-4025
407/838-2300

Human Resources Information:
Karen McCluskey
Employment Manager/Human Resources
NationsBank
205 Datura St.
West Palm Beach, FL 33401

Winter Haven

SunTrust Bank/Mid-Florida, N.A.
595 Cypress Gardens Blvd.
Winter Haven, FL 33880-4472
941/297-6800

Human Resources Information:
Barbara Austin
Assistant Vice President/Human Resources
SunTrust Bank/Mid-Florida, N.A.
P.O. Box 1380
Winter Haven, FL 33882-1380

Georgia

Atlanta

First Union National Bank of Georgia
999 Peachtree St.
Atlanta, GA 30309-3964
404/827-7100

Human Resources Information:
Calvin S. Stowell, Jr.
Senior Vice President/Human Resources
First Union National Bank of Georgia
999 Peachtree St. NE, Ste. 1200
Atlanta, GA 30309-3964
404/827-7119

NationsBank of Georgia, N.A.
600 Peachtree St. NE
Atlanta, GA 30308
404/581-2121

Human Resources Information:
Geri Thomas
Senior Vice President/Personnel Division
NationsBank of Georgia, N.A.
600 Peachtree St. NE, 54th Fl.
Atlanta, GA 30308

Prudential Bank and Trust Company
2 Concourse Pkwy, Ste. 500
Atlanta, GA 30328
770/551-6700

Human Resources Information:
Nan Fogle
Senior Vice President/Human Resources
Prudential Bank and Trust Company
1 Ravinia Drive, Ste. 1000

Atlanta, GA 30346
770/604-7500

SouthTrust Bank of Georgia
2000 Riveredge Pkwy.
Atlanta, GA 30328
770/951-4000

Human Resources Information:
Martha Lawrence, Banking Officer
Debra Wilkerson, Vice President/Human Resources
SouthTrust Bank of Georgia
2000 Riveredge Pkwy.
Atlanta, GA 30328
770/951-4011
770/951-4287 (fax)

SunTrust Bank of Atlanta
25 Park Place NE
Atlanta, GA 30303
404/588-7711

Human Resources Information:
Carolyn Cartwright
Senior Vice President and
Director/Personnel
SunTrust Bank of Atlanta
P.O. Box 4418
Atlanta, GA 30302-4418
Attn: M/C 0019
404/588-7086

Wachovia Bank of Georgia, N.A.
191 Peachtree St. NE
Atlanta, GA 30303
404/332-5000

Human Resources Information:
Marsha Calhoun

Senior Vice President/Human Resources
Wachovia Bank of Georgia, N.A.
191 Peachtree St. NE
Atlanta, GA 30303
Attn: M/C GA1200
404/841-8532

Columbus

Columbus Bank and Trust Company
1148 Broadway
Columbus, GA 31901
706/649-2311

Human Resources Information:
Helen Johnson
Director of Employment Services
Synovus Employment Services
P.O. Box 120
Columbus, GA 31902
706/649-4708

Hawaii

Honolulu

Bank of Hawaii
130 Merchant St.
Honolulu, HI 96813
808/847-8888

Human Resources Information:
Duane D. Feekin
Executive Vice President and Director/Human Resources
Bank of Hawaii
Human Resources Division
P.O. Box 2900

Honolulu, HI 96846

Central Pacific Bank
220 S. King St.
Honolulu, HI 96813-4530
808/544-0500

Human Resources Information:
Rita Flynn
Vice President and Manager/Human
Resources Division
Central Pacific Bank
P.O. Box 3590
Honolulu, HI 96811

First Hawaiian Bank
1132 Bishop St.
Honolulu, HI 96813-3501
808/525-7000

Human Resources Information:
Sheila Sumiea
Senior Vice President/Human Re-
sources
First Hawaiian Bank
P.O. Box 3200
Honolulu, HI 96847
Attn: Human Resources

Idaho

Boise

First Security Bank of Idaho, N.A.
119 N. Ninth St.
Boise, ID 83702
208/393-4000

Human Resources Information:
Laurie Bergey

Manager of Recruitment and Staffing
First Security Bank of Idaho, N.A.
P.O. Box 7069
Boise, ID 83730
208/393-4773

Key Bank of Idaho
702 W. Idaho St.
Boise, ID 83702-8901
208/334-7000

Human Resources Information:
Julie Eng
Human Resources State Manager
Key Bank of Idaho
702 W. Idaho St.
Boise, ID 83702
208/334-7081

U.S. Bank of Idaho
101 S. Capitol Blvd.
Boise, ID 83702
208/383-7000

Human Resources Information:
Attn: Human Resources Department
U.S. Bank of Idaho
P O Box 8247
Boise, ID 83733
208/383-7764

Illinois

Bannockburn

First of America Bank Illinois, N.A.
2595 Waukegan Rd.
Bannockburn, IL 60015
847/362-3000

Human Resources Information:
Leslie Koscinski
Human Resources Recruiter
First of America Bank Illinois, N.A.
325 N. Milwaukee Ave.
Libertyville, IL 60048

Chicago

**American National Bank and
Trust Company**
33 N. LaSalle St.
Chicago, IL 60690
312/661-5000

Human Resources Information:
Attn: Human Resources Department
American National Bank and Trust
Company
33 N. LaSalle St., Sixteenth Fl.
Chicago, IL 60690

Bank of America Illinois
231 S. LaSalle St.
Chicago, IL 60697
312/828-2345

Human Resources Information:
Mark Flynn
Senior Vice President/Eastern Center
Manager of Human Resources
Bank of America Illinois
200 W. Jackson St., Eighth Fl.
Chicago, IL 60697

Cole Taylor Bank
850 W. Jackson Blvd.
Chicago, IL 60607
312/738-2000

Human Resources Information:
Jan Doiel
Assistant Vice President and Staffing
Manager/Human Resources
Cole Taylor Bank
350 E. Dundee Rd., Ste. 201
Wheeling, IL 60090
847/459-5784 (fax)

Corus Bank
2401 N. Halsted St.
Chicago, IL 60614-2496
773/935-6000

Human Resources Information:
Thomas Grace
Director/Human Resources
Corus Bank
4800 N. Western Ave.
Chicago, IL 60625

First Chicago NBD
1 First National Plaza
Chicago, IL 60670
312/732-4000

Human Resources Information:
Tim Moen
Executive Vice President/Human Resources
First Chicago NBD
1 First National Plaza
Ninth Fl., Ste. 0548
Chicago, IL 60670-0548

Firstar Bank Illinois
30 N. Michigan Ave., Ste. 410
Chicago, IL 60602-3402

312/641-1000

Human Resources Information:
Ramona Grauzinis
Vice President/Human Resources
Firstar Bank Illinois
30 N. Michigan Ave., Ste. 410
Chicago, IL 60602

Harris Trust and Savings Bank
111 W. Monroe St.
Chicago, IL 60603-4003
312/461-2121

Human Resources Information:
Karen Stoeller
Vice President/Human Resources
Harris Trust and Savings Bank
P.O. Box 755
Chicago, IL 60690
312/461-7655

**LaSalle Bank (formerly Columbia
National Bank of Chicago)**
5250 N. Harlem Ave.
Chicago, IL 60656-1888
773/775-6800

Human Resources Information:
Dennis Johnson
Vice President/Human Resources
LaSalle Bank
135 S. LaSalle St.
Chicago, IL 60603
Attn: HR Department

**LaSalle Bank, N.A. (formerly
LaSalle Northwest National Bank)**
4747 W. Irving Park Rd.
Chicago, IL 60641-2700

773/777-7700

Human Resources Information:
Tim Janisch
Vice President/Human Resources Di-
rector
LaSalle Bank, N.A.
4747 W. Irving Park Rd.
Chicago, IL 60641

LaSalle Bank NI
3201 N. Ashland Ave.
Chicago, IL 60657-2182
312/525-2180

Human Resources Information:
Ronda Abramson
Vice President and Director/Human
Resources
LaSalle Bank NI
3201 N. Ashland Ave.
Chicago, IL 60657-2182

LaSalle National Bank
135 S. LaSalle St.
Chicago, IL 60674
312/443-2000

Human Resources Information:
Attn: Abn Amro Human Resources
LaSalle National Bank
135 S. LaSalle St., Ste. 3300
Chicago, IL 60603
312/904-6600 (jobline)

Marquette National Bank
6316 S. Western Ave.
Chicago, IL 60636-2491
773/476-5100

Human Resources Information:
Patrick F. Donovan
Vice President/Human Resources
Marquette National Bank
820 S. Harlem Ave.
Bridgeview, IL 60455

Northern Trust Company
50 S. LaSalle St.
Chicago, IL 60675
312/630-6000

Human Resources Information:
William N. Setterstrom
Senior Vice President/Human Resources
Northern Trust Company
181 W. Madison St., MB-5
Chicago, IL 60675

U.S. Bancorp (formerly First Bank, N.A.)
410 N. Michigan Ave.
Chicago, IL 60611
800/846-4646

Human Resources Information:
Robert H. Sayre
Executive Vice President/Human Resources
U.S. Bancorp
601 Second Ave. S.
Minneapolis, MN 55402-4302
Attn: M/S MPSP 3003

Crystal Lake

Grand National Bank
265 Virginia St.
Crystal Lake, IL 60014-3444

815/459-4600

Human Resources Information:
Denna Czaban
Director/Human Resources
Grand National Bank
P.O. Box 2367
Crystal Lake, IL 60039

Elmhurst

Old Kent Bank
105 S. York St.
Elmhurst, IL 60126-3454
630/941-5200

Human Resources Information:
John Starkey
Vice President/Human Resources
Old Kent Bank
105 S. York St.
Elmhurst, IL 60126-3454
630/941-5476

Evanston

Bank One, Chicago, N.A.
800 Davis St.
Evanston, IL 60201-4439
847/866-5500

Human Resources Information:
Pam Jackson
Vice President/Human Resources Manager
Bank One, Chicago, N.A.
111 N. Canal, Fifteenth Fl.
Chicago, IL 60606

Evergreen Park

First National Bank of Evergreen Park
3101 W. 95th St.
Evergreen Park, IL 60805
708/422-6700

Human Resources Information:
Ruth Gilke
Assistant Vice President/Human Resources
First National Bank of Evergreen Park
3101 W. 95th St.
Evergreen Park, IL 60805

Franklin Park

LaSalle Bank - Illinois
3044 Rose St.
Franklin Park, IL 60131-2776
847/202-3333

Human Resources Information:
Nancy Nottoli
Senior Vice President/Human Resources Regional Manager
LaSalle Bank - Illinois
4242 N. Harlem Ave.
Norridge, IL 60634
708/583-7689

Moline

First Midwest Bank, N.A.
506 Fifteenth St.
Moline, IL 61265-2159
309/797-7500

Human Resources Information:
Lisa Fuhlman
Vice President/Human Resources
First Midwest Bank, N.A.
506 Fifteenth St.
Moline, IL 61265-2159

Peoria

Commerce Bank
416 Main St.
Peoria, IL 61602-1103
309/676-1311

Human Resources Information:
Vicky Barlett
Human Resources Manager
Commerce Bank
416 Main St.
Peoria, IL 61602

Rockford

AMCORE Bank N.A., Rockford
501 Seventh St.
Rockford, IL 61104-1242
815/968-2241

Human Resources Information:
Wanda Liptow
Vice President and Manager/Human Resources
AMCORE Bank N.A., Rockford
P.O. Box 1537
Rockford, IL 61110

Tinley Park

Heritage Bank

17500 S. Oak Park Ave.
Tinley Park, IL 60477-3900
708/532-8000

Human Resources Information:
William White
Representative II/Human Resources
Heritage Bank
17500 S. Oak Park Ave.
Tinley Park, IL 60477

Urbana

Busey Bank
201 W. Main
Urbana, IL 61801-2693
217/384-4500

Human Resources Information:
Lisa Davis
Director/Human Resources
Busey Bank
208 W. Main
Urbana, IL 61801

Wheaton

First National Bank of Chicago
211 S. Wheaton Ave.
Wheaton, IL 60187
312/732-4000

Human Resources Information:
Tamara Lee Baloun
Vice President/Senior Human Re-
sources Specialist
First National Bank of Chicago
1 N. State, Ste. 0008
Chicago, IL 60670
312/407-4590

Indiana

Evansville

**Citizens National Bank of Evans-
ville**
20 NW Third St.
Evansville, IN 47708
812/464-3400

Human Resources Information:
John M. Oberhelman
Senior Vice President/Human Re-
sources
Citizens National Bank of Evansville
P.O. Box 778
Evansville, IN 47705-0778

Old National Bank in Evansville
420 Main St.
Evansville, IN 47708-1503
812/464-1200

Human Resources Information:
Jane Wittmer
Vice President/Human Resources Di-
rector
Old National Bank in Evansville
420 Main St., Eighth Fl.
Evansville, IN 47708-1503

Ft. Wayne

Fort Wayne National Bank
110 W. Berry St.
Ft. Wayne, IN 46802-2311
219/426-0555

Human Resources Information:

David H. Swanson
Vice President/Human Resources
Fort Wayne National Bank
P.O. Box 110
Ft. Wayne, IN 46801

Norwest Bank Indiana, N.A.
111 E. Wayne St.
Ft. Wayne, IN 46802-2405
219/461-6000

Human Resources Information:
B. DuWayne Blilie
Senior Vice Prsiedent/Regional Human Resources Director
Norwest Bank Indiana, N.A.
P.O. Box 960
Ft. Wayne, IN 46801-6624
219/461-6335

Indianapolis

Bank One, Indianapolis, N.A.
Bank One Tower
111 Monument Cir.
Indianapolis, IN 46277-0107
317/321-3000

Human Resources Information:
Starr L. McCoy
Vice President/Employment Manager
Bank One, Indianapolis, N.A.
Bank One Center/Tower
111 Monument Cir., Ste. 711
Indianapolis, IN 46277-0107
317/321-7986
317/321-1541 (fax)

Fifth Third Bank of Central Indiana
251 N. Illinois St., Ste. 1000
Indianapolis, IN 46204-2904
317/383-2300

Human Resources Information:
Theresa Shearer
Director/Human Resources
Fifth Third Bank of Central Indiana
251 N. Illinois St., Ste. 1000
Indianapolis, IN 46204

First of America Bank Indiana
5300 Crawfordsville Rd.
Indianapolis, IN 46224
317/767-6000

Human Resources Information:
Gerald Wright
Vice President/Human Resources
First of America Bank Indiana
101 W. Ohio Street, Ste. 220
Indianapolis, IN 46204

National City Bank, Indiana
101 W. Washington St.
Indianapolis, IN 46255-5500
317/267-7000

Human Resources Information:
Judith A. Muessig
Senior Vice President/Human Resources
National City Bank, Indiana
101 W. Washington St., Ste. 808E
Indianapolis, IN 46255-5500

NBD Bank, N.A.
1 Indiana Square
Indianapolis, IN 46266-0100
317/266-6000

Human Resources Information:
Robert O'Neal
First Vice President/Human Resources
NBD Bank, N.A.

1 Indiana Square, Ste. 7193
Indianapolis, IN 46266-0100

Lafayette

Bank One, Lafayette, N.A.
201 Main St.
Lafayette, IN 47901-1277
317/423-0300

Human Resources Information:
Judy Potts
Vice President/Human Resources
Bank One, Lafayette, N.A.
P.O. Box 380
Lafayette, IN 47902

Noblesville

Huntington National Bank of Indiana
949 E. Conner St.
Noblesville, IN 46060
317/776-4212

Human Resources Information:
Stephanie Cheetham
Vice President/Human Resources
Huntington National Bank of Indiana
201 N. Illinois St., Ste. 1800
Indianapolis, IN 46204

South Bend

First Source Bank
100 N. Michigan St.
South Bend, IN 46634
219/235-2000

Human Resources Information:
Dan L. Craft
Senior Vice President/Human Resources
First Source Bank
P.O. Box 1602
South Bend, IN 46634

Key Bank of Indiana
202 S. Michigan St.
South Bend, IN 46601-2021
219/237-5200

Human Resources Information:
Cedric Buchanon
Vice President/Human Resources
Key Bank of Indiana
202 S. Michigan St.
South Bend, IN 46601-2021

Valley American Bank and Trust Company
101 N. Main St.
South Bend, IN 46601-1631
219/256-6000

Human Resources Information:
Jacqueline Walton
Human Resources Director
Valley American Bank and Trust Company
P.O. Box 328
South Bend, IN 46624-0328
219/237-4695

Terre Haute

Terre Haute First National Bank
1 First Financial Plaza

Terre Haute, IN 47807-3225
812/238-6000

Human Resources Information:
Sharon Braun
Vice President/Human Resources Officer
Terre Haute First National Bank
1401 S. Third St.
P.O. Box 2122
Terre Haute, IN 47802

Iowa

Des Moines

Brenton Bank
400 Locust St., Ste. 200
Des Moines, IA 50309-0891
515/237-5100

Human Resources Information:
Mary Sweeney
Vice President/Human Resources
Brenton Bank
6800 Lake Drive, Ste. 250
West Des Moines, IA 50266

Firstar Bank Iowa
520 Walnut St.
Des Moines, IA 50309
515/245-6100

Human Resources Information:
Jan Burch
Vice President/Human Resources
Firstar Bank Iowa
520 Walnut St.
Des Moines, IA 50309
515/245-6278

Norwest Bank Iowa, N.A.
666 Walnut St.
Des Moines, IA 50309-3904
515/245-3131

Human Resources Information:
Vicki K. Butler
Senior Vice President and
Manager/Human Resources
Norwest Bank Iowa, N.A.
P.O. Box 837
Des Moines, IA 50304
Attn: M/S 4049

Kansas

Overland Park

Mercantile Bank
9900 W. 87th St.
Overland Park, KS 66212-4799
816/472-6372

Human Resources Information:
Elaine Diller
Senior Vice President/Human Resources Manager
Mercantile Bank
P.O. Box 419147
Kansas City, MO 64141
816/360-6140

Wichita

BANK IV Kansas, N.A.
100 N. Broadway
Wichita, KS 67202-2212
316/261-4444

Human Resources Information:
Rich Jiwanlal

Director of Human Resources
BANK IV Kansas, N.A.
P.O. Box 4
Wichita, KS 67201

INTRUST Bank, N.A.
105 N. Main St.
Wichita, KS 67202-1412
316/383-1111

Human Resources Information:
Gary Proffit
Vice President/Human Resources
INTRUST Bank, N.A.
P.O. Box 1
Wichita, KS 67201

Kentucky

Covington

**Fifth Third Bank of Northern
Kentucky**
535 Madison Ave.
Covington, KY 41011
606/283-8500

Human Resources Information:
Michelle Heeb
Human Resources Manager
Fifth Third Bank of Northern Kentucky
P.O. Box 427
Florence, KY 41042

Lexington

Bank One, Lexington, N.A.
201 E. Main St.

Lexington, KY 40507-2002
606/231-1000

Human Resources Information:
Roberta Dale
Employment Representative
Bank One, Lexington, N.A.
220 E. Reynolds Rd.
Lexington, KY 40517

Louisville

Bank One Kentucky, N.A.
416 West Jefferson
Louisville, KY 40202-3244
502/566-2000

Human Resources Information:
Lisa Morley
Senior Vice President/Human Resources
Bank One, Kentucky, N.A.
P.O. Box 32500
Louisville, KY 40232

Fifth Third Bank of Kentucky
200 W. Broad St.
Louisville, KY 40202
502/562-5215

Human Resources Information:
Susan Stocker
Human Resources Manager
Fifth Third Bank of Kentucky
401 S. Fourth Ave.
Louisville, KY 40202

**Mid-America Bank of Louisville
and Trust Company**

500 W. Broadway
Louisville, KY 40202-2210
502/589-3351

Human Resources Information:
William D. Moore, Jr.
Senior Vice President/Human Resources
Mid-America Bank of Louisville and Trust Company
P.O. Box 1101
Louisville, KY 40201

National City Bank, Kentucky
101 S. Fifth St.
Louisville, KY 40202
502/581-4200

Human Resources Information:
Twila May
Senior Vice President/Human Resources Director
National City Bank, Kentucky
P.O. Box 36000, Seventh Fl.
Louisville, KY 40233

PNC Bank, Kentucky, Inc.
500 W. Jefferson St.
Louisville, KY 40202
800/626-6505

Human Resources Information:
PNC Bank, N.A.
Attn: Human Resources Department
500 W. Jefferson St., Eighth Fl.
Louisville, KY 40202

Republic Bank and Trust Company

601 W. Market St.
Louisville, KY 40202-2700
502/584-3600

Human Resources Information:
Ruth Gillespie
Senior Vice President/Human Resources Director
Republic Bank and Trust Company
601 W. Market St., Fifth Fl.
Louisville, KY 40202

Paducah

Peoples First National Bank and Trust
Kentucky Ave. and Fourth St.
Paducah, KY 42001
502/441-1200

Human Resources Information:
Palmer Warren
Employment Manager/Human Resources
Peoples First Corporation
P.O. Box 2200
Paducah, KY 42002-2200

<u>Louisiana</u>

Baton Rouge

Bank One
451 Florida St.
Baton Rouge, LA 70801-1705
504/332-4011

Human Resources Information:
Mike Zaunbrecher

Executive Vice President/Human Resources
Bank One
P.O. Box 3399
Baton Rouge, LA 70821

City National Bank of Baton Rouge
445 North Blvd.
Baton Rouge, LA 70802-5707
504/387-2151

Human Resources Information:
Attn: Human Resources Department
City National Bank of Baton Rouge
P.O. Box 1231
Baton Rouge, LA 70821

Regions Bank of Louisiana
5353 Essen Lane, Ste. 500
Baton Rouge, LA 70809
504/767-9300

Human Resources Information:
Janet Lucia
Personnel Officer
Regions Bank of Louisiana
P.O. Box 250
New Roads, LA 70760

New Orleans

First National Bank of Commerce
210 Baronne St.
New Orleans, LA 70112
504/561-1371

Human Resources Information:
Barry M. Mulroy
Executive Vice President/Human Resources

First National Bank of Commerce
P.O. Box 60279
New Orleans, LA 70160

Hibernia National Bank
313 Carondelet St.
New Orleans, LA 70130-3178
504/533-5712

Human Resources Information:
Michael Zainey
Director/Human Resources
Hibernia National Bank
P.O. Box 61540
New Orleans, LA 70161
504/533-2852

Whitney National Bank
228 St. Charles Ave.
New Orleans, LA 70130-2615
504/586-7272

Human Resources Information:
Paul Bergeron
Vice President and Director/Human Resources
Whitney National Bank
P.O. Box 61260
New Orleans, LA 70161

Shreveport

Commercial National Bank in Shreveport
333 Texas St.
Shreveport, LA 71101-3666
318/429-1000

Human Resources Information:
Caroline F. Cunningham
Vice President/Human Resources

Manager
Commercial National Bank in
Shreveport
P.O. Box 21119
Shreveport, LA 71152

Maine

Portland

Key Bank of Maine
1 Canal Plaza
Portland, ME 04101
207/874-7000

Human Resources Information:
Betty A. Harvey
Senior Vice President/Human Re-
sources
Key Bank of Maine
1 Canal Plaza
Portland, ME 04101

Peoples Heritage Savings Bank
1 Portland Square
Portland, ME 04101-9057
207/761-8500

Human Resources Information:
Carol Mitchell
Executive Vice President/Human Re-
sources
Peoples Heritage Savings Bank
P.O. Box 9540
Portland, ME 04112

Maryland

Baltimore

Crestar Bank
1300 N. Charles St.
Baltimore, MD 21201
410/986-1500

Human Resources Information:
Suzan Garabedian
Vice President/Human Resources
Crestar Bank
120 E. Baltimore St.
Baltimore, MD 21202
Attn: M/C—CMD8023
410/986-1632
410/986-1628 (fax)

First National Bank of Maryland
25 S. Charles St.
Baltimore, MD 21201-3330
410/244-4000

Human Resources Information:
Attn: Human Resources Department
First National Bank of Maryland
110 S. Paca St., Eighth Fl.
Baltimore, MD 21201

**Mercantile-Safe Deposit and Trust
Company**
2 Hopkins Plaza
Baltimore, MD 21201
410/237-5900

Human Resources Information:
Hal Hamil
Vice President/Human Resources
Mercantile-Safe Deposit and Trust
Company
Operations Center
750 Old Hammonds Ferry Rd.
Linthicum Heights, MD 21090

Provident Bank of Maryland
114 E. Lexington St.
Baltimore, MD 21202-1725
410/281-7000

Human Resources Information:
Christine A. Pettingill
Manager and Director of Human Resources
Provident Bank of Maryland
114 E. Lexington St.
Baltimore, MD 21202-1725

Laurel

Citizens Bank of Maryland
14401 Sweitzer Lane
Laurel, MD 20707-2921
301/206-6000

Human Resources Information:
Jane Uphouse
Vice President and Director/Human Resources
Citizens Bank of Maryland
Attn: M/S724
14401 Sweitzer Lane
Laurel, MD 20707

Olney

Sandy Spring National Bank of Maryland
17801 Georgia Ave.
Olney, MD 20832-2267
301/774-6400

Human Resources Information:
James Farmer

Director/Human Resources
Sandy Spring National Bank of Maryland
17801 Georgia Ave.
Olney, MD 20832

Rockville

First Union National Bank of Maryland
110 Congressional Lane
Rockville, MD 20852
301/650-1045

Human Resources Information:
David H. Furman
Vice President and Human Resources Manager
First Union National Bank of Virginia
1970 Chain Bridge Rd., Fourth Fl.
McLean, VA 22102
703/760-6737

Massachusetts

Andover

Andover Bank
61 Main St.
Andover, MA 01810-0150
508/749-2000

Human Resources Information:
Barbara Conti
Senior Vice President/Human Resources
Andover Bank
P.O. Box 2005
Andover, MA 01810-0150

Boston

BankBoston (formerly Bank of Boston/Bank Boston)
100 Federal St.
Boston, MA 02110
800/788-5000

Human Resources Information:
Employment Department
BankBoston
100 Federal St.
MABOS 01-18-02
Boston, MA 02110
800/252-2808
617/434-0532 (fax)

Boston Safe Deposit and Trust Company
1 Boston Pl.
Boston, MA 02108-4402
617/722-7000

Human Resources Information:
Linda Kane
Manager/Human Resources
Boston Safe Deposit and Trust Company
1 Boston Pl.
Boston, MA 02108-4402
Attn: 024-006C

Citizens Bank of Massachusetts
55 Summer St.
Boston, MA 02110
617/482-2600

Human Resources Information:
Carole McDonough
Assistant Vice President/Human Resources
Citizens Bank of Massachusetts
55 Summer St.
Boston, MA 02110

First National Bank of Boston
100 Federal St.
Boston, MA 02110
617/434-2200

Human Resources Information:
Helen G. Drinan
Executive Vice President/Human Resources
First National Bank of Boston
100 Federal St.
Boston, MA 02110

State Street Bank and Trust Company
225 Franklin St.
Boston, MA 02110
617/786-3000

Human Resources Information:
Susan Schoonover
Vice President/Staffing Manager
State Street Bank and Trust Company
1776 Heritage Drive
North Quincy, MA 02171

USTrust
30 Court St.
Boston, MA 02108
617/726-7000

Human Resources Information:
Linda J. Lerner
Senior Vice President/Human Resources

USTrust
40 Court St., Eighth Fl.
Boston, MA 02108

Cambridge

Cambridge Savings Bank
1374 Massachusetts Ave.
Cambridge, MA 02138-3891
617/864-8700

Human Resources Information:
Marie Lodi
Vice President/Human Resources
Cambridge Savings Bank
1374 Massachusetts Ave.
Cambridge, MA 02138-3822

Haverhill

Family Bank, FSB
153 Merrimack St.
Haverhill, MA 01830-6107
508/374-1911

Human Resources Information:
Sandra Williams
Vice President/Human Resources
Family Bank, FSB
P.O. Box 431
Haverhill, MA 01831

Lawrence

First Essex Bank, FSB
296 Essex St.
Lawrence, MA 01840-1516
508/681-7500

Human Resources Information:
Cynthia Cross

Vice President/Human Resources
First Essex Bank, FSB
P.O. Box 1000
Lawrence, MA 01842

Lynn

Eastern Bank
270 Union St.
Lynn, MA 01901
617/599-2100

Human Resources Information:
Nancy Hutchinson-Stager, Senior
Vice President and Director/Human
Resources
John Bogdan, Assistant Vice Presi-
dent/Human Resources
Eastern Bank
112 Market St.
Lynn, MA 01901
617/596-4445 (fax)

Medford

Medford Savings Bank
29 High St.
Medford, MA 02155-3885
617/395-7700

Human Resources Information:
Jane Griffin
Vice President/Personnel Officer
Medford Savings Bank
P.O. Box 151
Medford, MA 02155-3885

Natick

Middlesex Savings Bank
6 Main St.

Natick, MA 01760-4506
508/653-0300

Human Resources Information:
George E. Tibbetts
Senior Vice President/Human Resources
Middlesex Savings Bank
6 Main St.
Natick, MA 01760

New Bedford

Compass Bank for Savings
791 Purchase St.
New Bedford, MA 02740
508/984-6000

Human Resources Information:
Linda M. Perron
Vice President/Human Resources
Compass Bank for Savings
141 N. Main St.
Fall River, MA 02720

Reading

MASSBANK for Savings
123 Haven St.
Reading, MA 01867
617/662-0100

Human Resources Information:
Margo Higgins
Assistant Vice President/Human Resources
MASSBANK for Savings
50 Central St.
Lowell, MA 01852
508/446-9360

508/446-9362 (fax)

Rockland

Rockland Trust Company
288 Union St.
Rockland, MA 02370-1896
617/878-6100

Human Resources Information:
Raymond G. Fuerschbach
Senior Vice President/Human Resources
Rockland Trust Company
288 Union St.
Rockland, MA 02370-1896

Salem

Salem Five Cents Savings Bank
210 Essex St.
Salem, MA 01970-3793
508/745-5555

Human Resources Information:
Louise Levesque
Senior Vice President/Human Resources
Salem Five Cents Savings Bank
210 Essex St.
Salem, MA 01970

Springfield

Fleet National Bank
1 Monarch Place
Springfield, MA 01102
800/833-6623

Human Resources Information:

Mary Scatamacchia
Human Resources Director
Fleet National Bank
1 Federal St.
Boston, MA 02109
Attn: MAOFD37B

Springfield Institution for Savings
1441 Main St.
Springfield, MA 01103-1406
413/748-8000

Human Resources Information:
Henry J. McWhinnie
Senior Vice President/Human Resources
Springfield Institution for Savings
P.O. Box 3034
Springfield, MA 01102-3034

Michigan

Ann Arbor

Republic Bank
122 S. Main St.
Ann Arbor, MI 48104-1922
517/789-4305

Human Resources Information:
Marilyn Ridenour
Assistant Vice President/Human Resources Representative
Republic Bank
306 W. Michigan Ave.
Jackson, MI 49204-0079

Detroit

Comerica Bank
1 Detroit Center
500 Woodward Ave.

Detroit, MI 48226-3369
800/521-1190

Human Resources Information:
Theodore Bennett
Senior Vice President/Human Resources Director
Comerica Bank
211 West Fort St., Second Fl.
Detroit, MI 48226
M/C: 3121

NBD Bank
611 Woodward Ave.
Detroit, MI 48226
313/225-1000

Human Resources Information:
Tim Moen
Executive Vice President/Human Resources
First Chicago NBD (formerly First National Bank of Chicago)
1 First National Plaza
Ninth Fl., Ste. 0548
Chicago, IL 60670-0548

Farmington Hills

Michigan National Bank
27777 Inkster Rd.
Farmington Hills, MI 48334
810/473-3000

Human Resources Information:
Joseph Fritzsche
Director of Human Resources
Michigan National Bank
27777 Inkster Rd.
Farmington Hills, MI 48334
Attn: M/C 10-69

Flint

Citizens Bank
1 Citizens Banking Center
Flint, MI 48502
810/766-7500

Human Resources Information:
Marilyn K. Allor
Senior Vice President/Human Resources Director
Citizens Bank
328 S. Saginaw St.
Flint, MI 48502
Attn: 001045
810/766-7580

Grand Rapids

Old Kent Bank
1 Vanderberg Center
Grand Rapids, MI 49503
616/771-5000

Human Resources Information:
Chuck Smeester
Senior Vice President/Corporate Operations
Old Kent Bank
CSC1, Attn: Corporate Operations
1850 E. Paris
Grand Rapids, MI 49546

Kalamazoo

First of America Bank Corporation
108 E. Michigan
Kalamazoo, MI 49007
616/376-9000

Human Resources Information:
Jennifer L. Crayner
Senior Recruiter
First of America Bank Corporation
K-A01-1G Corporate Staffing
225 N. Rose St.
Kalamazoo, MI 49006
616/376-7402
616/376-7410 (fax)

Monroe

Monroe Bank and Trust
102 E. Front St.
Monroe, MI 48161-2162
313/241-3431

Human Resources Information:
Rose Mary Johnson
Vice President/Human Resources
Monroe Bank and Trust
102 E. Front St., Third Fl.
Monroe, MI 48161

Troy

Huntington Banks of Michigan
801 W. Big Beaver Rd.
Troy, MI 48084
810/362-5000

Human Resources Information:
Patricia Herbst
Assistant Vice President/Human Resources
Huntington Banks of Michigan
801 W. Big Beaver Rd., Ste. 101
Troy, MI 48084

Zeeland

Huntington Bank (formerly FMB-First Michigan Bank)
101 E. Main St.
Zeeland, MI 49464-1779
616/355-9000

Human Resources Information:
Karen Yonker
Human Resources Generalist
Huntington Bank
1 Financial Plaza
Holland, MI 49423

Minnesota

Golden Valley

Marquette Bank
8200 Golden Valley Rd.
Golden Valley, MN 55427
612/797-8500

Human Resources Information:
Carol Jordan
Human Resources Generalist
Marquette Bank
P.O. Box 1000
Minneapolis, MN 55480-1000
612/948-5617

Minneapolis

Norwest Bank Minnesota, N.A.
Sixth St. and Marquette Ave.
Minneapolis, MN 55479
612/667-1234

Human Resources Information:
Stephen W. Hansen

Executive Vice President and Director/Human Resources
Norwest Corporation
Sixth St. and Marquette Ave.
Minneapolis, MN 55479-1023
Attn: Mail Station: 1023

U.S. Bancorp (formerly First Bank, N.A.)
601 Second Ave. S.
Minneapolis, MN 55402-4302
612/973-1111

Human Resources Information:
Attn: Human Resources Department
U.S. Bancorp
601 Second Ave. S., 21st Fl.
Minneapolis, MN 55402
612/973-2300

Rochester

Norwest Bank Minnesota South, N.A.
21 First St. SW
Rochester, MN 55902-3007
507/285-2800

Human Resources Information:
Elaine Eickhoff
Vice President/Human Resources
Norwest Bank Minnesota South, N.A.
21 First St. SW
P.O. Box 4500
Rochester, MN 55903
Attn: 3309

St. Paul

Firstar Bank of Minnesota, N.A.

101 E. Fifth St.
St. Paul, MN 55101
612/854-2211

Human Resources Information:
Cynthia Nihart
Assistant Vice President and Employment Consultant/Human Resources
Firstar Bank of Minnesota, N.A.
101 E. Fifth St., Seventh Fl.
St. Paul, MN 55101

Mississippi

Grenada

Union Planters Bank of Mississippi
108 S. Main St.
Grenada, MS 38901-4615
601/226-3141

Human Resources Information:
Karen West
Vice President/Human Resources Manager
Union Planters Bank of Mississippi
P.O. Box 947
Grenada, MS 38902-0947
601/227-2097 (fax)

Gulfport

Hancock Bank
1 Hancock Plaza
Gulfport, MS 39501-1947
601/868-4000

Human Resources Information:
Martha B. Peterman

Vice President/Personnel Director
Hancock Bank
P.O. Box 4019
Gulfport, MS 39502

Jackson

First American National Bank (formerly Deposit Guaranty National Bank)
1 Deposit Guaranty Plaza
Jackson, MS 39201
601/354-8211

Human Resources Information:
Susan Cain
Senior Vice President and Director/Human Resources
First American National Bank
P.O. Box 1200
Jackson, MS 39215
Attn: Susan Cain, Fifth Fl.

Trustmark National Bank
248 E. Capitol St.
Jackson, MS 39201-2502
601/354-5111

Human Resources Information:
Robert G. Spring
Senior Vice President/Human Resources Director
Trustmark National Bank
P.O. Box 291
Jackson, MS 39205

Tupelo

Bank of Mississippi
1 Mississippi Plaza
Tupelo, MS 38802

601/680-2000

Human Resources Information:
W. O. Jones
Senior Vice President and
Director/Human Resources
Bank of Mississippi
P.O. Box 789
Tupelo, MS 38802

The Peoples Bank and Trust Company
209 Troy St.
Tupelo, MS 38801-0209
601/680-1001

Human Resources Information:
Emily Patterson
First Vice President/Human Resources
The Peoples Bank and Trust Company
P.O. Box 709
Tupelo, MS 38802

Missouri

Brentwood

Magna Bank of Missouri
1401 S. Brentwood Blvd.
Brentwood, MO 63144
314/963-2600

Human Resources Information:
Les Mehrtens
Vice President and Director/Human Resources
Magna Group, Inc.
4820 W. Main
Belleville, IL 62226

618/257-3100

Clayton

Commerce Bank, N.A.
8000 Forsyth Blvd.
Clayton, MO 63105
314/726-2255

Human Resources Information:
Human Resources Information:
Attn: Human Resources
Commerce Bank, N.A.
8000 Forsyth Blvd., Ste. 900
Clayton, MD 63105

Kansas City

Bank Midwest, N.A.
1100 Main St.
Kansas City, MO 64105
816/471-9800

Human Resources Information:
Kelly Robinson
Personnel Director
Bank Midwest, N.A.
P.O. Box 26458
Kansas City, MO 64196-6458

Commerce Bank, N.A.
8000 Forsyth Blvd.
Clayton, MO 63105
816/234-2000

Human Resources Information:
Attn: Human Resources Department
Commerce Bank, N.A.
825 Main St.
Kansas City, MO 64141

NationsBank (formerly Boatmen's First National Bank of Kansas)
Tenth and Baltimore
Kansas City, MO 64133
816/221-2800

Human Resources Information:
Attn: Human Resources Department
NationsBank
14 W. Tenth St.
Kansas City, MO 64105

UMB Bank, N.A.
1010 Grand Ave.
Kansas City, MO 64106
816/860-7000

Human Resources Information:
James W. Rawlings
Senior Vice President and
Director/Human Resources
UMB Bank, N.A.
P.O. Box 419226
Kansas City, MO 64141-6226

Ladue

Mercantile Bank (formerly Mark Twain Bank)
8822 Ladue Rd.
Ladue, MO 63124
314/966-2530

Human Resources Information:
Mercantile Bank
Professional Recruiter, 02-0
P.O. Box 524
St. Louis, MO 63166
314/418-2525
jobs@mercantile.com E-mail
http://www.mercantile.com

Poplar Bluff

Mercantile Bank of St. Louis (formerly Mercantile Bank of Southeast Missouri)
P.O. Box 524
St. Louis, MO 63166-0524
573/785-4671

Human Resources Information:
Carol Sellers
Vice President/Human Resources
Manager
Mercantile Bank of St. Louis
P.O. Box 700
Poplar Bluff, MO 63902

Springfield

NationsBank (formerly Boatmen's Bank of Southern Missouri)
117 Park Central Square
Springfield, MO 65806
417/227-6000

Human Resources Information:
Cari Lindsey
Vice President/Human Resources
NationsBank
P.O. Box 1157
Springfield, MO 65801

St. Louis

Mercantile Bank of St. Louis, N.A.
Mercantile Tower
Seventh and Washington
St. Louis, MO 63101
314/425-2525

Human Resources Information:
Professional Recruiting
Mercantile Bank of St. Louis, N.A.
P.O. Box 524, Tram 02-0
St. Louis, MO 63166

NationsBank (formerly The Boat-men's National Bank of St. Louis)
1 Boatmen's Plaza
800 Market Street
St. Louis, MO 63101-2602
314/466-6000

Human Resources Information:
Attn: Employment
NationsBank
800 Market St.
MO1-800-03-01
St. Louis, MO 63101
314/466-7516

Southwest Bank of St. Louis
2301 S. Kingshighway Blvd.
St. Louis, MO 63110-3419
314/776-5200

Human Resources Information:
Donna R. Bess
Vice President/Human Resources
Southwest Bank of St. Louis
2301 S. Kingshighway Blvd.
St. Louis, MO 63110-3419

Montana

Billings

First Interstate BancSystem (for-merly First Interstate Bank of Commerce)

P.O. Box 30918
Billings, MT 59116
406/255-5000

Human Resources Information:
Human Asset Management Group
First Interstate BancSystem
P.O. Box 30918
Billings, MT 59116

Norwest Bank Montana, N.A.
175 N. 27th St.
Billings, MT 59101-2048
406/657-3405

Human Resources Information:
Kathy Fisher
Vice President/Human Resources
Manager
Norwest Bank Montana, N.A.
P.O. Box 30058
Billings, MT 59117
Attn: M/S 8013
406/657-3521

U.S. Bancorp (formerly First Bank Montana, N.A.)
303 N. Broadway
Billings, MT 59101-1239
406/657-8000

Human Resources Information:
Tom Manning
Vice President/Human Resources
U.S. Bancorp
303 N. Broadway
Billings, MT 59101
612/973-1111

Nebraska

Lincoln

National Bank of Commerce Trust and Savings Association
1248 O St.
Lincoln, NE 68508
402/434-4321

Human Resources Information:
Thomas L. Alexander
Senior Vice President/Human Resources
National Bank of Commerce Trust and Savings Association
1248 O Street, Third Fl.
Lincoln, NE 68508

Omaha

First Bank, N.A., Omaha
1700 Farnam St.
Omaha, NE 68102
402/348-6000

Human Resources Information:
Karol Lewallen, Officer and Corporate Manager/Human Resources
Becky Golden, Officer and Human Resources Generalist
First Bank, N.A., Omaha
1700 Farnam St.
Omaha, NE 68102
800/228-9175

First National Bank of Omaha
1 First National Center
Omaha, NE 68102
402/341-0500

Human Resources Information:
R. J. Urban
Vice President/Human Resources
First National Bank of Omaha
1 First National Center
1620 Dodge St.
Omaha, NE 68102

Norwest Bank Nebraska, N.A.
1919 Douglas St.
Omaha, NE 68102-1317
402/536-2420

Human Resources Information:
Sara Masters
Vice President/Human Resources Director
Norwest Bank Nebraska, N.A.
1919 Douglas St.
Omaha, NE 68102

Nevada

Las Vegas

Bank of America Nevada
300 S. Fourth St.
Las Vegas, NV 89101-6014
702/654-1000

Human Resources Information:
Laurie Burk
Senior Vice President/Human Resources Officer
Bank of America Nevada
Bank of America Plaza
300 S. Fourth Street, Second Fl.
Las Vegas, NV 89101
Attn: M/S 6731

Citibank Nevada, N.A.
8725 W. Sahara Ave.
Las Vegas, NV 89117
702/797-4444

Human Resources Information:
Joseph Manzo
Human Resources Director
Citibank Nevada, N.A.
8725 W. Sahara Ave.
The Lakes, NV 89117

Wells Fargo Bank, Nevada
3800 Howard Hughes Pkwy
Las Vegas, NV 89109
800/777-3000

Human Resources Information:
Regina Smith
Vice President and Human Re-
sources Consultant
Wells Fargo Bank, Nevada
P.O. Box 11007
Reno, NV 89520
702/334-1545

Reno

U.S. Bank of Nevada
1 E. Liberty St., First Fl.
Reno, NV 89501
702/688-3555

Human Resources Information:
Connie N. Brant
Human Resources Representative
U.S. Bank of Nevada
P.O. Box 171
Reno, NV 89504
M/S: NVR908
702/688-3502

New Hampshire

Concord

Providian National Bank
53 Regional Drive
Concord, NH 03301
603/225-1000

Human Resources Information:
Susan Piper
Director of Human Resources
Providian National Bank
53 Regional Drive, First Fl.
Concord, NH 03301

Keene

CFX Bank
100-102 Main Street
Keene, NH 03431-3757
603/352-2502

Human Resources Information:
Cindy Zett
Marketing Administrator
CFX Bank
P.O. Box 746
Keene, NH 03431

Manchester

Bank of New Hampshire
300 Franklin St.
Manchester, NH 03101
603/624-6600

Human Resources Information:
Maureen Donovan
Senior Vice President/Human Re-
sources
Bank of New Hampshire

P.O. Box 600
Manchester, NH 03105

Citizens Bank New Hampshire
875 Elm St.
Manchester, NH 03101
603/634-7000

Human Resources Information:
Ellen Sheil
Senior Vice President/Human Resources
Citizens Bank New Hampshire
875 Elm Street, Elm-4-2
Manchester, NH 03101

Fleet Bank of NH
1155 Elm St.
Manchester, NH 03101
603/485-6500

Human Resources Information:
Pat Parker
Vice President/Human Resources
Fleet Bank of NH
1155 Elm St.
Manchester, NH 03101

Tilton

**Providian National Bank (former-
ly First Deposit National Bank)**
295 Main St.
Tilton, NH 03276
603/286-4346

Human Resources Information:
Susan Piper
Director of Human Resources
Providian Bancorp
53 Regional Drive, First Fl.
Concord, NH 03301

New Jersey

Cherry Hill

Commerce Bank, N.A.
1701 Rte. 70 E.
Cherry Hill, NJ 08034
609/751-9000

Human Resources Information:
Rhonda Costello
Vice President and Director/Human
Resources
Commerce Bank, N.A.
Human Resources
1700 Horizon Way
Mount Laurel, NJ 08054
609/222-3080 (fax)

Ewing Township

New Jersey National Bank
370 Scotch Rd.
Ewing Township, NJ 08628
609/771-5700

Human Resources Information:
Vikram Dewan
Executive Vice President/Human Resources
CoreStates Financial Corporation
Center Square, W. Tower
1500 Market St., 39th Fl.
Philadelphia, PA 19102

Jersey City

Fleet Bank
10 Exchange Pl.
Jersey City, NJ 07302
201/547-7000

Human Resources Information:
Rich Greco
Executive Vice President/Human Resources
Fleet Bank
10 Exchange Place, 28th Fl.
Jersey City, NJ 07302

Provident Savings Bank
830 Bergen Ave.
Jersey City, NJ 07306-4599
201/333-1000

Human Resources Information:
Joanne Hynes
Vice President/Human Resources
Provident Savings Bank
830 Bergen Ave.
Jersey City, NJ 07306-4599

Trust Company of New Jersey
35 Journal Square
Jersey City, NJ 07306-4011
201/420-2500

Human Resources Information:
Robert McCarthy
Vice President/Human Resources
Trust Company of New Jersey
35 Journal Square, Ste. 301
Jersey City, NJ 07306-4011

Morristown

Chase Bank
225 South St.
Morristown, NJ 07960-5395
201/285-2484

Human Resources Information:
Linda Verdi
AVP/Employment Division
Chase Bank
4 Campus Drive
First Fl., Employment
Parsippany, NJ 07054
201/734-1061

Old Bridge

Amboy National Bank
3590 U.S. Hwy. 9
Old Bridge, NJ 08857-2894
908/591-8700

Human Resources Information:
Peggy Dembowski
Vice President/Human Resources
Amboy National Bank
P.O. Box 1076
Old Bridge, NJ 08857-2894

Paramus

Hudson City Savings Bank
W. 80 Century Rd.
Paramus, NJ 07652
201/967-1900

Human Resources Information:
Douglas Yingling
Vice President/Personnel Officer
Hudson City Savings Bank
W. 80 Century Rd.
Paramus, NJ 07652

Passaic

Valley National Bank

615 Main Ave.
Passaic, NJ 07055
201/777-1800

Human Resources Information:
Peter G. Verbout
Senior Vice President/Human Resources
Valley National Bank
1455 Valley Road
Wayne, NJ 07470

Plainfield

United National Bank
202 Park Ave.
Plainfield, NJ 07060
908/756-5000

Human Resources Information:
Charles E. Nunn, Jr.
Senior Vice President/Human Resources
United National Bank
1130 Route 22E
P.O. Box 6000
Bridgewater, NJ 08807-0010

Plainsboro Township

Merrill Lynch Bank and Trust Company
800 Scudders Mill Rd.
Plainsboro Township, NJ 08536-1697
609/282-2265

Human Resources Information:
Patrick Walsh
Senior Vice President/Human Resources

Merrill Lynch Bank and Trust Company
P.O. Box 9027
Princeton, NJ 08854
609/282-1400

Princeton

Custodial Trust Company
101 Carnegie Center
Princeton, NJ 08540
609/951-2300

Human Resources Information:
Steve Lacoff
Managing Director/Personnel
The Bear Stearns Company, Inc.
115 S. Jefferson Rd.
Whippany, NJ 07981

Summit Bank
301 Carnegie Center
Princeton, NJ 08543-2066
609/987-3412

Human Resources Information:
James Ferrier
Senior Vice President/Human Resources
Summit Bank
301 Carnegie Center
Princeton, NJ 08540
609/514-1358 (fax)

Union City

Hudson United Bank
3100 Bergenline Ave.
Union City, NJ 07087
201/348-2300

Human Resources Information:
Karen Foley
Senior Vice President/Human Resources
HUBCO, Inc.
1000 MacArthur Blvd.
Mahwah, NJ 07430

Warren

World Savings Bank, FSB
198 Washington Valley Road
Warren, NJ 07059
908/805-9800

Human Resources Information:
Joyce Erickson
Eastern Division HR Manager
World Savings Bank, FSB
377 Hoes Lane
Piscataway, NJ 08854
908/562-0303

West Paterson

Bank of New York (NJ)
385 Rifle Camp Rd.
West Paterson, NJ 07424
201/357-7000

Human Resources Information:
Tom Angers
Senior Vice President/Human Resources
Bank of New York (NJ)
48 Wall Street, Tenth Fl.
New York, NY 10286
973/357-7405

New Mexico

Albuquerque

Bank of America New Mexico, N.A.
201 Third St. NW
Albuquerque, NM 87102
505/889-1300

Human Resources Information:
Virginia Grant
Vice President/Human Resources
Consultant
Bank of America New Mexico, N.A.
P.O. Box 25000
Albuquerque, NM 87125

First Security Bank of New Mexico, N.A.
40 First Plaza
Third and Tijeras NW
Albuquerque, NM 87102-3355
505/765-4000

Human Resources Information:
Carole Herren
Manager of Human Resources
First Security Bank of New Mexico, N.A.
40 First Plaza
Third and Tijeras NW
Albuquerque, NM 87103

Norwest Bank New Mexico, N.A.
200 Lomas NW
Albuquerque, NM 87102
505/765-5000

Human Resources Information:
Attn: Human Resources, MS: 9320

Norwest Bank New Mexico, N.A.
200 Lomas NW
Albuquerque, NM 87102

**Sunwest Bank of Albuquerque,
N.A.**
303 Roma NW
Albuquerque, NM 87102
505/765-2211

Human Resources Information:
Sharon Wright
Senior Vice President/Human Resources
Sunwest Bank of Albuquerque, N.A.
P.O. Box 25500
Albuquerque, NM 87125-0500

New York

Albany

Fleet Bank of New York
69 State St.
Albany, NY 12201
518/447-4100

Human Resources Information:
John R. Madden
Senior Vice President/Human Resources
Fleet Bank of New York
69 State St.
Albany, NY 12207

Key Bank of New York
66 S. Pearl St.
Albany, NY 12207
518/486-8500

Human Resources Information:

Joe Pollino
Senior Vice President/Human Resources
Key Bank of New York
54 State Street, Tenth Fl.
Albany, NY 12207

Binghamton

BSB Bank and Trust Company
58-68 Exchange St.
Binghamton, NY 13902
607/779-2345

Human Resources Information:
Patricia A. Phelps
Vice President/Human Resources
BSB Bank and Trust Company
58-68 Exchange St.
Binghamton, NY 13901

Bronx

North Fork Bank
185 W. 231st St.
Bronx, NY 10463
516/298-5000

Human Resources Information:
George D. Carter
Vice President/Human Resources
North Fork Bank
170 Tulip Ave.
Floral Park, NY 11001

Brooklyn

Crossland Federal Savings Bank
211 Montague Street
Brooklyn, NY 11201
718/858-9100

Human Resources Information:
Lorie Goldstein
SVP and Employment
Counselor/Human Resources
Crossland Federal Savings Bank
1 Hanson Place
Brooklyn, NY 11243
212/525-7575 (fax)

**Dime Savings Bank of Williams-
burg**
209 Havemeyer Street
Brooklyn, NY 11211-6294
718/782-6200

Human Resources Information:
Myles McLoughlin
Assistant Vice President/Human Re-
sources
Dime Savings Bank of Williamsburg
209 Havemeyer Street
Brooklyn, NY 11211

Independence Savings Bank
130 Court St.
Brooklyn, NY 11201
718/624-6620

Human Resources Information:
Rosemary A. Traina
Vice President/Human Resources
Independence Savings Bank
195 Montague St., Twelfth Fl.
Brooklyn, NY 11201

Buffalo

Manufacturers and Traders Trust

Company
1 M&T Plaza, Eleventh Fl.
Buffalo, NY 14203
716/842-4200

Human Resources Information:
Ray E. Logan
Senior Vice President/Human Re-
sources
Manufacturers and Traders Trust
Company
1 M&T Plaza, Eleventh Fl.
Buffalo, NY 14203

Marine Midland Bank
1 Marine Midland Center, 24th Fl.
Buffalo, NY 14203
716/841-2424

Human Resources Information:
F. Christopher McLaughlin
Executive Vice President/Human Re-
sources
Marine Midland Bank
1 Marine Midland Center, 24th Fl.
Buffalo, NY 14203

Canton

Community Bank, N.A.
45-49 Court St.
Canton, NY 13617
315/386-4553

Human Resources Information:
Susan Abott
Vice President and Manager/Human
Resources
Community Bank, N.A.

5790 Widewater Pkwy.
Dewitt, NY 13214
315/445-2282

Fishkill

Pawling Savings Bank
1301 Route 52
Fishkill, NY 12524
914/855-1333

Human Resources Information:
Rose Mary Hyland
Human Resources Manager
Pawling Savings Bank
1301 Route 52
P.O. Box 7000
Fishkill, NY 12524
914/897-7400

Flushing

Queens County Savings Bank
38-25 Main St.
Flushing, NY 11354-5549
718/359-6400

Human Resources Information:
Donald Powell
Vice President/Human Resources
Queens County Savings Bank
38-25 Main St.
Flushing, NY 11354

Garden City

Dime Savings Bank of New York,
FSB
975 Franklin Ave.

Garden City, NY 11530
800/843-3463

Human Resources Information:
Arthur Bennett
Chief Human Resources Officer
Dime Savings Bank of New York,
FSB
EAB Plaza
Tenth Fl., East Tower
Uniondale, NY 11556

Roosevelt Savings Bank
1122 Franklin Ave.
Garden City, NY 11530-1602
516/742-9300

Human Resources Information:
Elaine Cordiello
Vice President/Human Resources
Roosevelt Savings Bank
1122 Franklin Ave.
Garden City, NY 11530-1602

Glens Falls

Evergreen Bank
237 Glen Street
Glens Falls, NY 12801-3507
518/792-1151

Human Resources Information:
Barbara B. Glenn
Director/Human Resources
Evergreen Bank
237 Glen Street
P.O. Box 318
Glens Falls, NY 12801

Goshen

MSB Bank
35 Matthew Street
Goshen, NY 10924
914/294-5194

Human Resources Information:
Jane Matheson
Vice President/Human Resources
MSB Bank
35 Matthew Street
Goshen, NY 10924

Jericho

Chase Bank
200 Jericho Quadrangle
Jericho, NY 11753
516/828-4000

Human Resources Information:
Joan Kish
Vice President/Human Resources
Chase Bank
200 Jericho, First Fl.
Jericho, NY 11753

Lake Success

Astoria Federal Savings (formerly Greater New York Savings Bank)
1 Astoria Federal Plaza
Lake Success, NY 11042
516/327-3000

Human Resources Information:
Attn: Recruiting
Astoria Federal Savings

1 Astoria Federal Plaza
Lake Success, NY 11042

Lockport

Lockport Savings Bank
55 East Ave.
Lockport, NY 14094-3785
716/434-6621

Human Resources Information:
Kathleen P. Monti
Senior Vice President/Human Resources
Lockport Savings Bank
P.O. Box 886
Lockport, NY 14095-0886

Lynbrook

Jamaica Savings Bank, FSB
303 Merrick Rd.
Lynbrook, NY 11563-2574
516/887-7000

Human Resources Information:
John J. Conroy
Senior Vice President/Human Resources
Jamaica Savings Bank, FSB
303 Merrick Rd.
Lynbrook, NY 11563

Mattituck

North Fork Bank
245 Love Lane
Mattituck, NY 11952
516/298-5000

Human Resources Information:
Karen Seelig
Senior Vice President/Human Resources
North Fork Bank
P.O. Box 8914
Melville, NY 11747

New York

Amalgamated Bank of New York
11-15 Union Square
New York, NY 10003
212/255-6200

Human Resources Information:
Joseph Muratore
Vice President/Human Resources
Amalgamated Bank of New York
11-15 Union Square
New York, NY 10003

Apple Bank for Savings
277 Park Ave., 40th Fl.
New York, NY 10172
212/224-6400

Human Resources Information:
Susan B. Goro
Senior Vice President/Human Resources
Apple Bank for Savings
277 Park Ave., 40th Fl.
New York, NY 10172

Atlantic Bank of New York
960 Ave. of the Americas
New York, NY 10001

212/695-5400

Human Resources Information:
Michael Protono
Senior Vice President and
Director/Human Resources
Atlantic Bank of New York
960 Sixth Avenue of the Americas
New York, NY 10001

Bank Leumi Trust Company of New York
579 Fifth Ave., Second Fl.
New York, NY 10017-1917
212/343-5000

Human Resources Information:
Herbert J. Small
Senior Vice President/Human Resources
Bank Leumi Trust Company of New York
579 Fifth Ave., Second Fl.
New York, NY 10017-1917

Bank of New York
48 Wall St.
New York, NY 10286
212/495-1784

Human Resources Information:
Attn: Personnel Department
101 Barclay Street, First Fl.
New York, NY 10286
212/815-4984

Bank of Tokyo Trust Company
1251 Ave of the Americas
New York, NY 10020

212/782-4000

Human Resources Information:
Carol Goldin
Senior Vice President and Manager/Human Resources
Bank of Tokyo Trust Company
1251 Ave of the Americas
New York, NY 10020

Bankers Trust Company
280 Park Ave.
New York, NY 10017
212/250-2500

Human Resources Information:
Mark Bieler
Senior Managing Director/Human Resources
Bankers Trust Company
130 Liberty Street, Twelfth Fl.
New York, NY 10006

Chase Bank
1 Chase Manhattan Plaza, 27th Fl.
New York, NY 10081
212/552-2222

Human Resources Information:
John J. Farrell
Executive Vice President/Human Resources
Chase Bank
270 Park Ave., Eighth Fl.
New York, NY 10017

Citibank, N.A.
399 Park Ave.
New York, NY 10043

212/559-1000

Human Resources Information:
Lawrence Phillips
Senior Human Resources Officer
Citibank, N.A.
153 E. 53rd St.
Citicorp Center, 23rd Fl.
New York, NY 10043

Commercial Bank of New York
301 Park Ave.
New York, NY 10022
212/308-9888

Human Resources Information:
Gerald Grez
Vice President/Human Resources
Commercial Bank of New York
320 Park Ave., Nineteenth Fl.
New York, NY 10022
212/735-0010

Depository Trust Company
55 Water St.
New York, NY 10041-0056
212/898-1200

Human Resources Information:
Tom C. Cardile
Senior Vice President/Human Resources
Depository Trust Company
55 Water St.
New York, NY 10041-0056

East New York Savings Bank
2644 Atlantic Ave.
New York, NY 11207

212/350-2500

Human Resources Information:
David Palmer
Vice President and Director/Human
Resources
East New York Savings Bank
350 Park Ave.
New York, NY 10022

Emigrant Savings Bank
5 E. 42nd St.
New York, NY 10017-6904
212/850-4000

Human Resources Information:
Edward Tully
Senior Vice President/Human Re-
sources Administrator
Emigrant Savings Bank
5 E. 42nd St., Seventh Fl.
New York, NY 10017

European American Bank
120 Broadway
New York, NY 10005
516/766-4650

Human Resources Information:
William Thornton
Senior Vice President and
Director/Human Resources
European American Bank
1 EAB Plaza
Uniondale, NY 11555-2819

Fuji Bank and Trust Company
2 World Trade Center, 82nd Fl.
New York, NY 10048-0001

212/898-2400

Human Resources Information:
Brian Thompson
Senior Vice President/Human Re-
sources
Fuji Bank and Trust Company
2 World Trade Center, 82nd Fl.
New York, NY 10048-0001

GreenPoint Bank
807 Manhattan Ave.
New York, NY 11222-2794
718/706-2900

Human Resources Information:
Tai Cheng
Staffing Manager
GreenPoint Bank
1981 Marcus Ave.
Lake Success, NY 11042

**IBJ Schroder Bank and Trust
Company**
1 State St.
New York, NY 10004-1506
212/858-2000

Human Resources Information:
Julie Jackson
Vice President/Human Resources
IBJ Schroder Bank and Trust Com-
pany
1 State St.
New York, NY 10004

**Industrial Bank of Japan Trust
Company**
245 Park Ave.

New York, NY 10167-0001
212/557-3535

Human Resources Information:
Paul Frank
Senior Vice President/Personnel Director
Industrial Bank of Japan Trust Company
245 Park Ave.
New York, NY 10167

Israel Discount Bank of New York
511 Fifth Ave.
New York, NY 10017-4997
212/551-8500

Human Resources Information:
Jarome Gottlied, Senior Vice President/Human Resources
Roger Maglio, First Vice President/Human Resources
Israel Discount Bank of New York
511 Fifth Ave.
New York, NY 10017

J.P. Morgan
60 Wall Street
New York, NY 10260
212/483-2323

Human Resources Information:
Herbert J. Hefke
Managing Director/Human Resources
J P Morgan
60 Wall Street
New York, NY 10260

LTCB Trust Company
165 Broadway
New York, NY 10006-1404
212/335-4900

Human Resources Information:
Francis Lynch
Joint General Manager
LTCB Trust Company
165 Broadway
New York, NY 10006

Merchants Bank of New York
434 Broadway
New York, NY 10013
212/973-6600

Human Resources Information:
Ruth T. Aimetti
Vice President/Human Resources
Merchants Bank of New York
275 Madison Ave.
New York, NY 10016

Republic National Bank of New York
452 Fifth Ave.
New York, NY 10018-2706
212/525-5000

Safra National Bank of New York
546 Fifth Ave.
New York, NY 10036
212/704-5500

Human Resources Information:
Jeanette Torres
Assistant Vice President and Director/Human Resources

Safra National Bank of New York
546 Fifth Ave.
New York, NY 10036

United States Trust Company of New York
114 W. 47th St.
New York, NY 10036-1532
212/852-1000

Human Resources Information:
Patricia W. McGuire
Managing Director/Human Resources
United States Trust Company of New York
114 W. 47th St.
New York, NY 10036-1532

Norwich

NBT Bank, N.A.
52 S. Broad St.
Norwich, NY 13815
607/337-6000

Human Resources Information:
Jane Neal
Senior Vice President and Director/Human Resources
NBT Bank, N.A.
P.O. Box 351
Norwich, NY 13815-0351

Pittsford

Citibank New York State
99 Garnsey Rd.
Pittsford, NY 14534-4532

716/248-7500

Human Resources Information:
Jeffrey Kendall
Lead Consultant for NY State Business
Citibank New York State
99 Garnsey Rd.
Pittsford, NY 14534-4532

Ridgewood

Ridgewood Savings Bank
71-02 Forest Ave.
Ridgewood, NY 11385-5697
718/240-4800

Human Resources Information:
Norman McNamee
Vice President/Human Resources
Ridgewood Savings Bank
71-02 Forest Ave., Fourth Fl.
Ridgewood, NY 11385-5697

Rochester

Rochester Community Savings Bank
40 Franklin St.
Rochester, NY 14604
716/258-3000

Human Resources Information:
Paula Dolan
Senior Vice President/Human Resources
Rochester Community Savings Bank
235 E. Main St.
Rochester, NY 14604

Roslyn

Roslyn Savings Bank
1400 Old Northern Blvd.
Roslyn, NY 11576-2154
516/621-6000

Human Resources Information:
Arthur W. Toohig
Senior Vice President/Human Resources
Roslyn Savings Bank
1400 Old Northern Blvd.
Roslyn, NY 11576-2154

Schenectady

Trustco Bank, N.A.
320 State St.
Schenectady, NY 12305
518/377-3311

Human Resources Information:
Sheri J. Parvis
Senior Personnel Officer
Trustco Bank, N.A.
192 Erie Blvd.
Schenectady, NY 12305

Staten Island

Richmond County Savings Bank
1214 Castleton Ave.
Staten Island, NY 10310
718/448-2800

Human Resources Information:
Dorothy Episcopia

Vice President/Human Resources
Richmond County Savings Bank
207 Taylor St.
Staten Island, NY 10310

Staten Island Savings Bank
15 Beach St.
Staten Island, NY 10304-2713
718/447-7900

Human Resources Information:
Catherine Arcuri
Assistant Vice President/Human Resources
Staten Island Savings Bank
45 Beach St.
Staten Island, NY 10304-2713

Syracuse

OnBank
101 S. Salina St.
Syracuse, NY 13202-1686
315/424-4400

Human Resources Information:
Thomas Del Duchetto
Vice President/Human Resources
OnBank and Trust Company
6350 Court Street Road
East Syracuse, NY 13057

Utica

Savings Bank of Utica
233 Genesee St.
Utica, NY 13501-2896
315/768-3000

Human Resources Information:
Ursula D. Flagg
Personnel Officer
Savings Bank of Utica
233 Genesee St.
Utica, NY 13501-2896

North Carolina

Charlotte

First Union National Bank
301 S. Tryon St.
Charlotte, NC 28288
704-374-6161

Human Resources Information:
Cheryl A. King, Staffing Specialist
Marye-Pat Kelly, VP/Personnel Planning and Assessment
First Union Corporation
1600 1 First Union Center
301 S. College Street
Charlotte, NC 28288-0953
704/374-2407 (fax)
cheryl.king@firstunion.com
704/374-2409

NationsBank, N.A.
101 S. Tryon Street
Charlotte, NC 28255
704/386-5000

Human Resources Information:
Charles Cooley
Principal Corporate Personnel Offi-
cer
NationsBank, N.A.
100 N. Tryon Street

Charlotte, NC 28255-0001

Concord

**SouthTrust Bank of North Caroli-
na**
40 Cabarrus Ave.
Concord, NC 28025-3452
704/788-3193

Human Resources Information:
Sandi Lewis
Human Resources Director
SouthTrust Bank of North Carolina
8604 Cliff Cameron Drive, Ste. 100
Charlotte, NC 28269

Durham

**Central Carolina Bank and Trust
Company**
111 Corcoran St.
Durham, NC 27701-3231
919/683-7777

Human Resources Information:
Kent Fawcett
Senior Vice President and
Director/Personnel
Central Carolina Bank and Trust
Company
P.O. Box 931
Durham, NC 27702
Attn: MO3-3

Raleigh

**First Citizens Bank and Trust
Company**

239 Fayetteville St.
Raleigh, NC 27604
919/755-7000

Human Resources Information:
Tracey Woods
Employment Manager
First Citizens Bank and Trust Company
2917 Highwood Blvd.
Raleigh, NC 27604

Triangle Bank
4800 Six Forks Road
Raleigh, NC 27609-5245
919/881-0455

Human Resources Information:
Mac Forde
Human Resources Director
Triangle Bank
4300 Glenwood Ave., Fourth Fl.
Raleigh, NC 27612
Ext. 130

Rocky Mount

Centura Bank
134 N. Church St.
Rocky Mount, NC 27804-5402
919/977-4400

Human Resources Information:
Leslie Rutledge, Jr.
Human Resources Division Head
Centura Bank
P.O. Box 1220
Rocky Mount, NC 27802

Whiteville

BB&T Bank (formerly UCB/Southern National)
127 W. Webster St.
Whiteville, NC 28472-4124
910/642-5131
910/914-9060

Human Resources Information:
Timothy R. Davis
Executive Vice President
BB&T Bank
200 W. Second Street
Winston Salem, NC 27101
910/733-2011
910/642-1215 (fax)

Winston-Salem

BB&T Bank (formerly BB&T/Southern National)
200 W. Second St.
Winston-Salem, NC 27101
910/733-2000

Human Resources Information:
Timothy R. Davis
Executive Vice President/Human Resources
BB&T Bank
200 W. Second St.
Winston-Salem, NC 27101

Wachovia Bank
100 N. Main St.
Winston-Salem, NC 27150
910/732-5209

Human Resources Information:
Kenneth L. Fleming
Director of Recruiting
Wachovia Bank
100 N. Main St.
Winston-Salem, NC 27150

North Dakota

Bismarck

Bank of North Dakota
700 E. Main Ave.
Bismarck, ND 58506
701/328-5600

Human Resources Information:
Kathy Ibach
Director/Human Resources and Marketing
Bank of North Dakota
P.O. Box 5509
Bismarck, ND 58506-5509

Fargo

Norwest Bank North Dakota, N.A.
406 Main Ave.
Fargo, ND 58126
701/293-4200

Human Resources Information:
Dale Hellevang
Senior Vice President/Human Resources Manager
Norwest Bank North Dakota, N.A.
406 Main Ave.
Fargo, ND 58126-7030

Ohio

Akron

Bank One, Akron, N.A.
50 S. Main St.
Akron, OH 44308
330/972-1000

Human Resources Information:
Sandra J. Pryor
Northeast Ohio Human Resources Manager
Bank One, Akron, N.A.
50 S. Main St.
Akron, OH 44308
330/972-1515

First Merit Corporation (formerly First National Bank of Ohio)
106 S. Main St.
Akron, OH
330/384-8000

Human Resources Information:
Attn: Human Resources Department
First Merit Corporation
III Cascade Plaza, Ste. 3
Akron, OH 44308

National City Bank, Northeast
1 Cascade Plaza
Akron, OH 44308-1136
330/375-8450

Human Resources Information:
Sally Beth
Vice President/Human Resources
National City Bank, Northeast

1 Cascade Plaza, Ninth Fl.
Akron, OH 44308-1136
330/375-8350

Cincinnati

Bank One, Cincinnati, N.A.
Bank One Towers
8044 Montgomery Rd.
Cincinnati, OH 45236
513/985-5000

Human Resources Information:
Carol Foltz
Vice President and Director/Human
Resources
Bank One, Cincinnati, N.A.
Bank One Towers
8044 Montgomery Rd., Ste. 555
Cincinnati, OH 45236
800/688-8530

Fifth Third Bank
38 Fountain Square Plaza
Cincinnati, OH 45263-0001
513/579-5300

Human Resources Information:
Daniel Keefe
Vice President and Director/Human
Resources
Fifth Third Bank
38 Fountain Square Plaza
Cincinnati, OH 45263

PNC Bank, Ohio, N.A.
201 E. Fifth St.
Cincinnati, OH 45201
513/651-8000

Human Resources Information:
Brian W. Trimborn
Vice President/Human Resources
PNC Bank, Ohio, N.A.
201 E. Fifth St.
Cincinnati, OH 45202

Provident Bank
1 E. Fourth St.
Cincinnati, OH 45202
513/579-2000

Human Resources Information:
Terry E. Henley
Senior Vice President/Human Re-
sources
Provident Bank
801 Linn St.
Cincinnati, OH 45203
Attn: M/S 550E

Star Bank, N.A.
425 Walnut St.
Cincinnati, OH 45202-3912
513/632-4000

Human Resources Information:
Steve Smith
Director of Human Resources
Star Bank, N.A.
425 Walnut St.
Cincinnati, OH 45202-3912
Attn: ML 2020

Cleveland

Bank One, Cleveland, N.A.
600 Superior Ave.

Cleveland, OH 44114
216/781-3333

Human Resources Information:
Sandra J. Pryor
Northeast Ohio Human Resources
Manager
Bank One, Cleveland, N.A.
50 S. Main St.
Akron, OH 44308

Fifth Third Bank of Northeastern Ohio
1404 E. Ninth Street
Cleveland, OH 44114
216/696-5300

Human Resources Information:
Jean Smith
Human Resources Manager
Fifth Third Bank of Northeastern
Ohio
1404 E. Ninth Street
Cleveland, OH 44114

Key Bank
127 Public Square
Cleveland, OH 44114
216/689-3000

Human Resources Information:
Bruce Murphy
Senior Vice President/Human Resources
Key Corp.
127 Public Square
Cleveland, OH 44114
Attn: M/S OH-01-27-0903

Key Bank USA
127 Public Square
Cleveland, OH 44114
800/872-5553

Human Resources Information:
Wendy Worthington, Human Resources Generalist
Key Bank USA
127 Public Square, Twelfth Fl.
Cleveland, OH 44114
Attn: Recruiting
888/539-7247

National City Bank
1900 E. Ninth St.
Cleveland, OH 44114
216/575-2000

Human Resources Information:
Charles Moomah
Senior Vice President/Human Resources
National City Bank
P.O. Box 5756
Cleveland, OH 44114-2042
216/575-2461

Columbus

Bank One, Columbus, N.A.
100 E. Broad St.
Columbus, OH 43271-0160
614/248-5800

Human Resources Information:
Bank One Staffing
Bank One, Columbus, N.A.
800 Brooksedge Drive

Columbus, OH 43271

Fifth Third Bank of Columbus
21 E. State St.
Columbus, OH 43215-3707
614/341-2595

Human Resources Information:
Attn: Human Resources
Fifth Third Bank of Columbus
21 E. State St.
Columbus, OH 43215

Huntington National Bank
41 S. High St.
Columbus, OH 43287
614/480-8300

Human Resources Information:
Attn: Human Resources
Huntington National Bank
41 S. High St.
Columbus, OH 43215
614/480-5627 (jobline)

National City Bank, Columbus
155 E. Broad Street
Columbus, OH 43215-3609
614/463-7100

Human Resources Information:
Terri Kitz
Senior Vice President/Human Re-
sources
National City Bank, Columbus
155 E. Broad Street
Columbus, OH 43251
614/463-7444

Dayton

Bank One, Dayton, N.A.
Kettering Tower
Dayton, OH 45401-1103
513/449-8600

Human Resources Information:
Carol Foltz
Vice President and Director/Human
Resources
Bank One, Dayton, N.A.
Kettering Tower
Dayton, OH 45401-1103

National City Bank, Dayton
6 N. Main St.
Dayton, OH 45412
937/226-2000

Human Resources Information:
Jill Wallace
Vice President/Human Resources
National City Bank, Dayton
6 N. Main St.
Dayton, OH 45412-2000
937/224-6699

Hamilton

**First National Bank of Southwest-
ern Ohio**
300 High St.
Hamilton, OH 45011
513/867-4700

Human Resources Information:
Brian Moriarty
Senior Vice President/Human Re-

sources
First National Bank of Southwestern
Ohio
P.O. Box 476
Hamilton, OH 45012

Lima

Bank One, Lima
121 W. High Street
Lima, OH 45801-4340
419/221-5000

Human Resources Information:
Brendala Anspaugh
Senior Vice President/Human Resources
Bank One, Lima
121 W. High Street
Lima, OH 45801
419/221-5033

Newark

The Park National Bank
50 N. Third Street
Newark, OH 43055-5548
614/349-8451

Human Resources Information:
Human Resources Department
The Park National Bank
P.O. Box 3500
Newark, OH 43058
Attn: Donna Stasel

Piqua

Fifth Third Bank of Western Ohio

123 Market St.
Piqua, OH 45356-1117
513/773-1212

Human Resources Information:
Sharon R. Haney
Vice President/Human Resources
Fifth Third Bank of Western Ohio
123 Market Street
Piqua, OH 45356

Salineville

The Citizens Banking Company
10 E. Main Street
Salineville, OH 43945-1134
330/679-2328

Human Resources Information:
Nancy Trombetta
Vice President/Human Resources Director
The Citizens Banking Company
10 E. Main Street
Salineville, OH 43945

Toledo

Fifth Third Bank of Northwestern Ohio
606 Madison Ave.
Toledo, OH 43604-1102
419/259-7890

Human Resources Information:
Carol J. McAnall
Vice President/Personnel
Fifth Third Bank of Northwestern Ohio

606 Madison Ave.
Toledo, OH 43604

National City Bank, Northwest
405 Madison Ave.
Toledo, OH 43604-1207
419/259-7700

Human Resources Information:
Karen Matthews
Human Resources Administrator
National City Bank, Northwest
405 Madison Ave., Sixth Fl.
Toledo, OH 43604

Warren

The Second National Bank of Warren
108 Main Ave., SW
Warren, OH 44481-1010
330/841-0123

Human Resources Information:
Karen Herrmann
Human Resources Manager
The Second National Bank of Warren
108 Main Ave., SW
Warren, OH 44482

Youngstown

Bank One, Youngstown, N.A.
6 Federal Plaza W.
Youngstown, OH 44503-1410
330/744-5041

Human Resources Information:

Sandra Pryor
Northeast Ohio Human Resources
Manager
Bank One, Youngstown, N.A.
50 S. Main St.
Akron, OH 44308

Oklahoma

Oklahoma City

BancFirst
101 N. Broadway
Oklahoma City, OK 73102-8405
405/270-1000

Human Resources Information:
Mike Rogers
Vice President/Human Resources
BancFirst
P.O. Box 26788
Oklahoma City, OK 73126-0788

Bank One (formerly Liberty Bank and Trust Company of Oklahoma)
100 N. Broadway
Oklahoma City, OK 73102
405/231-6000

Human Resources Information:
Daniel L. Shelton
Senior Vice President/Human Resources
Bank One
100 N. Broadway
Oklahoma City, OK 73102
405/231-6145 (fax)

NationsBank (formerly Boatmen's

First National Bank of Oklahoma)
211 N. Robinson
Oklahoma City, OK 73102-7404
405/230-4000

Human Resources Information:
LeAnne Edwards
Associate Center Manager
NationsBank
Trans America Square
401 N. Tryon Street
Charlotte, NC 28255
MC: NC1-021-02-02
800/866-9999 Bank Associate Center

Tulsa

Bank of Oklahoma, N.A.
Bank of Oklahoma Tower
Tulsa, OK 74103
918/588-6000

Human Resources Information:
Attn: Human Resources Department
Bank of Oklahoma, N.A.
P.O. Box 2300
Tulsa, OK 74192

Bank One (formerly Liberty Bank and Trust Company of Tulsa)
15 E. Fifth St.
Tulsa, OK 74103
918/586-1000

Human Resources Information:
Carol Allbritton-Waugh
Administrator/Employment
Bank One

P.O. Box 1
Tulsa, OK 74193-0001

NationsBank (formerly Bank IV Oklahoma, N.A.)
515 S. Boulder Ave.
Tulsa, OK 74103-4207
918/591-8444

Human Resources Information:
Jane Lambeth
Senior Vice President and
Director/Human Resources
NationsBank
515 S. Boulder Ave., Tenth Fl.
Tulsa, OK 74103-4207
918/591-8394

Oregon

Portland

Bank of America Oregon
121 SW Morrison St.
Portland, OR 97204
503/275-1429

Human Resources Information:
Diane Corra
Vice President/Recruiting Resources
Bank of America Oregon
800 Fifth Ave., 33rd Fl.
Seattle, WA 98104
503/275-1155

Key Corp (formerly Key Bank of Oregon)
1211 SW Fifth Ave.
Portland, OR 97204

503/790-7500

Human Resources Information:
Attn: Human Resources Department
Key Corp
1211 SW Fifth Ave., Ste. 550
Portland, OR 97204

U.S. Bank
111 SW Fifth Ave.
Portland, OR 97204
503/275-7393

Human Resources Information:
Mike Jennings
Executive Vice President/Human Resources
U.S. Bancorp
P.O. Box 8837
Portland, OR 97208
503/275-3650 or 800/524-0129

Wells Fargo Bank
1300 SW Fifth Ave.
Portland, OR 97201-5667
800/869-3557

Human Resources Information:
Katie Iverson
Senior Vice President/Regional HR Manager
Wells Fargo Bank
1300 SW Fifth Ave.
Portland, OR 97201
Attn: MAC 6101131
503/226-1701 (fax)

<u>**Pennsylvania**</u>

Altoona

Mid-State Bank and Trust Company
1130 Twelfth Ave.
Altoona, PA 16601-3428
814/946-6600

Human Resources Information:
Deborah C. Locke
Manager/Human Resources Services
Mid-State Bank and Trust Company
1331 Twelfth Ave., First Fl.
Altoona, PA 16601

Avondale

First Union National Bank
102 Pennsylvania Ave.
Avondale, PA 19311
201/565-3200

Human Resources Information:
William Karmen
Executive Vice President/Human Resources
First Union National Bank
550 Broad St.
Newark, NJ 07102

Boyertown

National Penn Bank
Philadelphia and Reading Avenues,
First Fl.
Boyertown, PA 19512
610/367-6001

Human Resources Information:

Sharon L. Weaver
Senior Vice President/Human Resources
National Penn Bank
P.O. Box 547
Boyertown, PA 19512-0547

Flourtown

Firstrust Savings Bank
1800 Bethlehem Pike
Flourtown, PA 19031
215/722-2000

Human Resources Information:
Edward Benz
Senior Vice President/Corporate Administration
Firstrust Savings Bank
1931 Cottman Ave.
Philadelphia, PA 19111
215/728-8422

Greensburg

Mellon Bank, N.A.
1 N. Main St.
Greensburg, PA 15601
412/832-5900

Human Resources Information:
Mellon Bank, N.A.
1 Mellon Bank Center
Room 700
Pittsburgh, PA 15258
412/234-5000

Greenville

First National Bank of Pennsylvania
166 Main St.
Greenville, PA 16125
412/588-6770

Human Resources Information:
Kevin Bennett
Personnel Officer
First National Bank of Pennsylvania
4140 E. State St.
Hermitage, PA 16148

Harrisburg

Dauphin Deposit (Holding Company: Allied Irish Bancshares/First Maryland Bancorp)
213 Market St.
Harrisburg, PA 17105
717/255-2121

Human Resources Information:
Jenny Pritsch
Human Resources Central Division Manager
Dauphin Deposit Corporation
213 Market St.
Harrisburg, PA 17105
717/255-2385
717/237-6153 (fax)

Diane Murphy
Director/Human Resources
First Maryland Bancorp
Baltimore, MD 21201
Attn: M/C 109-803

Haverford

Jefferson Bank
551 W. Lancaster Ave.
Haverford, PA 19041-1419
610/525-9865

Human Resources Information:
Mary Ciarone
Vice President/Human Resources
Jefferson Bank
2 Jefferson Bank Center
Downingtown, PA 19335-0901
610/269-6500

Horsham

Frankford Bank, N.A.
601 Dresher Rd.
Horsham, PA 19044
215/956-7000

Human Resources Information:
Margaret Stairiker
Director/Human Resources
Frankford Bank, N.A.
601 Dresher Rd., Third Fl.
Horsham, PA 19044

Indiana

Deposit Bank
601 Philadelphia Street
Indiana, PA 15701-3903
412/349-3400

Human Resources Information:
David Alberg
Vice President/Human Resources
Deposit Bank

P.O. Box 607A
Dubois, PA 15801

S&T Bank
800 Philadelphia St.
Indiana, PA 15701
412/349-2900

Human Resources Information:
Samuel D. Scott
Vice President/Human Resources
S&T Bank
324 N. Fourth St.
Indiana, PA 15701

Johnstown

Johnstown Bank and Trust Company
532-534 Main Street
Johnstown, PA 15901-2093
814/532-3000

Human Resources Information:
William P. McKinney
Vice President/Human Resources
Johnstown Bank and Trust Company
532-534 Main Street
Johnstown, PA 15901

United States National Bank in Johnstown
216 Franklin St.
Johnstown, PA 15901
814/533-5300

Human Resources Information:
Michael Komara
Vice President/Human Resources

United States National Bank in Johnstown
P.O. Box 520
Johnstown, PA 15907

USBANCORP Trust Company
216 Franklin St.
Johnstown, PA 15901-1887
814/533-5397

Human Resources Information:
Michael Komara
Vice President/Human Resources
USBANCORP Trust Company
P.O. Box 520
Johnstown, PA 15907

Lancaster

Fulton Bank
1 Penn Square, 7 N. Queen St.
Lancaster, PA 17602-2823
717/291-2411

Human Resources Information:
Craig H. Hill
Senior Vice President and
Director/Human Resources
Fulton Bank
P.O. Box 4887
Lancaster, PA 17602

Lititz

Farmers First Bank
9 E. Main Street
Lititz, PA 17543-1926
717/626-4721

Human Resources Information:
Edward Balderston, Jr.
Senior Vice President/Administrative
Services
Farmers First Bank
24 N. Cedar Street
Lititz, PA 17543

First Western Bank, N.A.
101 E. Washington St
New Castle, PA 16101-3725
412/652-5511

Human Resources Information:
Rich Rausch
Vice President and Director/Human
Resources
First Western Bank, N.A.
101 E. Washington St
New Castle, PA 16103

Philadelphia

Beneficial Mutual Savings Bank
1200 Chestnut St.
Philadelphia, PA 19107
215/864-6000

Human Resources Information:
Joseph Vetter
Vice President/Personnel Director
Beneficial Mutual Savings Bank
White Building, Attn: Personnel
Dept., Fourth Fl.
105 S. Twelfth St.
Philadelphia, PA 19107

CoreStates Bank, N.A.
Broad and Chestnut Streets

Philadelphia, PA 19101
215/973-3100

Human Resources Information:
Vikram Dewan
Executive Vice President/Human Resources
CoreStates Financial Corporation
Center Square, West Tower
1500 Market St., 39th Fl.
Philadelphia, PA 19102
215/786-7105

Pittsburgh

National City Bank of Pennsylvania
300 Fourth Ave.
Pittsburgh, PA 15278
412/644-8111

Human Resources Information:
National City Bank of Pennsylvania
Attn: Human Resources Department
20 Stanwix Street
Pittsburgh, PA 15222
412/644-8111

PNC Bank
1 PNC Plaza
Fifth and Wood Streets
Pittsburgh, PA 15265
412/762-2000

Human Resources Information:
Resume Coordinator
PNC Bank
620 Liberty Ave.
Pittsburgh, PA 15222

412/762-2256
412/768-4146 (fax)
resumes@pncbank.com

Pottsville

Pennsylvania National Bank and Trust Company
1 S. Centre St.
Pottsville, PA 11354-5549
717/622-4200

Human Resources Information:
Martina A. Roos
Vice President/Human Resources
Pennsylvania National Bank and
Trust Company
1 S. Centre St.
P.O. Box 1150
Pottsville, PA 17901

Williamsport

Northern Central Bank
102 W. Fourth St.
Williamsport, PA 17701
717/326-2611

Human Resources Information:
Thomas P. Hurwitz
Vice President/Human Resources
Northern Central Bank
P.O. Box 3068
Williamsport, PA 17701

Wyomissing

Sovereign Bank (formerly Bankers Savings)

1134 Berkshire Blvd.
Wyomissing, PA 19610
732/442-4100

Human Resources Information:
Team Member Services
Sovereign Bank
P.O. Box 727
Toms River, NJ 08724

York

York Bank and Trust Company
107 W. Market St.
York, PA 17405
717/843-8651

Human Resources Information:
Gary Shaffer
Vice President/Human Resources
Manager
York Bank and Trust Company
1123 N. George St.
York, PA 17404

Rhode Island

Providence

Citizens Savings Bank
1 Citizens Plaza
Providence, RI 02903-1339
401/456-7000

Human Resources Information:
Cal Ballard
Vice President/Human Resources
Citizens Savings Bank
1 Citizens Drive

Riverside, RI 02915

Citizens Trust Company
1 Citizens Plaza
Providence, RI 02903-1339
401/456-7000

Human Resources Information:
Cal Ballard
Vice President/Human Resources
Citizens Trust Company
1 Citizens Drive
Riverside, RI 02915

Fleet Bank
111 Westminster Street
Providence, RI 02903
401/278-6000

Human Resources Information:
Fleet Bank
Fleet Resume Acceptance Center
111 Westminster Street
Providence, RI 02903
401/278-3489 (fax)
resumes@fleet.com
http://www.fleet.com

Rhode Island Hospital Trust National Bank
1 Hospital Trust Plaza
Providence, RI 02903-2401
401/278-8000

Human Resources Information:
John Cassidy
Senior Vice President/Human Resources
Rhode Island Hospital Trust National

Bank
15 Westminster St.
Providence, RI 02903-2401

South Carolina

Columbia

**First Citizens Bank and Trust
Company of South Carolina**
1230 Main St
Columbia, SC 29201-3248
803/771-8700

Human Resources Information:
Carnie Hipp
Senior Vice President/Human Re-
sources Director
First Citizens Bank and Trust Com-
pany of South Carolina
P.O. Box 29
Columbia, SC 29202

**Wachovia Bank of South Carolina,
N.A.**
1426 Main St.
Columbia, SC 29226
803/765-3000

Human Resources Information:
Jeffrey R. Scott
Senior Vice President/Human Re-
sources
Wachovia Bank of South Carolina,
N.A.
1426 Main St.
Columbia, SC 29226
803/765-4333 (fax)

Greenville

BB&T of South Carolina
301 College St.
Greenville, SC 29601
864/242-8026

Human Resources Information:
Pat Mitchell, Vice President/Human
Resources
Annette Whelchel, Employment Spe-
cialist
BB&T of South Carolina
P.O. Box 408
Greenville, SC 29602

Carolina First Bank
102 S. Main St.
Greenville, SC 29601-2711
864/255-7900

Human Resources Information:
Melvin Sinclair
Senior Vice President/Human Re-
sources
Carolina First Bank
200 E. Camperdown Way
P.O. Box 1029
Greenville, SC 29601

**First Union National Bank of
South Carolina**
1 Shelter Centre
Greenville, SC 29601-2127
864/255-8000

Human Resources Information:
Julie Sizer
VP/Human Resources and Relation-

ship Manager
First Union National Bank of South
Carolina
P.O. Box 1329
Greenville, SC 29602

Sumter

National Bank of South Carolina
1 Broad St.
Sumter, SC 29150
803/778-8550

Human Resources Information:
Lott L. Pruitt
Senior Vice President/Human Re-
sources
National Bank of South Carolina
P.O. Drawer 1457
Columbia, SC 29202

South Dakota

Sioux Falls

Citibank South Dakota, N.A.
701 E. 60th St. N.
Sioux Falls, SD 57117
605/331-2626

Human Resources Information:
Jim Coyne
Human Resources Director
Citibank South Dakota, N.A.
701 E. 60th St. N.
Sioux Falls, SD 57117
Attn: 3105

First Bank of South Dakota, N.A.

141 N. Main Ave.
Sioux Falls, SD 57102
605/339-8600

Human Resources Information:
Sharon Schroeder
Human Resources Manager
First Bank of South Dakota, N.A.
P.O. Box 5308
Sioux Falls, SD 57117-5308

Hurley State Bank
811 E. Tenth St.
Sioux Falls, SD 57103
605/336-5661

Human Resources Information:
Renee Storm
Human Resources Manager
Hurley State Bank
811 E. Tenth St.
Sioux Falls, SD 57103

Norwest Bank South Dakota, N.A.
101 N. Phillips Ave.
Sioux Falls, SD 57102-0543
605/339-7332

Human Resources Information:
Charles J. Janssen
Senior Vice President/Human Re-
sources
Norwest Bank South Dakota, N.A.
101 N. Phillips Ave., Ste. 200
P.O. Box 5128
Sioux Falls, SD 57117-5128

Tennessee

Chattanooga

AmSouth Bank of Tennessee
601 Market Center
Chattanooga, TN 37402
423/756-4600

Human Resources Information:
Shirley Brown
Personnel Director
AmSouth Bank of Tennessee
601 Market Center
Chattanooga, TN 37402

SunTrust Bank
736 Market St.
Chattanooga, TN 37402-4803
423/757-3011

Human Resources Information:
Patricia P. Hyde
Senior Vice President/Human Resources
SunTrust Bank
P.O. Box 1638
Chattanooga, TN 37401
M/S: Human Resources-MO820

Knoxville

SunTrust Bank, East Tennessee, N.A.
700 E. Hill Ave.
Knoxville, TN 37915-2562
423/544-2509

Human Resources Information:
Catherine H. Dodson
Senior Vice President/Human Resources
SunTrust Bank, East Tennessee, N.A.
700 E. Hill Ave.
Knoxville, TN 37915-2562

Memphis

First Tennessee Bank, N.A.
165 Madison Ave.
Memphis, TN 38103
901/523-4444

Human Resources Information:
Attn: Employment Services
First Tennessee Bank, N.A.
Personnel Division
P.O. Box 84
Memphis, TN 38101-8460

National Bank of Commerce
1 Commerce Square
Memphis, TN 38150-0002
901/523-3434

Human Resources Information:
Karen Allen
Vice President and Employment Assistant
National Bank of Commerce
Human Resources
1 Commerce Square, Sixth Fl.
Memphis, TN 38150

NationsBank (formerly Boatmen's Bank of Tennessee)
6060 Poplar Ave.
Memphis, TN 38119
901/433-6200

Human Resources Information:
Janice Russel
Personnel Manager
NationsBank
6060 Poplar Ave., Ste. 410
Memphis, TN 38119
901/541-8650

Union Planters National Bank
6200 Poplar Ave.
Memphis, TN 38119
901/580-6000

Human Resources Information:
John Oakes
Director/Corporate Human Resources
Union Planters Corporation
7130 Goodlett Farms Pkwy. - A1E
Cordova, TN 38018

Nashville

First American National Bank
First American Center
Nashville, TN 37237-0602
615/748-2000

Human Resources Information:
Melissa Buffington
Executive Vice President and Director/Human Resources
First American National Bank
300 Union Street
Nashville, TN 37237-1704

First Union National Bank of Tennessee

First Union Tower
150 Fourth Ave. N.
Nashville, TN 37219-2419
615/251-9200

Human Resources Information:
Gari Cowan
Vice President/Human Resources Manager
First Union National Bank of Tennessee
First Union Tower
150 Fourth Ave. N., Third Fl.
Nashville, TN 37219-2419

NationsBank of Tennessee
1 NationsBank Plaza
Nashville, TN 37239-1697
615/749-3333

Human Resources Information:
Attn: Corporate Recruiter
NationsBank of Tennessee
1 NationsBank Plaza, Fifth Fl.
Nashville, TN 37239-1694
M/C: TN1-100-05-15

SunTrust Bank
201 Fourth Ave. N.
Nashville, TN 37219
615/748-4000

Human Resources Information:
Thomas Van Etten
First Vice President/Human Resources
SunTrust Bank
P.O. Box 305110
Nashville, TN 37230-5110

Union Planters Bank of Middle Tennessee
401 Union St.
Nashville, TN 37219-8958
615/244-0571

Human Resources Information:
Jan Walker
Vice President/Human Resources
Union Planters Bank of Middle Tennessee
401 Union St., Ninth Fl.
Nashville, TN 37219-8958

Texas

Amarillo

Amarillo National Bank
Plaza One, Fifth and Taylor
Amarillo, TX 79101-1566
806/378-8000

Human Resources Information:
Attn: Personnel
Amarillo National Bank
P.O. Box 1
Amarillo, TX 79105-0001

NationsBank (formerly Boatmen's First National Bank of Amarillo)
Eighth and Taylor
Amarillo, TX 79180
806/378-1400

Human Resources Information:
Stan Harrison
Senior Vice President/Human Resources
NationsBank
P.O. Box 1331
Amarillo, TX 79180
806/378-1887

Brownsville

Mercantile Bank
835 E. Levee
Brownsville, TX 78520-5149
210/546-2421

Human Resources Information:
Genie Trevino
Vice President/Human Resources
Mercantile Bank
P.O. Box 2219
Brownsville, TX 78522-2219

Channelview

Prime Bank
811 Sheldon Rd.
Channelview, TX 77530-3511
713/209-6200

Human Resources Information:
Karen Sue Kirk
Personnel Manager
Prime Bank
P.O. Box 21129
Houston, TX 77226-1129
713/209-6099 (fax)

Dallas

Bank One, Texas, N.A.
1717 Main St., Sixth Fl.

Dallas, TX 75201
214/290-2000

Human Resources Information:
R. Philip Kenny
Director/Human Resources
Bank One, Dallas
1717 Main St., Sixth Fl.
Dallas, TX 75201
Attn: Human Resources

Comerica Bank Texas
1909 Woodall Rogers Freeway
Dallas, TX 75201-2239
214/841-1400

Human Resources Information:
Lisa J. Murray
Senior Vice President/Human Resources
Comerica Bank Texas
P.O. Box 650282
Dallas, TX 75265-0282
Attn: 6507

NationsBank of Texas, N.A.
901 Main St., 47th Fl.
Dallas, TX 75202
214/508-6262

Human Resources Information:
Carl Melella
Senior Vice President/Personnel
NationsBank of Texas, N.A.
901 Main St., 47th Fl.
Dallas, TX 75202
214/508-1443

El Paso

Norwest Bank El Paso
221 N. Kansas
El Paso, TX 79901
915/532-9922

Human Resources Information:
Carol Nichols
Vice President and Manager/Human Resources
Norwest Bank El Paso
P.O. Box 1072
El Paso, TX 79958
915/546-4743

Ft. Worth

Norwest Bank (formerly Central Bank and Trust)
777 W. Rosedale
Ft. Worth, TX 76104-4627
817/347-8800

Human Resources Information:
Sandra Walker
West Texas Vice President/Human Resources
Norwest Bank
777 W. Rosedale
Ft. Worth, TX 76104
817/347-8129

Houston

Compass Bank, Houston
24 Greenway Plaza, Ste. 1402
Houston, TX 77046-2401
713/621-3336

Human Resources Information:
Larry Lowers
Senior Vice President/Human Resources
Compass Bank, Houston
P.O. Box 4444
Houston, TX 77210-4444
713/831-5693

Southwest Bank of Texas
4295 San Felipe
Houston, TX 77027
713/235-8800

Human Resources Information:
Kim Zabin
Vice President/Human Resources Director
Southwest Bank of Texas
P.O. Box 27459
Houston, TX 77227-7459

Texas Commerce Bank, N.A.
712 Main St.
Houston, TX 77002
713/236-4865

Human Resources Information:
Ann V. Rogers
Director/Human Resources
Texas Commerce Bank, N.A.
P.O. Box 2558
Houston, TX 77252-8029

Wells Fargo Bank (Texas)
Houston Central
1000 Louisiana St.
Houston, TX 77002-5008
713/250-1911

Human Resources Information:
Ken Jernigan
Vice President and Manager/Human Resources
Wells Fargo Bank (Texas)
Houston Central
1000 Louisiana Street
Houston, TX 77002
713/250-1666

Irving

Bank of America Texas, N.A.
1925 W. John Carpenter Freeway
Irving, TX 75063-3297
214/444-5555

Human Resources Information:
Bill Crozier
Senior Vice President/Human Resources
Bank of America Texas, N.A.
P.O. Box 619005
Dallas, TX 75261-9005

Laredo

International Bank of Commerce
1200 San Bernardo St.
Laredo, TX 78040-6301
210/722-7611

Human Resources Information:
Rosalinda Ramirez
Vice President/Human Resources
International Bank of Commerce
P.O. Drawer 1359
Laredo, TX 78040

Laredo National Bank
700 San Bernardo St.
Laredo, TX 78040-5025
210/723-1151

Human Resources Information:
Javier Lozano
Senior Vice President/Human Resources
Laredo National Bank
P.O. Box 59
Laredo, TX 78042

Lubbock

Norwest Bank Texas, N.A.
1500 Broadway
Lubbock, TX 79401
806/765-8861

Human Resources Information:
Patsy Martin
SVP/Texas Regional Human Resources Manager
Norwest Bank Texas, N.A.
16414 San Pedro, Ste. 800
San Antonio, TX 78232-9770
210/856-8827

McAllen

Texas State Bank
3900 N. Tenth Street
McAllen, TX 78501-1719
210/631-5401

Human Resources Information:
Gary Gulbrandsen

First Vice President/Human Resources
Texas State Bank
P.O. Box 4797
McAllen, TX 78502

San Antonio

Frost National Bank
100 W. Houston St.
San Antonio, TX 78296
210/220-4011

Human Resources Information:
Jim Eckel
Senior Vice President/Personnel
Frost National Bank
P.O. Box 1600
San Antonio, TX 78296

Victoria

Norwest Bank Texas, South Central
1 O'Connor Plaza
Victoria, TX 77902
512/573-5151

Human Resources Information:
Patsy Martin
SVP/Texas Regional Human Resources Manager
Norwest Bank Texas, South Central
16414 San Pedro, Ste. 800
San Antonio, TX 78232-9770
210/856-8827

Utah

Ogden

First Security Bank of Utah, N.A.
2404 Washington Blvd.
Ogden, UT 84401
801/626-9500

Human Resources Information:
David Edmunds
Vice President/Human Resources
First Security Bank of Utah, N.A.
381 E. Broadway, Garden Level
Salt Lake City, UT 84111

Salt Lake City

Bank One, Utah, N.A.
185 S. State St.
Salt Lake City, UT 84111
801/481-5000

Human Resources Information:
Kathy Brown
Human Resources Manager
Bank One, Utah, N.A.
50 W. Broadway, Ste. 506
Salt Lake City, UT 84101

Key Bank of Utah
Key Bank Tower
50 S. Main St., Ste.1901
Salt Lake City, UT 84144-0452
801/535-1000

Human Resources Information:
Tina A. Moerer
Vice President/Human Resources
State Manager
Key Bank of Utah

Key Bank Tower
50 S. Main St., Ste.1901
Salt Lake City, UT 84114
801/535-1040

Zions First National Bank
1 S. Main St.
Salt Lake City, UT 84111
801/524-4711

Human Resources Information:
Richard Crandall
Vice President/Human Resources Director
Zions Bancorporation
1 S. Main Street, Ste. 800
Salt Lake City, UT 84111

Sandy

MountainWest Financial Corporation
855 E. 9400 South
Sandy, UT 84094
801/566-4161

Human Resources Information:
Karen Dworniczek
Human Resources Manager
MountainWest Financial Corporation
280 W. 10200 S.
Sandy, UT 84070-4154

Vermont

Brattleboro

Vermont National Bank
100 Main St.

Brattleboro, VT 05301-3032
802/257-7151

Human Resources Information:
Kathleen K. Brooks
Vice President/Human Resources
Vermont National Bank
P.O. Box 804
Brattleboro, VT 05302

Burlington

Chittenden Trust Company
2 Burlington Square
Burlington, VT 05401-4442
802/658-4000

Human Resources Information:
Attn: Human Resources Department
Chittenden Trust Bank
2 Burlington Square
Burlington, VT 05402

Virginia

Charlottesville

**Wachovia Corporation (formerly
Jefferson National Bank)**
123 E. Main St.
Charlottesville, VA 22902-5283
804/972-1100

Human Resources Information:
Susan Stafford
Senior Vice President and
Director/Human Resources
Wachovia Corporation
P.O. Box 711

Charlottesville, VA 22902

Falls Church

First Virginia Bank
6400 Arlington Blvd., Seventh Fl..
Falls Church, VA 22042-2336
703/241-4000

Human Resources Information:
Clifford Wilson
Vice President/Human Resources
First Virginia Bank
6400 Arlington Blvd., Seventh Fl..
Falls Church, VA 22042-2336

McLean

Riggs Bank
6805 Old Dominion Drive
McLean, VA 22101
703/506-2706

Human Resources Information:
Annie Knight
Manager/Retail Staff Planning
Riggs Bank
6805 Old Dominion Drive, Second
Fl.
McLean, VA 22101
Attn: VA07
202/835-0318

Richmond

Crestar Bank
919 E. Main St.
Richmond, VA 23219
804/782-5000

Human Resources Information:
James Kelley
Senior Vice President/Human Resources
Crestar Bank
P.O. Box 26665
Richmond, VA 23261
804/270-8880
Fax resumes to: 804/270-8828

First Union (formerly Signet Bank/Virginia)
7 N. Eighth St.
Richmond, VA 23219
804/747-2000

Human Resources Information:
H. Nathanial Taylor
Executive Vice President/Human Resources
First Union
7 N. Eighth St.
Richmond, VA 23219
800/388-8388 (HR Service Center)

Wachovia Corporation (formerly Central Fidelity National Bank)
Central Fidelity Bank Bldg.
Richmond, VA 23219
804/782-4000

Human Resources Information:
Charlene Meinhard
Human Resources Manager
Wachovia Corporation
1021 E. Cary Street
Richmond, VA 23219

Roanoke

First Union National Bank of Virginia
201 S. Jefferson
Roanoke, VA 24011
540/563-7000

Human Resources Information:
David H. Furman
Vice President/Human Resources Manager
First Union National Bank of Virginia
1970 Chain Bridge Rd., Fourth Fl.
McLean, VA 22102
703/760-6737

Washington

Seattle

Key Bank of Washington
Corporate Office
109 Pacific Ave.
Seattle, WA 98124
206/684-6550
800/305-5292

Human Resources Information:
Bob Haas, NW Region Executive
Sandy Hedington, Vice President/Human Resources
Key Bank of Washington
P.O. Box 90
Seattle, WA 98111

SeaFirst Bank
701 Fifth Ave.

Seattle, WA 98124
206/358-3000

Human Resources Information:
Attn: Recruiting Resources
SeaFirst Bank
P.O. Box 3977
Seattle, WA 98124

U.S. Bank of Washington, N.A.
1420 Fifth Ave.
Seattle, WA 98101-2391
206/344-3795
800/524-0129

Human Resources Information:
Linda Sincoff
Human Resources Manager
U.S. Bank of Washington, N.A.
P.O. Box 720
Seattle, WA 98111
M/S: WWH-631
206/344-3619

Washington Mutual Bank
1201 Third Ave.
Seattle, WA 98101
206/461-2000

Human Resources Information:
M. Lynn Ryder
Senior Vice President/Human Re-
sources
Washington Mutual Bank
1201 Third Ave.
Seattle, WA 98101
M/S: WMT1501

Spokane

Washington Trust Bank
717 W. Sprague Ave.
Spokane, WA 99204-2127
509/353-4122

Human Resources Information:
Drew MacAfee
Senior Vice President/Operations
Administration
Washington Trust Bank
P.O. Box 2127
Spokane, WA 99210

Tacoma

Key Bank of Washington
1119 Pacific Ave.
Tacoma, WA 98102-4374
253/305-7750
800/539-8189

Human Resources Information:
Debra McCormick
Human Resources Manager
Key Bank of Washington
P.O. Box 11500
Tacoma, WA 98411
Attn: M/C WA-31-10-5348

West Virginia

Charleston

Huntington National Bank of West Virginia
1 Commerce Square
Charleston, WV 25322
304/348-5000

Human Resources Information:
Richard D. Wallace
Vice President/Human Resources
Huntington National Bank of West
Virginia
P.O. Box 633
Charleston, WV 25322

One Valley Bank, N.A.
1 Valley Square
Charleston, WV 25301
304/348-7000

Human Resources Information:
Bernice Day Deen
Senior Vice President/Human Re-
sources Division Head
1 Valley Bank, N.A.
P.O. Box 1793
Charleston, WV 25326

Huntington

Bank One, West Virginia, N.A.
1000 Fifth Ave.
Huntington, WV 25701
304/526-4200

Human Resources Information:
Sandra Fenger
State Vice President/Human Re-
sources Director
Bank One, West Virginia, N.A.
P.O. Box 179
Huntington, WV 25706

Parkersburg

United National Bank
514 Market St.
Parkersburg, WV 26101
304/424-8800

Human Resources Information:
Jack C. Stokes
Senior Vice President/Human Re-
sources
United National Bank
P.O. Box 1508
Parkersburg, WV 26102

Wisconsin

Green Bay

Associated Bank Green Bay, N.A.
200 N. Adams St.
Green Bay, WI 54301
920/433-3200

Human Resources Information:
Pat A. O'Keefe
Vice President/Human Resources Di-
rector
Associated Bank Green Bay, N.A.
P.O. Box 19006
Green Bay, WI 54307-9006

Madison

Firstar Bank Madison, N.A.
1 S. Pinckney St.
Madison, WI 53703-2808
608/252-4000

Human Resources Information:
Jennifer N. Kramer

First Vice President and Director/Human Resources
Firstar Bank Madison, N.A.
Capital Square Office
1 S. Pinckney Street
Madison, WI 53703

M&I Bank
1 W. Main St.
Madison, WI 53703-3327
608/238-9373

Human Resources Information:
James Harrison
Senior Vice President/Human Resources
M&I Madison Bank
1 W. Main St.
Madison, WI 53703

Milwaukee

Bank One, Milwaukee, N.A.
111 E. Wisconsin Ave.
Milwaukee, WI 53202-4803
414/765-3000

Human Resources Information:
Michael E. Leske
Senior Vice President and
Director/Human Resources
Bank One, Milwaukee, N.A.
111 E. Wisconsin Ave., Twelfth Fl.
Milwaukee, WI 53202-4803

First Bank, N.A.
201 W. Wisconsin Ave.
Milwaukee, WI 53259-0001
414/227-6000

Human Resources Information:
Mary Ellen DeHaven
Vice President/Human Resources
First Bank, N.A.
201 W. Wisconsin Ave.
Milwaukee, WI 53259
414/227-5930

Firstar Bank Milwaukee, N.A.
777 E. Wisconsin Ave.
Milwaukee, WI 53202-5302
414/765-4321

Human Resources Information:
Dennis R. Fredrickson
Senior Vice President/Human Resources
Firstar Bank Milwaukee, N.A.
777 E. Wisconsin Ave.
Milwaukee, WI 53202-5302
Attn: M/C JSS2

M&I Bank
770 N. Water St.
Milwaukee, WI 53202-3593
414/765-7700

Human Resources Information:
Gary Strelow
SVP and Corporate Director/Human Resources
M&I Bank
770 N. Water St., NW, Eighth Fl.
Milwaukee, WI 53202-3593

Norwest Bank Wisconsin, N.A.
735 W. Wisconsin Ave.
Milwaukee, WI 53201

414/276-6500

Human Resources Information:
David Van Wartingen
Senior Vice President/Human Resources
Norwest Bank Wisconsin, N.A.
636 Wisconsin Ave.
P.O. Box 171
Sheboygan, WI 53082-0171
414/459-2110

Wyoming

Casper

Norwest Bank Wyoming, N.A.
234 E. First St.
Casper, WY 82601
307/266-1100

Human Resources Information:
Kathy Fisher
Vice President/Human Resources
Manager
Norwest Bank Wyoming, N.A.
P.O. Box 30058
Billings, MT 59117
Attn: M/S 8013

Cheyenne

Key Bank of Wyoming
1800 Carey Ave.
Cheyenne, WY 82001
307/771-3400

Human Resources Information:
Richard Rodriquez

Vice President/Human Resources
Key Bank of Wyoming
1800 Carey Ave.
Cheyenne, WY 82001

Outside the U.S.

Canada

Ontario

Citizens Business Bank
701 N. Haven Ave.
Ontario, CA 91764-4903
909/980-4030

Human Resources Information:
Michael Thompson
Director/Human Resources
Citizens Business Bank
P.O. Box 51000
Ontario, CA 91761

Puerto Rico

Hato Rey

Banco Popular de Puerto Rico
209 Munoz Rivera Ave.
Hato Rey, PR 00918
809/765-9800

Human Resources Information:
Eduardo Rodriguez
Vice President/Director of Human Resources
Banco Popular de Puerto Rico
P.O. Box 362708
San Juan, PR 00936-2708

Banco Santander, Puerto Rico
Avenue Ponce de Leon 207
Hato Rey, PR 00918
809/759-7070

Human Resources Information:
Estrella Miranda
Senior Vice President/Human Resources
Banco Santander, Puerto Rico
P.O. Box 362589
San Juan, PR 00936-2589

Oriental Trust
Munoz Rivera 268
Hato Rey, PR 00919
787/766-1986

Human Resources Information:
Enrique Rubiano
Vice President/Human Resources
Oriental Trust
P.O. Box 191429
San Juan, PR 00919

Scotiabank de Puerto Rico
273 Ponce de Leon Ave.
Hato Rey, PR 00917
787/758-8989

Human Resources Information:
Eva Mundo
Human Resources Manager
Scotiabank de Puerto Rico
P.O. Box 362230
San Juan, PR 00936-2230

Humacao

Oriental Bank and Trust
State Road 908
Humacao, PR 00791
787/850-2000

Human Resources Information:
Jeanne Forbs
Vice President/Human Resources
Oriental Bank and Trust
P.O. Box 1429
Hato Rey, PR 00919

Roig Commercial Bank
Carreras and Georgetti Street
Humacao, PR 00791
787/852-1010

Human Resources Information:
Jorge Surillo
Senior Vice President/Human Resources
Roig Commercial Bank
P.O. Box 457
Humacao, PR 00792

Mayaguez

Westernbank Puerto Rico
19 W. McKinley St.
Mayaguez, PR 00680
809/834-8000

Human Resources Information:
Jose A. Ruiz
Vice President/Branch Supervision
Westernbank Puerto Rico
P.O. Box 1180
Mayaguez, PR 00681-1180

Ponce

PonceBank
Villa and Concordia Streets
Ponce, PR 00731
809/844-8100

Human Resources Information:
Wanda Goyco
Vice President/Human Resources
PonceBank
P.O. Box 1024
Ponce, PR 00733-1024

San Juan

Banco Bilbao Vizcaya Puerto Rico
Ponce de Leon Ave. and Parque
San Juan, PR 00936-4745
809/724-3717

Human Resources Information:
Clarissa Perez
Vice President/Human Resources
Banco Bilbao Vizcaya Puerto Rico
P.O. Box 364745
San Juan, PR 00936-4745

Santurce

FirstBank Puerto Rico
1519 Ponce de Leon Ave.
Santurce, PR 00908
809/729-8200

Human Resources Information:
Aida M. Garcia
Senior Vice President/Human Re-
sources
FirstBank Puerto Rico
P.O. Box 9146
Santurce, PR 00908

DIRECTORY OF OUTSOURCERS AND OTHER COMPANIES SELLING PRODUCTS AND SERVICES TO BANKS

Banks constitute an industry specialty for many companies. The major accounting firms, office products companies, and computer hardware and software firms all target the banking industry. And outsourcers, especially, need people able to sell to banks and able to provide services previously performed inside banks. Who can better sell to bankers and who can better develop products and services for banks than former bankers?

The following companies have demonstrated an interest in getting to bankers. They advertise heavily in banking publications, or are known to employ people with banking experience and skills. As with the preceding list of the top 500 U.S. banks, this information may become quickly outdated. Calling to ascertain names of hiring executives and to verify addresses before writing or sending resumes could eliminate wasted effort and misdirected inquiries.

Consulting/Accounting

Andersen Consulting
1345 Sixth Ave.
New York, NY 10105
212/708-4400

Andersen Worldwide
1330 W. 43rd St.
Chicago, IL 60609-3308
312/580-0069

Arthur Andersen LLP

33 W. Monroe St.
Chicago, IL 60603
312/580-0033

Arthur Andersen LLP
1345 Avenue of the Americas, Ste. 13
New York, NY 10105
212/708-4000

Atlantic Data Services, Inc.
1 Batterymarch ParkQuincy, MA 02169
617/770-3333

703/836-4101

Austin Financial Services, Inc.
(AFSI)
3450 W. Central Ave., Ste. 124
Toledo, OH 43606-1401
419/531-9559

Bank Compensation Strategies
Group
3600 W. 80th St., Ste. 205
Minneapolis, MN 55431
612/893-6767

Business Banking Board Company
600 New Hampshire Ave. NW
Washington, DC 20037
202/672-5600

Coopers and Lybrand
1301 Avenue of the Americas
New York, NY 10019-6013
212/259-1000

Deloitte and Touche
2 World Financial Center, Ste. 9
New York, NY 07921
212/436-4814

Director Resource Group
89 Culpeper St.
Warrenton, VA 22186
504/341-7135

Ely and Company, Inc.
108 N. Alfred St.
Alexandria, VA 22314

Family Business Group
800 Marquette Ave., Ste. 1300
Minneapolis, MN 55402-2839
612/376-9376

GRA, Thompson White and Company
6740 Antioch Road, Ste. 100
Shawnee Mission, KS 66204
913/677-3383

Hay Management
1500 K St. NW, Ste. 1000
Washington DC, 20005
202/637-6600

Hellmold Associates
640 Fifth Ave., Thirteenth Fl.
New York, NY 10019
212/424-1900

IBM Corporation
Armonk, NY 10604
800/426-3333

Jay Alix and Associates
4000 Town Center, Ste. 500
Southfield, MI 48075
248/358-4420

KPMG Peat Marwick
345 Park Ave.
New York, NY 10154
212/758-9700

M ONE
2813 E. Camelback
Phoenix, AZ 85016
602/957-7479

McKensey and Company
55 E. 52nd St., 23rd Fl.
New York, NY 10022
212/446-7000

Price Waterhouse
1177 Avenue of the Americas
New York, NY 10036
212/596-7000

Prime Consulting Group
2 Concourse Pkwy., Ste. 650
Norcross, GA 30093
770/416-7299

Response Analysis
230 Fourth Ave. N.
Nashville, TN 37219
615/248-2020

Right Associates
1818 Market St.
Philadelphia, PA 19103-3614
215/988-1588

Ronald H. Rovig and Company
2426 Sweetwater Country Club Drive
Apopka, FL 32712
407/880-2310

Sendero
7272 E. Indian School Road, Ste.
300
Scottsdale, AZ 85251
602/941-8112

The Directors' Network, Inc.
685 Fifth Ave., Ste. 601
New York, NY 10022
212/754-3086

Thomson Financial Publishing
4709 W. Golf Rd.
Skokie, IL 60076-1253
800/443-2824

Towers Perrin
100 Summit Lake Drive
Valhala, NY 10595
914/745-4000

Financial Investment / Financial Service Providers

Aegon Insurance Group of Companies
4333 Edgewood Road NE
Cedar Rapids, IA 52499
319/363-8511

Affiliated Financial Services
7840 E. Berry Place, Ste. 200
Englewood, CO 80111
303/770-4429

AIM Fund Management Company
11 Greenway Plaza, Ste. 1919
Houston, TX 77046
800/659-1005

AIM Fund Management Company
11 Greenway Plaza, Ste. 1919
Houston, TX 77046
800/659-1005

Alliance Fund Distributors
1345 Avenue of the Americas, Ste.
37
New York, NY 10105
212/969-1000

Alliance Fund Distributors
1345 Avenue of the Americas, Ste.
37
New York, NY 10105
212/969-1000

ALPS Mutual Funds Service, Inc.
370 Seventeenth St., Ste. 2700
Denver, CO 80202
303/623-2577

American Bankers Insurance Group
11222 Quail Roost Drive
Miami, FL 33157
305/253-2244

American Express
200 Vessey St., Ste. 24
New York, NY 10285-3130
212/640-2000

American Funds Distributor
135 S. State College Blvd.
Brea, CA 92821-5804
714/529-5828

American Skandia
1 Corporate Dr., Ste. 10
Shelton, CT 06484
203/926-1888

AMERISTAR Investment Management
First American Center, 315 Deaderick St.
Nashville, TN 37237
615/748-2000

Bennington Capital Management
1420 Fifth Ave., Ste. 3130
Seatle, WA 98101
206/224-7420

BHC Securities, Inc.
2005 Market St., Twelfth Fl.
Philadelphia, PA 19103-3212
215/636-3000

Bisys Group, Inc.
Overlook at Great Notch, 150 Clove Rd.
Little Falls, NJ 07424
973/812-8600

Bisys Group, Inc.
Overlook at Great Notch, 150 Clove

Road
Little Falls, NJ 07424
973/812-8600

Bull and Bear Service Center, Inc.
11 Hanover Square, Twelfth Fl.
New York, NY 10005
212/785-0900

Calvert Group
4550 Montgomery Ave., Ste. 1000N
Bethesda, MD 20814
800/368-2750

Charles Schwab and Company, Inc.
101 Montgomery St.
San Francisco, CA 94104
415/627-7000

CIT Group/Credit Finance
1211 Avenue of the Americas
New York, NY 10036
212/

Colonial Group, Inc.
1 Financial Center
Boston, MA 02111
617/426-3750

Commerce Data Service
1 Commerce Square
Memphis, TN 38150
901/523-3630

DeCelle, Inc.
1525 Washington St.

Braintree, MA 02184
617/848-6951

Discover Card Services
2500 Lake Cook Road
Riverwoods, IL 60015
847/405-0900

Dreyfus Bank Services
200 Park Ave., Eighth Fl.
New York, NY 10166
212/922-6000

Eaton Vance Mutual Funds
24 Federal St.
Boston, MA 02110
617/482-8260

Essex Corporation
825 Third Ave., Ste. 37
New York, NY 10022
212/371-0303

Fidelity Investments
Institutional Services Company, 82
Devonshire St.
Boston, MA 02119-3614
800/544-8888

FIMCO
111 E. Kilbourn Ave., Ste. 1850
Milwaukee, WI 53202-6611
414/224-5900

Financial Network Investment Corporation

2780 Skypark Dr., Ste. 300
Torrance, CA 90505
310/326-3100

First Data Merchant Service
1401 NW 136th Ave.
Sunrise, FL 33323
954/785-2100

First Data Resources
10825 Farnham Dr.
Omaha, NE 68154
402/222-7050

Fortis
6053 Hudson Road
St. Paul, MN 55125
612/739-6840

Frank Russell Trust Company
909 A St.
Tacoma, WA 98401
253/572-9500

Franklin Templeton Distributors, Inc.
777 Mariners Island Blvd
San Mateo, CA 94404
415/378-2300

Funds Distributor, Inc.
60 State St.
Boston, MA 02109
617/221-7930

Furman/Selz
230 Park Ave., Ste. 13

New York, NY 10169
212/309-8200

GE Capital Mortgage Corporation
6601 Six Forks Rd.
Raleigh, NC 27615-6519
919/846-4100

General Motors Acceptance Corporation
3044 W. Grand Blvd., Ste. 240
Detroit, MI 48202
313/556-1022

GMAC/RFC Residential Funding
8500 Normandale Lake Rd., Ste. 600
Minneapolis, MN 55437
612/921-2131

GNA Corporation
601 Union St.
Seattle, WA 98101
206/625-1755

Heartland Funds
790 N. Milwaukee St.
Milwaukee, WI 53202
800/432-7856

IDS Advisory Group, Inc.
80 S. Eighth St.
Minneapolis, MN 55402
612/671-3112

Independent Financial Marketing
Group, Inc.

244 Westchester Ave.
White Plains, NY 10604
914/997-5600

Integrity Investments, Inc.
3004 W. Viewmont Way W.
Seattle, WA 98199
206/286-0113

Invesco Funds
101 Federal St., Twentieth Fl.
Boston, MA 02110
617/345-8200

Invesco Funds Group, Inc.
7800 E. Union Ave., Ste. 220
Denver, CO 80237
303/930-6300

Invest Financial Corporation
2701 N. Rocky Point Dr., Seventh
Fl.
Tampa, FL 33607
800/473-4732

Investment Centers of Americas
212 N. Fourth St.
Bismarck, ND 58501
701/255-6060

Investment Company Institute
1401 H. St. NW, Ste. 1200
Washington, DC 20005
202/326-5800

Investment Management (MFS)

500 Boylston St.
Boston, MA 02116
617/954-5000

Investors Trust
601 Union St., Ste. 5600
Seattle, WA 98111
206/625-1755

James Mitchell and Company
9710 Scranton Rd., Ste. 100
San Diego, CA 92121
619/450-0055

John Alden Life Insurance Company
7300 NW Nineteenth St., Ste. 200
Miami, FL 33126-1208
305/715-1255

John Hancock Funds
101 Huntington Ave.
Boston, MA 02199
617/375-1760

John Nuveen and Company, Inc.
333 W. Wacker Dr., 31st Fl.
Chicago, IL 60606
312/917-7700

Kemper Distributors
Kemper Financial Services, 120 S.
LaSalle St.
Chicago, IL 60603
312/781-6871

Kemper Financial Services

120 S. LaSalle St., Twentieth Fl.
Chicago, IL 60601
800/537-6001

Kennedy Wilson, Inc.
3110 Main St.
Santa Monica, CA 90405
800/822-6665

Liberty Financial
Federal Reserve Plaza, 600 Atlantic
Ave., Ste. 24
Boston, MA 02210
617/722-6000

Liberty Mutual Insurance Group
175 Berkeley St.
Boston, MA 02117
617/357-9500

Liberty Securities Corporation
Federal Reserve Plaza, 600 Atlantic
Ave.
Boston, MA 02210-2214
617/722-6050

LPL Financial
440 Commercial St.
Boston, MA 02109
617/720-4977

Marketing One, Inc.
851 SW Sixth Ave.
Portland, OR 97204
503/220-3302

MasterCard International
2000 Purchase St.
Purchase, NY 10577
914/249-4600

Nationwide Life Insurance Company
1 Nationwide Plaza
Columbus, OH 43215-2220
614/249-7831

Nationwide Mutual Insurance Company
1 Nationwide Plaza
Columbus, OH 43215
614/249-7855

Oppenheimer Funds Management
Corporation
2 World Trade Center, 34th Fl.
New York, NY 10048-0203
212/323-0666

Pacific Mutual
700 Newport Center Drive
Newport Beach, CA 92660
717/640-3011

Phoenix Systems, Inc.
2970 Clairmont Rd., Ste. 900
Atlanta, GA 30329
404/633-2466

Pilgrim America
9606 E. Vialinda
Scottsdale, AZ 85258
800/336-3436

Pioneer Distribution Funds, Inc.
60 State St.
Boston, MA 02109-1820
800/622-1262

Pioneer Funds Distributor
60 State St.
Boston, MA 02109
800/622-1262

PrimeVest Financial Services
400 First St. S., Ste. 300
St. Cloud, MN 56301-3600
320/656-9066

Primus
5209 Linbar Dr., Ste. 615
Nashville, TN 37215-0395
615/333-0059

Prudential Securities
1 New York Plaza, Eighteenth Fl.
New York, NY 10004
212/778-1000

Putnam Investments
1 Post Office Square, Seventh Fl.
Boston, MA 02109
617/292-1000

Putnam Investments
1 Post Office Square
Boston, MA 02109
617/292-1000

Scudder, Stevens and Clark
345 Park Ave., Ste. 25
New York, NY 10154-0010
212/326-6200

Scudder, Stevens and Clark
2 International Place
Boston, MA 02110
617/295-1000

SEI Corporation
680 E. Swedesford Road
Wayne, PA 19087-1658
610/254-2361

T. Rowe Price Associates
100 E. Pratt St.
Baltimore, MD 21202
410/547-2308

Thomson Financial Publishing
4709 W. Golf Rd.
Skokie, IL 60076-1253
800/443-2824

Thornburg Management Company
119 E. Marcy, Ste. 202
Santa Fee, NM 87501
505/984-0200

Unitech Systems, Inc.
1240 E. Diehl Rd., Ste. 3
Naperville, IL 60563
630/505-1800

Van Eck Global

99 Park Ave., Ste. 8
New York City, NY 10016
914/941-7098

Van Kampen American Capital
1 Parkview Plaza
Oak Brook, IL 60181
708/684-6171

Van Kampen American Capital
1 Park View Plaza
Oak Brook Terrace, IL 60181
708/684-6171

Visa International
PO Box 1700
Herndon, VA 20172
703/742-5000

VISA International
900 Metro Center Blvd.
San Mateo, CA 94404
415/432-3200

Voyageur Funds
90 S. Seventh St., Ste. 4400
Minneapolis, MN 55402-4115
612/376-7000

Wachovia Bank and Trust Company,
NA
301 N. Main St.
Winston-Salem, NC 27150
919/770-5000

Western National Corporation

5555 San Felipe, Ste. 900
Houston, TX 77056
713/888-7800

Wright Investor Services, Inc.
1000 Lafayette Blvd.
Bridgeport, CT 06604
203/333-6666

Insurance

AIG
70 Pine St., Ste. 58
New York, NY 10270
212/770-7107

American Re-Insurance Company
American Re Plaza, 555 College
Road E.
Princeton, NJ 08543-5241
609/243-4200

Amerin
200 E. Randolph Dr., 49th Fl.
Chicago, IL 60601-7125
312/540-0078

BancInsure
5005 N. Lincoln Blvd.
Oklahoma City, OK 73105
405/524-0118

Bankers Insurance Center
1122 21st St. NW, Ste. 200
Washington, DC 20036
800/334-2242

Chubb and Son, Inc.
15 Mountain View Road
Warren, NJ 07059
908/903-2000

CNA
180 Maiden Ln., Fifteenth Fl.
New York, NY 10038
212/440-3000

Executive Risk
82 Hopmeadow St.
Simsbury, CT 06070-7683
860/408-2000

Fidelity and Deposit Company
300 Saint Paul Pl.
Baltimore, MD 21202
410/539-0800

Great American Insurance Companies
1515 Woodfield Rd., Ste. 850
Schaumburg, IL 60173
847/330-6800

Hampton Corporate Strategy Group
2111 Wilson Blvd., Ste. 700
Arlington, VA 22201
703/351-5028

J and H Marsh and McLennan
125 Broad St.
New York, NY 10004
212/574-7283

Kemper National Insurance Company
3401 Enterprise Pkwy.
Beachwood, OH 44122/7340
216-514/3801

Lexington Insurance Company
200 State St., Ste. 5
Boston, MA 02109
617/330-1100

Matterhorn Bank Programs, Inc.
9515 Deereco Rd., Ste. 4
Lutherville, MD 21093
410/821-9500

Minet
1114 Avenue of the Americas
New York, NY 10036-7703
212/782-6000

Northland Insurance Companies
1295 Northland Drive
St. Paul, MN 55120-1139
800/237-9334

Reliance National
77 Water St., Ste. 21
New York, NY 10005
212/968-0710

Scarborough
10 S. LaSalle St., Ste. 10
Chicago, IL 60603
312/630-7420

St. Paul Companies
385 Washington St.
St. Paul, MN 55102-1309
612/310-7911

Stogniew and Associates
12225 28th St. N.
St. Petersburg, FL 33716
813/572-7400

TBA Insurance Company
8200 Anderson Blvd.
Fort Worth, TX 76120
817/265-2000

USF&G Corporation
100 Light St.
Baltimore, MD 21202
410/547-3000

Zurich Direct, Inc.
The Zurich Towers, 1400 American
Lane
Schaumburg, IL 60173-5452
847/969-3500

Investment Banks

A.G. Edwards and Sons, Inc.
1 N. Jefferson Ave.
St. Louis, MO 63103
314/289-3000

Advest Financial Institute
200 Liberty St., 30th Fl.

New York, NY 10281-1013
212/786-0600

Alex Brown, Inc.
1 South St.
Baltimore, MD 21202
410/727-1700

Alex Sheshunoff Management Services
98 San Jacinto Blvd., Ste. 1900
Austin, TX 78701
512/472-4000

Allen C. Ewing and Company
50 N. Laura St., Ste. 3625
Jacksonville, FL 32202
904/354-5573

Austin Associates, Inc.
7205 W. Central Ave.
Toledo, OH 43617
419/841-8521

Baxter Fentriss
9100 Arboretum Pkwy., Ste. 280
Richmond, VA 23236
804/323-7540

Bear, Stearns and Company, Inc.
245 Park Ave., Fourth Fl.
New York, NY 10167
212/272-2000

Berkshire Capital Corporation
399 Park Ave., 28th Fl.

New York, NY 10022
212/207-8200

Berwind Financial Group
1500 Market St., Ste. 3000
Philadelphia, PA 19102
215/563-2800

Brown, Brothers Harriman
59 Wall St.
New York, NY 10005
212/483-1818

Capital Planning Advisory Group
71 Executive Drive
Princeton, NJ 08540-1529
609/497-7500

Capital Resources Funding Group,
Inc.
826 Ninth St., Ste. 100
Greeley, CO 80632-1444
970/356-9822

Chaffe and Associates, Inc.
220 Camp St., Fifth Fl.
New Orleans, LA 70130
504/524-1801

Charles Webb and Company
211 Bradenton Ave.
Dublin, OH 43017-3541
614/766-8400

Chase Securities, Inc.
270 Park Ave., Ninth Fl.

New York, NY 10017
212/270-6000

Chicago Dearborn Company
208 S. LaSalle St., Ste. 1000
Chicago, IL 60604-1003
312/855-7600

Constellation Financial Management
Company
52 Vanderbilt Ave.
New York, NY 10017
212/557-5500

Corestates Investment Advisors
1500 Market St.
Philadelphia, PA 19107
215/786-7070

CS First Boston Group, Inc.
55 E. 52nd St.
New York, NY 10055
212/909-2000

Dain Bosworth
60 S. Sixth St.
Minneapolis, MN 55402
612/371-2711

Danielson Associates, Inc.
6110 Executive Blvd., Ste. 504
Rockville, MD 20852
301/468-4884

David A. Noyes and Company
107 N. Pennsylvania St.

Indianapolis, IN 46204
317/634-6563

Dillon, Read and Company
535 Madison Ave., Ste. 15
New York, NY 10022
212/906-7000

Donaldson Lufkin and Jenrette
277 Park Ave.
New York, NY 10172
212/892-3000

Eagle Asset Management
880 Carillon Pkwy.
St. Petersburg, FL 33716
813/573-3800

EVEREN Securities
77 W. Wacker Dr., Ste. 3100
Chicago, IL 60601
312/574-6000

Financial Capital Resources LLP
21 Eastbrook Bend, Ste. 116
Peachtree City, GA 30269
770/487-6650

Friedman Billings Ramsey and Company
1001 Nineteenth St. N.
Arlington, VA 22209
703/312-9500

Geneva Company
5 Park Plaza

Irvine, CA 92714
714/756-2200

Goldman, Sachs and Company
85 Broad St., Ste. 27
New York, NY 10004
212/902-1000

Hilliard Lyons
455 S. Fourth Ave., Ste. 1700
Louisville, KY 40232-2760
502/588-8400

Hoefer and Arnett
353 Sacramento St., Ste. 1000
San Francisco, CA 94111
415/362-7111

Hopper Soliday and Company, Inc.
1703 Oregon Pike
Lancaster, PA 17604
717/560-3015

Hovde Financial, Inc.
1826 Jefferson Place NW
Washington, DC 20036
202/775-8109

Howe Barnes Investments, Inc.
135 S. LaSalle St., Ste. 1500
Chicago, IL 60603
312/655-3000

J.C. Bradford and Company
330 Commerce St
Nashville, TN 37201

615/748-9000

Janney Montgomery Scott, Inc.
1801 Market St.
Philadelphia, PA 19103
215/665-6000

JP Morgan
60 Wall St.
New York, NY 10260-0060
212/483-2323

Keefe and Keefe International, Inc.
375 Park Ave., Ste. 3108
New York, NY 01052
212/688-1112

Keefe, Bruyette and Woods
2 World Trade Center, Ste. 8566
New York, NY 10048
212/323-8300

Kemper Securities
231 S. Jefferson St.
Chicago, IL 60661-5613
312/454-3220

Lazard Freres
120 Broadway, Ste. 901
New York, NY 10012
212/346-2500

Legg Mason
1747 Pennsylvania Ave. NW
Washington, DC 20006-4691
202/452-4000

Lehman Brothers
3 World Financial Center
New York, NY 10285-0001
212/526-7000

LSC Financial Services, Inc.
Davis Road at Oakwood Ln.
Valley Forge, PA 19482
610/783-5488

M.A. Schapiro and Company
1 Chase Manhattan Plaza
New York, NY 10005-1436
212/425-6600

McConnell, Budd and Downes, Inc.
365 South St.
Morristown, NJ 07960-7339
201/538-7800

McDonald and Company
800 Superior Ave.
Cleveland, OH 44114-2601
216/443-2300

Mercer Capital Management, Inc.
5860 Ridgeway Center Parkway, Ste.
410
Memphis, TN 38120-4030
901/685-2120

Merrill Lynch
World Financial Center, North Tower
New York, NY 10281-1325
212/449-1000

Montgomery Securities
600 Montgomery St.
San Francisco, CA 94111-2777
415/627-2000

Morgan Guaranty Trust Company
9 W. 57th St.
New York, NY 10019-2701
212/483-2323

Morgan, Keegan and Company, Inc.
Morgan Keegan Tower
Memphis, TN 38103-2196
901/524-4100

Morgan, Stanley and Company
1585 Broadway
New York, NY 10036
212/703-4000

Morgen-Walke Associates, Inc.
380 Lexington Ave., 50th Fl.
New York, NY 10168-0002
212/850-5600

Northeast Capital and Advisory
80 State St., Ninth Fl.
Albany, NY 12207-2505
518/426-0100

Oppenheimer and Company, Inc.
Oppenheimer Tower, World Financial Center
New York, NY 10281-3798
212/667-7000

Piper Jaffray, Inc.
222 S. Ninth St
Minneapolis, MN 55402-3389
612/342-6322

Professional Bank Services, Inc.
The 1000 Building, 6200 Dutch-
man's Lane, Ste. 305
Louisville, KY 40205-3285
502/451-6633

Prudential Securities
1 New York Plaza, Eighteenth Fl.
New York, NY 10004-1998
212/778-1000

Raffensperger Hughes and Company,
Inc.
20 N. Meridian St.
Indianapolis, IN 46201
800/382-1126

Raymond James Financial, Inc.
880 Carillon Pkwy.
St. Petersburg, FL 33716-1100
813/573-3800

Robert W. Baird and Company
777 E. Wisconsin Ave.
Milwaukee, WI 53201-5391
414/765-3500

Robinson Humphrey Company, Inc.
Atlanta Financial Center, 3333
Peachtree Road NE, Ste. 7

Atlanta, GA 30326-1070
404/266-6000

Rodman and Renshaw
Sears Tower, 233 S. Wacker Drive,
Ste. 4500
Chicago, IL 60606-6363
312/526-2000

Roney and Company
1 Griswald
Detroit, MI 48226-3401
313/963-6700

RP Financial, LC
1700 N. Moore St., Ste. 2210
Arlington, VA 22209-1903
703/528-1700

Ryan, Beck and Company
10 Main St.
West Orange, NJ 07052-5414
201/325-3000

Salomon Brothers
Seven World Trade Center
New York, NY 10048-1102
212/783-7000

Sandler O'Neill
747 Middle Neck Road
Great Neck, NY 11024-1929
516/829-3410

Sandler O'Neill
2 World Trade Center, 104th Fl.

New York, NY 10048-0678
212/446-7900

Schroder Wertheim and Company
787 Seventh Ave.
New York, NY 10019-6018
212/492-6000

Schroder Wertheim and Company
787 Seventh Ave.
New York, NY 10019-6018
212/492-6000

Scott and Stringfellow, Inc.
909 E. Main St.
Richmond, VA 23219-3002
804/643-1811

Smith Barney
388 Greenwich St., Ste. 31
New York, NY 10013-2375
212/816-6000

Southard Financial
665 Oakleaf Office Lane
Memphis, TN 38117-4812
901/761-7500

State Street Boston Corporation
225 Franklin St.
Quincy, MA 02110-2804
617/786-3000

Stephen, Inc.
111 Center St.
Little Rock, AR 72201-4402

501/377-2000

Stifel, Nicolaus and Company, Inc.
500 N. Broadway, Ste. 1500
St. Louis, MO 63102-2188
314/342-2000

T. Stephen Johnson
9755 Dogwood Rd., Ste. 310
Roswell, GA 30075-7021
770/998-6491

The Findley Company
1470 N. Hundley
Anaheim, CA 92806-1322
714/630-6195

Trident Financial
4601 Six Forks Rd., Ste. 400
Raleigh, NC 27609-5210
919/781-8900

Tucker Anthony, Inc
1 Beacon St
Boston, MA 02108-3176
617/725-2000

UBS Securities
299 Park Ave.
New York, NY 10171-0002
212/821-3905

US Banking Alliance
2 Concourse Pkwy., Ste. 650
Atlanta, GA 30328
770/395-2400

W. Y. Campbell
200 Renaissance Center, 26th Fl.
Detroit, MI 48243-1203
313/259-3040

Wasserstein and Perrella
31 W. 52nd St.
New York, NY 10019-6163
212/969-2700

Wheat First Butcher Singer
901 E. Byrd St
Richmond, VA 23219-4069
804/649-2311

William Blair and Company
135 S. LaSalle St., Ste. 2900
Chicago, IL 60603-5307
312/236-1600

Miscellaneous

American Bankers Association
1120 Connecticut Ave. NW
Washington, DC 20036
202/663-5000

American Stock Exchange
86 Trinity Place
New York, NY 10006-1881
212/306-1000

Bank Administration Institute
1 N. Franklin St.
Chicago, IL 60606-0943

MasterCard
2000 Purchase St.
Purchase, NY 10577
914/249-4600

NASDAQ Stock Market, Inc.
1735 K St. NW
Washington, DC 20006-1504
202/728-8000

New York Stock Exchange, Inc.
11 Wall St.
New York, NY 10005
212/656-3000

Rand McNally and Company
Financial Publicity Division, 8255 N.
Central Park
Skokie, IL 60676
847/329-6516

Response Analysis
230 Fourth Ave. N., Ste. 501
Nashville, TN 37219
615/248-2020

S and L Securities
410 E. Main St.
Charlottesville, NC 22902
804/977-1600

Security First Network Bank, FSB
3390 Peachtree Road NE, Ste. 1700
Atlanta, GA 30326-1108
404/812-6300

Sheshunoff Information Services
505 Barton Springs Rd., Ste. 1200
Austin, TX 78704
800/505-8333

Tax Shop
5422 Carrier Dr., Ste. 201
Orlando, FL 32819
407/352-3370

Thomson Financial Publishing
4709 W. Golf Road
Skokie, IL 60076-1253
800/443-2824

Thomson Financial Publishing
4709 W. Golf Road
Skokie, IL 60076-1253
800/443-2824

Mortgage Industry

Advanta Mortgage USA
16875 W. Bernardo Drive
San Diego, CA 92127
619/674-1800

Countrywide Funding Corporation
155 N. Lake Ave., Dept. 24
Pasadena, CA 91109
818/304-8400

Fannie Mae
3900 Wisconsin Ave., NW
Washington, DC 20016-2899
202/752-7000

312/553-4600

Bank Building Corporation
13537 Barrett Parkway Dr., Ste. 215
Manchester, MO 63021
314/821-2265

Bankers Systems, Inc.
6815 Saukview Drive
St. Cloud, MN 56303
612/251-3060

Bauer Financial Reports, Inc.
2655 LeJeune Road
Coral Gables, FL 33134
305/445-9500

Boston Ventures, Inc.
21 Custom House St.
Boston, MA 02110
617/737-3700

Brink's Incorporated
1 Thorndale Circle
Darien, CT 06820
203/662-7800

Chicago Board of Trade
141 W. Jackson, Ste. 2280
Chicago, IL 60604
312/435-3500

Chicago Mercantile Exchange
30 S. Wacker
Chicago, IL 60606
312/930-1000

D. F. King and Company
77 Water St.
New York, NY 10005
212/269-5550

Dun and Bradstreet Business
1 Diamond Hill Road
Murray Hill, NJ 07974-0027
908/665-5000

FISI Madison Financial
P.O. Box 40726
Nashville, TN 37204
615/371-2779

International Banking Technology
1770 Indian Trail Rd., Ste. 300
Norcross, GA 30093
770/381-2023

J. J. Kenny Company
65 Broadway, 21th Fl.
New York, NY 10006
212/770-4000

John H. Harland Company
2939 Miller Road
Decatur, GA 30035
770/981-1502

Laurel Management Partners
1 Maritime Plaza
San Francisco, CA 94111
415/288-0544

Federal Home Loan Mortgage
8200 Jones Branch Drive
McLean, VA 22102-3107
703/903-2000

GE Capital Mortgage Corporation
6601 Six Forks Rd.
Raleigh, NC 27615-6519
919/846-4100

GMAC Residential Funding
8500 Normandale Lake Blvd., Ste.
600
Bloomington, MN 55437
612/921-2131

Mortgage Banker's Association
1125 Fifteenth St. NW
Washington, DC 20005
202/861-6500

Technology

ADP Financial Services
275 Wyman St., Ste. 200
Waltman, MA 02154
617/890-2400

Affiliated Computer Services, Inc.
2828 N. Haskell Ave.
Dallas, TX 75204-2909
214/841-6289

Affinity Processing Corporation
1333 Main St., Ste. 101
Columbia, SC 29201-3201

803/254-9006

Alltel Information Services
4001 Rodney Parham Road
Little Rock, AR 72212-2442
501/220-5100

Anacomp
3060 Peachtree Road
Atlanta, GA 30305
404/262-2667

Antinori Software, Inc.
1201 Peachtree St., NE
Atlanta, GA 30361-3500
404/873-6740

BancTec, Inc.
4435 Spring Valley Rd.
Dallas, TX 56301
972/341-4000

Bankers Systems, Inc.
P. O. Box 1457
St. Cloud, MN 56301
800/397-2341

Bell and Howell Mail Processing
Systems
795 Roble Road
Allentown, PA 18103
610/264-4510

Bisys Group, Inc.
Overlook at Great Notch, 150 Clove
Road
Little Falls, NJ 07424

973/812-8600

Broadway and Seymour
128 S. Tryon St.
Charlotte, NC 28202-5050
800/274-9287

Brokers Transaction Services
9 N. Federal Ave.
Mason City, IA 50402-1501
515/424-1488

Business Enterprises
449 N. State Road, Ste. 434
Altamonte Springs, FL 32714
407/865-7933

CFI Pro Service, Inc.
440 SW Sixth Ave., Ste. 200
Portland, OR 97204-1608
503/274-7280

Checkfree Corporation
4411 E. Jones Bridge Road
Norcross, GA 30092
770/840-1615

Computer Associates International, Inc.
1 Computer Associates Plaza
Islandia, NY 11788-7001
516/342-5224

Diebold, Inc.
5995 Mayfair Road
Canton, OH 44720
800/999-3600

Digital Equipment Corporation
200 Forest St.
Marlborough, MA 01752
508/467-6211

EDS
128 S. George St.
York, PA 17403
717/845-5602

EIS
1351 Washington Blvd
Stanford, CT 06902
203/354-4800

EMC Corporation
171 South St.
Hopkinton, MA 01748
508/435-1000

Fair Isaac
120 N. Redwood Dr
San Rafael, CA 94903-1996
415/472-2211

First Commerce Technologies
1248 O St., Ste. 600
Lincoln, NE 68508
800/742-7633

First Data Resources, Inc.
10825 Farnam Drive
Omaha, NE 68154
402/222-7909

Firstar Leasing Service

777 E. Wisconsin Ave
Milwaukee, WI 53202
414/765-5624

FIS, Inc.
401 S. Magnolia Ave.
Orlando, FL 32801-3392
800/234-7015

Fiserv Solutions
255 Fiserv Drive
Brookfield, WI 53008-0979
800/872-7882

GFS Gallagher Financial Systems,
Inc.
5110 Maryland Way, Ste. 280
Brentwood, TN 37027
615/221-7300

Hewlett Packard Company
3000 Hanover St.
Palo Alto, CA 94304-1181
415/857-1501

Hogan Systems
5525 LBJ Freeway
Dallas, TX 75240
972/386-0020

IA Corporation
Watergate Tower 1, 1900 Powell St.
Emeryville, CA 94608
510/450-7000

IBM Corporation
Armonk, NY 10504

800/426-3333

Information Technology, Inc.
1345 Old Cheney Road
Lincoln, NE 68512
402/423-2682

INTEL Corporation
3065 Bowers Ave.
Santa Clara, CA 95051
408/987-8080

Interlinq Software Corporation
11255 Kirkland Way
Kirkland, WA 98033
800/569-1234

International Banking Technologies
1770 Indian Trail Road, Ste. 300
Norcross, GA 30093
770/381-2023

Jack Henry and Associates
663 W. Hwy. 60
Monett, MO 65708
800/299-4001

Kirchman Corporation
711 E. Altamonte Drive
Altamonte Springs, FL 32701
407/831-3001

LeapFrog Technologies
1731 N. Elm St., Ste. 100
Commerce, GA 30529
706/369-8288

Lexmark International
740 New Circle Road
Lexington, KY 40511
606/232-2000

M & I Data Services, Inc.
4900 W. Brown Deer Road
Milwaukee, WI 53202
414/357-2290

Microsoft
1 Microsoft Way
Redmond, WA 98052
425/882-8080

NCR Community Bank Solutions
1529 Brwon St.
Dayton, OH 45479-0002
937/445-6611

NCS Assessment Services
5605 Green Circle Drive
Hopkins, MN 55343-9602
612/939-5900

Olivetti North America
22425 E. Appleway Ave.
Liberty Lake, WA 99019-9534
509/927-5600

Peerless Group
1212 E. Arapaho Road
Richardson, TX 75081
800/353-5513

Phoenix Systems, Inc.
2970 Clairmont Road, Ste. 900
Atlanta, GA 30329

404/633-2466

Premier Solutions
333 Technology Drive
Malvern, PA 19355
610/251-6500

Profitstar, Inc.
11128 John Galt Blvd., Ste. 350
Omaha, NE 68137
800/356-9099

Sanchez Computer Associates
40 Valley Stream Pkwy.
Malvern, PA 19355
610/296-8877

Sendero Corporation
7272 E. Indian School Road, Ste.
300
Scottsdale, AZ 85251
602/941-8112

Sun Microsystems
2550 Garcia Ave.
Mountain View, CA 94043
415/960-3200

Thomson Financial Publishing
4709 W. Golf Road
Skokie, IL 60076-1253
800/443-2824

Unisys
1100 Corporate Dr.
Farmington, NY 14425
215/986-2324

Visa International
900 Metro Center Blvd.
San Mateo, CA 94402
415/432-3200

Telecommunications

AT&T Affiliates
Atlanta, GA 30301
800/367-7225

ALLTEL Information Services, Inc.
2200 Lucien Way
Maitland, FL 32751
407/875-1818

BellSouth Corporation
1155 Mount Vernon Hwy.
Atlanta, GA 30338-5441
770/399-4588

MCI
1650 Tyson's Blvd.
McLean, VA 22102
703/506-6002

MCI Communications Corporation
1801 Pennsylvania Ave. NW
Washington, DC 20006
202/872-1600

MCI Telecommunications
2560 N. First St.
San Jose, CA 95131-1015
408/922-0250

NCR Community Bank Solutions
1529 Brown St.

Dayton, OH 45479-0002
937/445-66rint
8140 Ward Pkwy.
Kansas City, MO 64114
913/624-3000

INDEX

Reader Comments

The authors and editors of this book welcome reader comments. If you have something to say about *Career Alternatives for Bankers*—a comment, a correction, a compliment—send it to Lee Wilson, Editor, Magellan Press, Inc., P.O. Box 121075, Nashville, TN 37212.

Book Orders

If you cannot find *Career Alternatives for Bankers* at your local bookstore, you may order additional copies directly from the publisher in two ways.

1. Call 800/624-5359 to pay with a credit card.
or
2. Use the order blank below (or a photocopy) to pay by check.

Please send *Career Alternatives for Bankers* in the quantity indicated. Number of copies _____

Ship to:

_____
(institution or individual)

_____
(street address)

_____
(city, state, zip)

Amount enclosed: $_____
Send $37.95 ($34.95 plus $3.00 shipping) **per copy orderd.**
Make check payable to Magellan Press, Inc.

Mail check and order blank to:
Magellan Press, Inc.
P.O. Box 121075
Nashville, TN 37212